Imagining Interest in Political Thought

Stephen G. Engelmann

Imagining Interest in Political Thought

Origins of Economic Rationality

Duke University Press   Durham and London 2003

For my mother and father, and for Sophia

Contents

Acknowledgments

The debts I have incurred in writing this book are enormous, and will never be paid. They go back to kitchen talk with Florian Bail, and to my time at Reed College and Queen's University, where teachers and fellow students pushed me to keep learning. I was first given the freedom to explore many of the book's themes at Johns Hopkins University under the supervision of Richard Flathman, the very best advisor and interlocutor one could hope to have. Kirstie McClure prodded me to improve my historical and theoretical skills—as well as my writing—while William Connolly, J.G.A. Pocock, and Ali Khan provided additional guidance. Other early helpers included Lanfranco Blanchetti, James Crimmins, Kaveh Ehsani, Charles Euchner, John Maltese, Rina Palumbo, and Meg Russett, as well as John Guillory, David Harvey, and the late Sharon Stephens. Arguments were later tested at conferences in the United States and Canada, and in seminars and workshops at the University of Illinois at Chicago and the University of Chicago. Chapter 4 appeared in *Utilitas* 13:4 (November 2001). I am grateful to Yoshio Nagai and his colleagues from the Japanese Society for Utilitarian Studies for their invitation to present a draft of chapter 5; ideas for chapter 7 were developed at the invitation of the International Society for Utilitarian Studies Bentham Seminar at University College London. Philip Schofield and the staff of the Bentham Project at UCL are wonderful hosts. I am indebted to conversations with them, and to responses from numerous discussants and audiences. The book itself could not have been written without the support of my colleagues and students in the Department of Political Science at UIC, and without the time provided by the Department, by grants from the Office of the Vice Chancellor for Research, and by a sabbatical leave from the University. Valerie Johnson, Marla Lane, Amalia Pallares, and Daniel Thomas were especially important sources of tips, aid, and comfort. I thank the University College London library for permission to quote from the Bentham Collection, the University of Michigan's Early English Books Online service for its rich store of seventeenth-century writings, and the UIC library and its staff for access to a wealth of their own and others' materials. Jeffrey Johnson's loyal and ultra-competent assistance at a late stage was invaluable. I thank Raphael Allen for his early and steady faith in the project. He and Fred Kameny and their colleagues at Duke University Press have consistently provided the intelligent and patient guidance I needed to produce a relatively brief and, I hope, readable text.

Several individuals read and commented on specific chapters, including Isaac Balbus, Mark Canuel, Doris Graber, David Hasen, Don Herzog, Meredith McGill, Sophia Mihic, Norma Moruzzi, Andrew Parker, Gordon Schochet, Mildred Schwartz, and Elizabeth Wingrove. I have never even met David Burchell, but he graciously gave helpful comments on chapter 5 upon request. My friend Stephen Schwartz always responded quickly and generously when asked to check and correct French translations. I am grateful to Balbus and Canuel for their careful readings of the entire manuscript, as I am to two anonymous readers for Duke University Press. At different times three wonderfully talented thinkers and writers—McGill, Mihic, and Wingrove—worked around the clock on parts of the manuscript, and tried to make some of their talent rub off on me. Any moments of excellence in what follows should be credited to their insistent criticism.

Conversations with several old and new friends in different walks of life have aided my efforts, as has the indulgent support of a close extended family— parents Fred and Mary, brothers John and Peter, in-laws, cousins, aunts and uncles, "family friends," the Reed gang, and more—and above all Sophia, and our new companion Mia. I hope that this study, despite all of its omissions and remaining obscurities, reflects in some way the compassionate collective intelligence of the plural circles in which I have been privileged to travel. This book investigates the emergence of modern utility and the political use to which use has been put; in other words, it engages underexplored features of the commodity form. My own fortunate experience at the hands of others, and the existence of this text itself, speak to the power of a different relation—the continuing circulation of the gift.

Imagining Interest in Political Thought

1 Introduction

To make sense of contemporary politics, we must first make sense of neoliberalism. By promoting markets as the preferred regulatory mechanism of everyday life, neoliberal doctrines turn states into enforcers of a global financial and trade regime. Although these "privatizing" trends put governmental power into the hands of economic actors lacking democratic accountability, they have attracted only minimal attention from American political theorists. The problem can be attributed in part to the predominance of a liberal tradition that puts the individual subject and freedom of choice at its center. Encompassing both theories of normative liberalism and explicitly economistic rational-choice theory, this tradition orients political theorists toward assessments of whether government preserves and enhances individual choice or restricts and erodes it. The liberal tradition is ill equipped to appreciate choice itself as government, and thus it is ill suited to a clear appraisal of neoliberal reform.

"Neoliberalism" is a contested term primarily used by critics of the politics that it names. My own use invokes a complex of theories, proposals, and policies that by and large activate interest-governed choice in the pursuit of collective efficiency. Efficiency calls, wherever feasible, for the "private" ownership of (material and spiritual) goods and for an increase in the scope and intensity of profitable transactions among owners. Some see neoliberalism as a throwback to classical liberal theory and practice, but this view is misleading. Classical liberalism viewed market exchange as a distinct sphere and mode of practice. Its political economy was a study and pursuit of collective wealth. And its orientation was juridical; its rule was a matter of law. Neoliberalism's market is by contrast without boundaries, and its political economy is a study and pursuit of collective value, not wealth. Its orientation is scientific and governmental; its rule is not so much a matter of sovereign law as a matter of regulatory policy.

Neoliberalism is rightly associated with the Chicago School of economics and with the New Right reforms of the Thatcher and Reagan years (minus much of the latter's substantial cultural-conservative baggage). What distinguishes the Chicago School, and the work of its leading theorist Gary Becker, is not that it promotes free markets, but that it applies market analysis to all areas of life. It would be a mistake, however, to associate neoliberalism narrowly with the Right, and not only because Clinton and Blair extended and advanced programs of neoliberal reform. The neoliberal story is not only a story of rightist mobilization and leftist capitulation. That we privilege, for example, choice, value, and policy over right, wealth, and law is also the product of discursive shifts in which the movements of the New Left played a powerful role. The forward-looking, self-actualizing individual, guided by a liberated and liberating imagination, has taken up a permanent place in contemporary government. Neoliberal government renews the mobilization of individual *interest*—in all its spiritual, creative, and altruistic manifestations as well as its crass, routine, and selfish ones.

To grasp neoliberal government we need to unlearn some of our current approaches to politics and the theoretical frames that guide them. Theory is a way of seeing, and Americans tend to see government in a state that intervenes in the spheres of society and economy for better (welfare liberalism) or for worse (market liberalism). To understand neoliberalism we require another way of seeing, one that does not focus on distinctions among state, society, and economy and notices instead that markets are always regulated and that they always govern conduct. The mode of government advanced by neoliberalism is rather peculiar in its circumvention of sovereignty: here government serves neither the people nor a ruler but instead an *economy*. And while this economy's agencies include transnational corporations, international organizations, and even nation-states, it also requires millions of individuals acting as self-inspecting governors of themselves—consumers making self-empowering and self-realizing choices in the pursuit of their interests. The economism of the neoliberal political order thus implicates not only governing institutions and policies, but in addition, the very intelligibility of a "choosing" subject. Any attempt to understand this economism will fail if it adheres to the conceptual-izations of self and society, market and state, and intervention and noninter-vention that characterize contemporary liberal debate. Indeed, in their focus on agency, the preoccupations of many American political theorists risk facilitat-ing rather than comprehending neoliberal politics. What we need is an account of how individual imagination and initiative are coordinated in the pursuit of interest. In short, what we need is a reconceptualization of economy.

In this study I present a historical and analytical framework that enables us to see self and society themselves as organized economies. I argue that the tradition of Anglophone liberalism, and in particular the apparently illiberal liberalism of Jeremy Bentham, articulates a mode of government centered on what I call *monistic interest*. "Interest" may call to mind a particular desire for or connec-tion to something or someone. Monistic interest, by contrast, subordinates this notion of plural attachments and concerns to a logic of commensurability. Bentham almost always writes "interest" in the singular rather than the plural because any interest that directs individuals or communities—that is, any self-interest or public interest—is already an aggregate of commensurable goods. Monistic interest depends on the imagination, not only to construct commen-surables that can be balanced and thus maximized, but also to produce expecta-tions. And while monistic interest is thus always prospective—it works through individuals perpetually imagining their future—its prospects are shaped to fit with one another in a system that governs by coordinating the self-government of its members.

In the course of elaborating this system of government I develop four re-lated arguments. First, although interest—especially economic interest—calls to mind the worldly and the material, monistic interest comes out of a tradition of introspection. Eighteenth-century philosophy commonly invokes a complex plurality only to arrange it into imagined economies that are themselves under-girded by monistic interest. My analysis will trace puzzling correspondences between eighteenth-century and contemporary theory. Second, I argue that the rationality specific to monistic interest—economic rationality—is not merely instrumental. Instrumental reason finds the most efficient means to fixed and given ends. Economic reason is more comprehensive: all ends as well as means are subordinated to a calculus that weighs priorities against one another and against present and future resources. I maintain that only by appreciating how economic reason directs ends as well as means can we see how monistic interest governs. Third, the polity governed by monistic interest structures expecta-tions; the imagination is stimulated, and confirmed or disconfirmed, in the service of aggregate interest. I argue that the imagination, which is often seen as preceding or transcending politics, has become a target for and instrument of government. Fourth, I demonstrate a curious continuity between monistic interest and the logic of reason of state (*raison d'état*). Ideas of the interest of the individual and the interest of society are complementary, and both derive from arguments first applied to early modern states. Rather than critical sociology's account of market encroachment on society or lifeworld, I will tell a more directly political tale of the origins of a particular regime of security: the emergence and proliferation of economy *as* government.[1]

Understanding my first argument, which insists that we notice the role of introspection in the construction of interest, requires revisiting our very notion of "self-interest." By self-interest one often means one or more of the following: prudence, egoism, atomism, private utility, rational greed, whatever benefits the self or its circle of concern. These senses of interest presume that self-interest enters into and shapes relations with others. I will demonstrate, however, that self-interest is itself shaped and sustained by a relationship. Typically, we focus on what is *in* one's self-interest, expanding or contracting it or asking it to give way under certain circumstances. In order to understand self-interest as a species of monistic interest, however, we need to attend not to its multiple contents but to its singular form. If every interest is a relation, monistic interest is a reflexive relation that renders commensurable all other relations, thereby subordinating each of them, however construed, to its logic of economy. Monistic interest demands introspection, or what the third earl of Shaftesbury calls "home-Survey": the self's inspection of its internal economy.[2] Introspection draws boundaries between inside and outside; monistic interest, in its designation of what counts, additionally points to what is real and what is not—what is, for example, merely imagined. I show through my reading of Bentham how these ostensibly foundational distinctions are drawn and how the full force of the imagination is put at the heart of the interest relation, making it really matter, and making it matter at the expense of specific commitments, connections, or needs. The commonly assumed viscerality of Benthamic interest is belied when he notes that "it is no otherwise than through the medium of the *imagination*, that any pleasure, or pain, is capable of operating in the character of a *motive*."[3] The reflexivity endemic to monistic interest is fully present in contemporary rational-choice theory. Consider for example James Coleman's axiom for all individual and group action: "The two parts of the structure of the simplest possible actor correspond to what I have called . . . the object self . . . and the acting self . . . ; interests constitute the linkage between the two."[4]

Monistic interest allows Bentham and his heirs to exploit and reproduce a subject-centered way of seeing that facilitates our insertion into a broader economy. I argue that the "simplest possible actor" is not so much a structural premise as a structural effect, and thus the social theory that identifies this actor as a premise serves as a branch of the government that it studies.

The notion of economy that animates neoliberal theory has roots in what we think of as moral or psychological theories of interest. In this book, I retrace these connections through discussions of Shaftesbury and Bentham.[5] These writers are typically contrasted as theorists of natural altruism (Shaftesbury) and egoism (Bentham). I argue that they are better seen as having initiated the framework for such oppositions by emphasizing the arrangement of self and society as economies. In contrasting egoism and altruism we accept the pre-arrangement of a personal and social economy, and the problematic of intro-spection in which these economies are grounded. But a concern with the fit between self and society renders invisible the monistic interest that structures both as economies. I argue that the self-society dyad—which posits a self and a public interest served respectively by egoism and altruism—squeezes out alter-native conceptions of private and public such as those that are unconcerned with the interior of the self or those that understand the private as one's stake in the public. In my treatment of the English seventeenth century I look behind the opposition between self and public interest, to explore what is imposed and what is excluded by that pairing.

The history of changes in the meaning of interest offers insights into changes in the forms of interested life. Despite the continuing complexities and multiple senses of "interest," formerly dominant juridical and existential meanings are currently overshadowed by psychological and prospective uses. The term has strikingly recent and pan-European origins, and derives from the Latin *inter esse*: to be between.[6] The rise of monistic interest suggests a turn away from relations between interested beings. In their accounts of interest, Shaftesbury's introspective hedonism sets the stage for Bentham's own fantastic materialism: both theorists foreground and yet retreat from the viscerality of feeling bodies and their plural concerns. Pleasure and pain in Bentham's scheme are the aesthetic pleasures and pains of Shaftesbury's spectator self, retooled as visions of the future. My reading of Bentham offers an important challenge to his rational-choice heirs *and* their critics, both of whom tend to read him as a crude materialist. I demonstrate that just as Shaftesbury's *Inquiry Concerning Virtue, or Merit* (1699, 1711) counters religious enthusiasm with a secularism that extols the pleasures of introspection, so too Bentham's *An Introduction to* the *Principles of Morals and Legislation* (1780, 1789) and *A Table of the Springs of Action* (1815, 1817) attack the imaginary creations of discourse only to locate materiality in the imagination.[7]

Even the most sophisticated of Bentham's revisionist interpreters have not questioned his appeal to the self-evident viscerality of pleasure and pain. My alternative reading suggests that pain and pleasure for Bentham, like preferences for microeconomists today, are elements of a rhetoric that facilitates our insertion into a project of government and participation in it. The constituents of interest—pain, pleasure, and more generally preference—are taken to name the pre-existing reality to which the economic polity responds. In arguing, by contrast, that the elements of interest are imaginatively composed, I am not asserting that they are merely imaginary. According to Bentham, interest can only be made up of "expectations," a subset of imaginings that are accompanied by a "sentiment of belief" in their probable occurrence.[8] These prospects are produced and arranged by systems of what he calls direct and indirect legislation.[9] Expectations are grounded and secured by a range of institutional measures that join the crucial initiative of the motivated self to the interest of the whole. Thus the process of prospectively imagining the things and relations between us as economic commensurables is a critical dimension of government. And theories that model this process perform a function of government.

Monistic interest is made up of the individual's imagined expectations, and these are constructed by the very regime that maximizes them. The regime is no less liberal for this: it does not frustrate individual goals with collective ones; rather, only individual interests count. The construction of interests is not the work of a self-serving manipulative state; rather, the state is only one cluster of myriad "public" and "private" agencies that produce and coordinate expectations. Moreover, the state is itself subject to a very strict economic regulation. In place of a liberal vision in which government appears only as a protector of the free pursuit of interest, I argue that the free pursuit of interest is itself a mode of government, one that deploys individual imagination and choice as its agents.

It might seem that government through choice is purely instrumental—that the rationality of monistic interest is the "slave of the passions," in David Hume's provocative phrase.[10] Economic government cannot be properly understood, however, if economic reason is confused with instrumental reason. And indeed, many critics conflate the two. Instrumental reason calculates the best or most efficient means to given ends. Economic reason's efficiency is more than instrumental: it moves beyond means to consider the efficiency of ends. According to critics of rational choice, the economic actor is beholden to a set of arbitrary preferences that are merely given and accepted without question; the extent of his or her rational practice involves finding and implementing the best way to satisfy these preferences. From the perspective of critical theory, the economic polity is a kind of technocracy that eschews collective reflection on the ends it pursues, and that focuses only on the continuous improvement of the means to those ends. I maintain, however, that the Kantian assumptions that often inspire such critiques are too confining to appreciate the specificity of economic reason.[11] Armed with Kantian assumptions, one is too likely to approach monistic interest as a kind of incomplete rationality and suggest that its problem is its lack of critical self-consciousness.

At first glance, it does seem as though economic reason directs me to find the most efficient means to do what I wish, whatever that might be. But economic reason turns out to be more complex. Let's assume, for example, that winter weather makes me miserable and I want to escape it. My project, if I approach it instrumentally, is simply to figure out the quickest and most effortless way to accomplish this unquestioned goal. If I approach the problem economically, however, I need to think in terms of a budgeting of fungible and finite resources of time and money, and to think in terms of timing—all of which ideally will involve a thorough reflection on all my other goals and relations. It is entirely possible that rather than subordinate these other goals to my desire to get away, I'll subordinate this desire to them and never go—even though going may be entirely possible in a world of available means, ranging from buying a flight on credit to hitchhiking. Nothing about this process changes if we alter the goal in the example from escaping winter weather to going to a friend in desperate need. Instrumental reason does not challenge ends: it is subordinate to whatever sense of desire or duty rules my will. But for economic reason no desire or duty, no matter how powerful, is sovereign.

Economic reason's challenge to ends is why preference rankings are so important in microeconomic models: my ends, and not only my means, need to be made commensurable with one another. All desires, duties, whims, and preoccupations are brought into an economy of weighed preferences.[12] But any hostility to this apparent reductionism is likely to distract attention from how very demanding the discipline of economic reason is. The good instrumental actor has merely to reflect on alternative means and their relative effectiveness. The good economic actor, however, has to consider these simultaneously with all alternative means to all alternative ends, and simultaneously with the probable collateral consequences of action that produce multiplier and foreclosure effects among these means and ends, and all against the background of a survey of available resources and probable effects on resources. But even as this process might appear to be endless, in fact the process imposes efficiency on decision making itself: economic rationality demands a consideration of the costs of consideration. The potential range and even depth of economic reflection suggest that instead of opposing it to a fuller rationality, we might do better to see economic reason as itself a form of critical self-consciousness. Granted, this form might be parodic—but we fail to understand economic reason if we miss the disciplined self-awareness that it promotes.[13]

Just as no duty or desire is sovereign for the economic actor, similarly no constitution or dominant will is sovereign for the economic polity. Monistic interest circumvents or domesticates sovereign instrumentality to serve economy. I argue that the works of Machiavelli and Hobbes—high-canonical suspects in the development of the theory of the modern state—are not the places to look for a theoretical elaboration of monistic interest. Neither, I claim, is Hume, that arch-suspect in the development of theories of civil society. By looking to received figures and categories we miss the specificity of economic government. For the aggregate interest as for self-interest, any ruling will (no matter how democratic) or rule of custom or law (no matter how republican) must be captured and secured by the logic of economy. This was the reforming task of Bentham's constitutional writings, just as it is the reforming task of the law and economics movement today.[14] Thus we go astray when we try to understand neoliberalism in terms of sovereignty and constitutionalism—when we think that it is about "who rules" or "how much" rulers should rule. Instead, neoliberalism rules in the name of efficiency. My contention is that for neoliberalism, as for Bentham, democracy and individual rights as we know them are not ends in themselves: they are simply the best available means to subject sovereignty to economy in complex societies. We misunderstand neoliberalism if we think that it tilts toward "the sovereignty of the individual" and away from "the sovereignty of the collective." For economic government, the devices of sovereignty are adjustable tools that must enable, without themselves interfering with, the security of expectations and the maximization of interest.[15]

The distinction between sovereignty and government has been well articulated by Michel Foucault. Broadly speaking, sovereignty is a "deductive" or limiting juridical power of right and law, which has no end beyond the preservation of sovereign order; government is a "productive" or constitutive power of policy and incentive, which has as its end the good of the governed. Sovereignty dictates prohibitions and permissions but is otherwise unconcerned with conduct; government doesn't dictate so much as orchestrate conduct. For Foucault, modern Western states have combined sovereignty and government in regimes that have relied for their functioning and reproduction on the presupposition, improvement, and spread of discipline, or training.[16] Foucault's concept of government—analytically separated, as it is, from the state— proves useful for understanding the de-centered economic rule of monistic interest. When it comes to appreciating Bentham, however, Foucault has been part of the problem: he has given new impetus to a vexing and continuing project of misreading. Focusing as he did on Bentham's notorious Panopticon, the Inspection House disciplinary technology of surveillance and self-surveillance, Foucault contributed to a dominant illiberal image of Bentham. Especially in the United States, where readers of Foucault often misinterpret discipline as sovereignty, Bentham is confirmed as a statist architect of unfreedom.[17] Bentham, however, was a strong defender of rights and liberties; he was dismissive only of natural rights, and his fiercest polemics were directed at state inefficiencies and infelicities.[18] Many of his proposals, including the Panopticon prison itself, embraced the "privatization" so much in favor today.[19] Bentham was not a promoter of the state but of government, and the same formula that dismisses him is what allows American theorists to minimize the significance to political theory of neoliberal reforms. Armed with a formula that juxtaposes free individuals against intervening coercive or enabling orders, we worry about Bentham's liberalism—but what we should interrogate instead is liberalism's Benthamism. To what extent does this formula's deductive framework not only misconstrue, but actively presuppose and facilitate, the constitutive power of economic government? To what extent, in other words, might such a formula play an important role in the economic polity's structuring of the very expectations through which it governs?

Liberalism's free individual has traditionally been figured as a subject of rights; neoliberalism has refined this subject to emphasize an individual who is free to *choose*. Under neoliberalism, individual and collective possibilities increasingly appear as a menu of calculable choices, and individuals become intelligible to themselves and others primarily as choosers. The tendency to embrace a sovereign agent of choice as one's starting assumption is especially strong in the United States today. Discourses of Right and Left have converged in recent years to promote choice: from self-help, to community empowerment, to the attack on bureaucracy and expertise, to lifestyle alternatives, to the niche-marketing and personalization of services and systems of security, to the renaming and new flexibility of labor, choice is the watchword. American political theory itself has recently given new emphasis to self-making. Several Commonwealth researchers, by contrast, have treated this emphasis itself as a symptom, by identifying the importance for neoliberal government of the construction and mobilization of an "enterprise self": the self-as-firm who treats himself or herself as what economists have called "human capital."[20] This enterprise self is increasingly manifest across classes and contexts. Among the affluent, work and play become blurred in practices that are treated as neither work nor play but as selective investments: from personal exercise regimens to "quality time" with loved ones to continuous education. And advocates of the poor and even the poor themselves have renewed the narrative that sees poverty not as an economic or political problem but as a behavioral and ultimately spiritual one. Poverty is seen as an effect of bad personal decisions that are themselves the effect of low self-esteem: it is a symptom of an underlying malaise demanding technologies of self-help.[21] As inequalities along many axes increase, everyone—no matter how positioned—is equally regarded, it seems, as someone who can benefit from good choices and suffer from bad ones. Even toddlers and the dying are represented as choice-making self-managers.

Much of the theory and practice informed by discourses of choice implicitly undermines the shared assumption of a sovereign chooser by suggesting the need not only to generate and advertise choices, but to generate and orchestrate a chooser who wants to and can make good choices. Discourses of choice not only map out prospects for improvement or advancement or pleasurable living; they also exhort their targets to be the future-oriented improvers or advancers or pleasure seekers they are ostensibly assumed to be. Here we see an important example of how the economic polity structures expectations: a fundamental expectation generated by discourses of choice is the expectation of the importance of choice itself. The guidance and exhortation that construct the persistent centrality of choice do not occur in a vacuum. Many elements need to be in place for them to resonate. The neoliberal focus on choice presupposes, even as it refines, a system that diffuses goals of maximization within framing economies. Monistic interest models and reproduces such a system. Monistic interest sets the stage for subjects to be continuously intelligible to themselves as choosers.

I can understand myself as a chooser in importantly different ways, of course: as a responsible maker and keeper of commitments, as a chooser of rebellion rather than obedience, and so on. These self-understandings might conform or conflict with the project of choice for the maximization of interest. I argue that the discourses promoting the rise of monistic interest in the English seventeenth century tended to domesticate the less governable construals of choice that they initially relied on, in particular those articulated as antinomian conscience. The reconfiguring of conscience as an adaptable and prudent, rather than rigid or enthusiastic, organ of expectant self-interest was a crucial moment in the prehistory of economic government. Only on this basis could an emerging economic polity reliably structure expectations in the name of each and all. In my reading of Bentham I show how the interest of the self-interested self is arranged by the regime that serves it, through the landscaping of the imagined terrain of prospects. Again, although the state plays an important part, sanctions of state are only one class of factors here. Other sanctions—for example, those provided by what we would now call "the market" and "norms"—are also important. State personnel are themselves organized in accordance with what Bentham called the "junction-of-interests prescribing principle": well applied, this makes it in the interest of state actors to choose that which promotes the aggregate interest.[22]

Economic government does not emanate from a central point.[23] I argue, however, that an incipient logic of economic government was first consolidated in sixteenth- and seventeenth-century Continental writings on reason of state. Reason of state disciplined early modern statecraft and sovereignty, directing rulers to preserve and augment the interest of the state. Reason of state took up and regularized the natural-law justification of prerogative in cases of life-preserving necessity, so that the distinction between matters of necessity and matters of convenience was obliterated when it came to affairs of state.[24] Reason of state demanded a new knowledge of past and present, oriented entirely toward the future and positing a best interest that could be calculated to direct the decisions of statesmen.[25] But reason of state was contained by and served the ruling apparatus that it identified as the state. Monistic interest, by contrast, is concerned with the individual and aggregate interest, and not with the state as such. And it applies not only to statesmen in their capacities as statesmen but potentially to all individuals in their every affair. I argue that the logic of reason of state broke free of emerging state institutions during the long crisis of the seventeenth century. In a revised story of English exceptionalism, I identify the English civil wars as the site for the origins of a new critique of civil arrangements—not in the familiar terms of natural right, but in terms of a new language of necessity and convenience: the public interest. The English "public interest" expressed the adaptation of reason of state to a scene of national apocalypse. Whereas reason of state opposed conscience, the public interest was grounded in it. The struggle to imagine, stabilize, and realize the public interest, and to domesticate the consciences animated by it, proliferated a new logic of rule among individuals. It has recently been argued that the rights-bearing subject was derived by analogy from the rights of states in war and peace.[26] I argue similarly that the subject of interest can be traced to arguments initially applied to states.[27]

Interest of state is monistic with regard to internal affairs, but plural with regard to external affairs. Other states cannot be assimilated into an economy; dealing with them requires a strategic rather than a managerial approach. Not so with the public interest: unlike interest of state, it has no outside. When the public interest was reduced from a contested theologico-political to a contested civil category, and then to a broadly recognized aggregate whole, and when the attack on religious enthusiasm tied conscience to prudence, conditions were ripe for the appearance of economies of self and society ruled by monistic interest. Monistic interest has coexisted, though not always comfortably, with the juridical structures we associate with the liberal state. I demonstrate through Bentham that the logic of economy works to convert laws into tactics of government. The implications of this conversion for contemporary neoliberalism are profound. Like Bentham, neoliberal critics question existing law and forms of rule from the standpoint of efficiency. In renewing the tension between economy and sovereignty, neoliberal reform seems to be paving the way for a global regime of security.[28]

Political theorists—mired as we generally are in defending and criticizing normative liberalisms—have not come to terms with a neoliberalism that continues to shift the ground under our feet.[29] If anything, political theory continues unwittingly to reproduce, in a number of different inflections, the economies of self and society on which monistic interest relies. And traditional history of political thought has tended to take some version of normative liberalism as its object of study, emphasizing its roots in natural rights and contract theory, or possibly civil society and the Scottish Enlightenment. Individual rights and civil society are either celebrated as attributes and sites of autonomy and voluntary cooperation, or castigated for their selfishness and competitiveness. Current efforts to understand global developments as expansions of rights and of civil society rehearse these interpretive limitations. In so doing, these efforts fail to grasp the particular mode of government that neoliberalism deploys.[30]

Not long ago, political theory paid more attention than it does today to utilitarianism, the utilitarian tradition, and the language of interest.[31] But John Rawls and his critics also shifted the terms of debate away from a more explicit engagement with economy. If anything, self and society have become more firmly anchored in subsequent discussions of agency, autonomy, and situatedness. In *A Theory of Justice*, Rawls dismissed "classical" utilitarianism—including Bentham—for lacking respect for persons in lumping them together and thus subordinating their rights to a conception of the good.[32] Rawls's alternative was a normative liberalism that takes organized economies of self and society for granted in a scheme derived from a sophisticated problem of rational choice. Prospective language, and especially the language of expectations, runs throughout *A Theory of Justice*, which deepens choice with added reflexivity by asking its readers to imagine themselves imagining themselves from behind a veil of ignorance. Here any plurality of interests is necessarily conceived of as a plurality of values or subjective goals. And thus something like monistic interest—which is not so much a particular conception of the good as it is a kind of all-purpose purpose—can serve as everyone's goal.[33] Astute critics such as Bonnie Honig have noted a powerful link between introspection and a particular scheme of government in Rawls's work.[34] Honig and others have called attention to the remainders generated and obscured by existing models of self and society, and have noted the conflictual dimensions of individual and collective life in response to theorists who aim to harmonize them out of existence. But conflict is appreciated in terms of the inevitable ruptures and dilemmas that it poses for the reflective subject, and thus choice as forward-looking self-making is confirmed by celebrating an ethic of self-overcoming.[35]

Even Joseph Raz, an especially acute critic of liberal monism, assumes and reinforces the outlines of the economies of self and society that sustain it. Raz argues that Rawls and other contemporary liberals have erred in attributing no intrinsic value to liberty and in refusing to acknowledge its plural sources and manifestations. According to him, liberalism capitulates to monism in the moment when, on pluralist grounds, it refuses to defend the priority of autonomy and so turns attention away from the conditions that effectively promote or suppress it. Raz wisely does not give much specification to liberal ideals that must, as he recognizes, necessarily remain open to diverse interpretations and continual revision. He is a fierce critic of presumptions of commensurability, and his attention to the "social forms" that condition liberty avoids pulling their plurality back into the introspective frame of a choosing subject.[36] But, engaged as he is in a normative-theoretical conversation, Raz still tends to assume that political theory requires the articulation and extension of a moral point of view.[37] Thus he inevitably replicates a procedure inaugurated by the likes of Shaftesbury and Bentham without recognizing, as Bentham does, that this procedure serves a particular project of government. "Who then is the moral person?" Raz asks. "What is the proper relationship between self-interest and moral concern?" Accepting the terms of the question, he answers that "the morally good person is he whose prosperity is so intertwined with the pursuit of goals which advance intrinsic values and the well-being of others that it is impossible to separate his personal well-being from his moral concerns."[38] These issues of the "personal" and the "moral" and their articulation are precisely Bentham's issues; their adoption as premises is a crucial condition for the shaping of politics to serve and produce monistic interest.

Bentham is usually read as a moral philosopher and normative political philosopher; I read him instead as a theorist of government who can help illuminate why it is that our normative perspectives leave us helpless when it comes to recognizing contemporary conditions.[39] Benthamic government is advanced by theories that promote work on a self and its relations to society. This includes even theories like Raz's and Honig's—theories that understand the self as plural or agonistic, and society as comprehending multiple forms or forces of normalization. The preoccupation with self and society and their articulation is not only a preoccupation in normative political theory; it has consumed political science as well. A wide range of choice theory has been directly concerned with economic government as both problem and solution: with how maximizing behavior can fail to generate maximums, and with how this problem can correct itself or be corrected, or at least improved, through policy or institutional design. Here too, theory aimed at disrupting this paradigm ends up by contributing to economic government. Most prominently, Robert Putnam's *Making Democracy Work* concludes that its research on multiple networks and their associative interests is about "social capital": a phenomenon that can ameliorate collective-action dilemmas.[40] Thus what might otherwise be represented as a complex plurality is treated as a fungible resource for securing aggregable expectations. Armies of researchers, many of whom see themselves as opponents of neoliberal trends, are not only busily identifying "levels" of social capital but making policy prescriptions aimed at enhancing it on the basis of their research. Bentham's theory of indirect legislation marks an early formulation of this idea: one that distinguishes positive trust building from sinister associations and that sees the potential for architectural work by officials, scientists, and moralists. Of course, for Bentham there is no dogmatic, qualitative distinction between "private" and "public" policing, as there is in work focused on rights, civil society, and their distinction from the state. The relevant question for Bentham is that asked by rigorous neoliberals today: which policy provides greater benefit at less cost?

Understanding Bentham, then, and understanding the origins and character of monistic interest, will help us to understand the grounds and mechanisms of neoliberal government. Even as neoliberalism reoccupies some of the categories of normative liberalism, it can remain remarkably deaf to liberalism's concerns: for example, it can erase or at least rework the principle of noninterference by recognizing only maximizing activity as free activity.[41] And neoliberalism happily absorbs and transforms some of the premises of sociological liberalism, replacing categories like intermediary associations with social capital, and roles and norms with preferences and signals. Liberalism is relatively helpless before the reoccupation of its categories, because this is less a usurpation of one tradition by another than a development within one tradition. "Liberalism," after all, names a family of doctrines that date not from the seventeenth century but from the nineteenth. Liberalism could not really consolidate as such until it implicitly smuggled in a utilitarian foundation.[42] Bentham is an emblematic transitional figure: a practitioner of neither normative theory nor social science, he was present at the origins of each. He can be read as an inspirational figure for each of the usual periodizations of the liberal state: from the Radical attack on feudal economic protection and political privilege, to the rise of the civil service and professions and the growth of the welfare state, to the contemporary attack on welfare and expertise and the trend toward privatization. My project here is not to read Bentham in terms of any or all of these historical moments, but instead to try to read historical developments in terms of Bentham. I argue that this is best done by reconceptualizing the history of liberal practice as phases in the history of monistic interest or economic government. Bentham's work is open to a range of appropriations; one way of reading this range is in terms of representations of "economy" itself. For Bentham, economy is closer to a formal than a representational principle; to the extent that he violates this formality, he does so in the name of the "four ends" of government: security, subsistence, abundance, and equality.[43] But with the rise of political economy or economics as a discipline, and with the emergence of "the economy," economy has become subject to competing, and arguably increasingly narrow, representations.

Economy must be reconceptualized rather than represented, and reconceptualized in terms of monistic interest. In chapter 2, "Against the Usual Story," I challenge canonical accounts of interest, and make the case for a focus on the specific rationality of monistic interest. I explore exemplary constructions of monistic interest in chapters 3, "Virtuous Economies," and 4, "Imagining Interest," which respectively offer readings of Shaftesbury and Bentham. In chapter 5, "State Rationality," I compare and contrast the economic rationality of monistic interest with the logic of *raison d'état*. The displacement of natural law and alternative representations of interest by public and self-interest is the subject of chapter 6, "The Public Interest." In a concluding chapter, "The Economic Polity," I consider further how an analysis of Bentham illuminates the logic of contemporary (neo)liberal government.

Bentham's essay on indirect legislation promotes fundamental rights, open government and vigorous debate, competitive markets, the hegemony of public opinion, and universal tattooing for identification purposes.[44] Just as it is a mistake to read this as a statist project, it is misleading to characterize it as "illiberal." The ideal that drives Benthamic self-government requires the proliferation of mechanisms that facilitate security: mechanisms that rely, for their proper functioning, on the robust exercise by individuals of their liberty in a relentlessly prospective society. Bentham recognized the usefulness of freedom, and thus theorized a mode of government that exalts the individual imagination and individual choice. And Bentham urged a forward-looking orientation that might sidestep the problem of loss that transcends cost.[45] Technologies of choice are proliferating today in systems ranging from voicemails to pensions; government through choice is a central theme of new management techniques aimed at improving the performances of individuals, households, and workplaces. Choice carries risk for systems and individuals, but risk is calculable.[46] Security is a recurrent preoccupation at all levels. This is no longer, however, the lateral security of groups and states. It is the prospective security of nested economies of governance, with politics understood as productive or unproductive interest-competition rather than as the struggle over incommensurables.[47]

In the following chapter I attack misconceptions about interest theory, especially in relation to major figures in the history of political thought. My purpose in doing so is to make the case for a focus on Shaftesbury and Bentham. This focus puts on display what is more difficult to extract from well-mined sources for the theoretical origins of contemporary politics—from, for example, English political jurisprudence or Scottish political economy.[48] My treatment of Shaftesbury and Bentham thus prompts the alternative histories of chapters 5 and 6. It puts on display the introspective economy that supports our bipolar gravitation toward self and society. In Shaftesbury's *Inquiry* and in a range of Bentham's texts we see how monistic interest translates the persistent plurality of our condition into a pluralism of value: value that can be understood subjectively as the vantage point of the individual imagination and objectively as a social aggregate. And particularly in Bentham's work, we see how this translation is fundamental to an ongoing project of government that attempts—however unsuccessfully and incompletely—to make fuller and fuller use of us through our celebrated freedom to choose.

2 Against the Usual Story

There is a story that springs to mind when we reflect on the concept of interest. If we are aware of the relative modernity of the term, we might think that its history simply reflects the passing of a theological world-view and the rise of a secular and scientific one. One version of this story is a narrative of progress: conflicts have always been conflicts between people and groups with competing interests, but it was necessary in pre-modern Europe to disguise the sources of conflict because of the hegemony of religious thinking and of the church. With the decline of this regime it became possible to acknowledge what had always been the case. The language of interest, on this account, frankly describes the real basis of conflict; it emerged as part of the pluralism and skepticism of an increasingly secular world of states no longer bound to the dictates of the Bible and of Rome. In the turmoil of Renaissance Italy, Machiavelli wrote as the first modern secular theorist who dared to say what was probably generally known: justice and the good are so many fine words deployed in games of interest, and the church is merely another player. Interest is, on this view, what any political analysis should always look to; interest identifies conflicts as involving the aspirations and choices of concrete, living, and striving individuals—whether alone or in groups. These aspirations and choices frequently clash, sometimes leading to violence; in other cases they are resolved through bargaining and strategic agreement. According to this progressive story, Hobbes was Machiavelli's more systematic successor, the first to understand how order and stability can be produced out of an apparently disordered and unstable interplay of interests. Hobbes cast off superstition and sentimentality in clearly seeing a perennial interest-based problem of collective action. And he offered a rational, if severe, solution to this problem: the absolute sovereign as third-party enforcer of rights and contracts.

Alternatively we might narrate many of the same details as a story of decline. Before the era of interest, politics was not a strategic game of individual or group competition for mere power and resources. It was instead an ongoing conversation and contest over the meaning of the good life, set in contexts that respected the limits on individual and group conduct imposed by natural law. On this view, interest was part of a secularizing movement that unleashed a dangerous amorality or immorality into human affairs. Now the ends of power and gain could justify the means to achieve them. Natural law, traditional authority, and any notion of the common good were forever undermined by perspectives that misunderstood the true foundations of individual and collective life. According to this account, Machiavelli justified immoral interest-based state action and princely striving after power, by means of a flawed account of the sources of political order. And the interest-theorist Hobbes justified tyranny by means of an unmoored theory of natural right and a false assumption of human atomism. In both stories, interest's modernity is associated with the likes of Machiavelli and Hobbes, and with the emergence of a new individualism that defines and underpins—for better or worse—the secular institutions of state and market, freed as they are from overarching moral concerns.

The usual story is, in many respects, poor history. But its biggest defect might be the way it assumes, whether in celebration or lamentation, that interest separates conduct from virtue. In other words, it isn't sufficiently attentive to the "virtue" in interest. This virtue might well clash with Christian virtue, but it probably carries even less resemblance to Machiavelli's neo-pagan *virtù*, to either princely virtuosity or to the republican virtue of *The Discourses*. Interest does, however, discipline and focus conduct, and it directs conduct in the pursuit of a good of some sort. Albert O. Hirschman, in *The Passions and the Interests*, has nicely demonstrated this disciplining quality of interest-pursuit.[1] Hirschman shows that one aim of early interest theory was to bridle, rather than liberate, the more dangerous ambitions of late medieval and early modern nobility—by trying to pit their moderate against their immoderate passions. He understands interest as part of an inadvertently revolutionary new scheme of self-government, and attends as I do to peculiar mutations and less prominent texts. Hirschman's question is different from mine, however. He asks how it is that once-reviled passions and pursuits—those related to economic gain—came eventually to be valorized. I ask instead how it is that all pursuits became comprehensible as economic pursuits in a different sense of "economic": that is, how they became governable according to economic rationality. Hirschman's question leads him to focus more on analyses of the passions and particular interests, and less on the civil prudence that is the original virtue in interest. I argue in chapter 5 that sixteenth-century civil prudence—the ethic of the reason of state—implied an interest of state, the forerunner of monistic interest. Hirschman's study of interest as a countervailing passion, by deemphasizing interest of state, obscures the distinction between particular interests and monistic interest. Thus, despite his intent, his work can reinforce the tendency to detach interest-pursuit from the broader regime that structures it. Hirschman's account might also leave us to conclude that interest's rationality is instrumental rather than economic, and so lead us to underestimate the extent of its discipline.

Hirschman does succeed, however, in estranging us from the usual story's high-canon account of interest, which combines flawed and often anachronistic interpretations with flawed assumptions about interest rationality. Machiavelli and Hobbes—neither of whom had much use for the language of interest—are probably better seen as writers to whom theorists of an interest-governed world *respond*. In what follows I briefly discuss Machiavelli and Hobbes to show their distance from interest theory. I also discuss David Hume as another prominent contender for how we might think about interest. Unlike Machiavelli and Hobbes, Hume finds the language of interest important. But Hume's interests are the calm passions analyzed by Hirschman or the plural and opaque interests of civil society: Humean interest is not monistic. I treat Machiavelli, Hobbes, and Hume to make the case for turning to Shaftesbury and Bentham in chapters 3 and 4. In chapters 5 and 6 I give my own account of the history of interest in the sixteenth and seventeenth centuries. Focusing as I do on Continental reason of state and the English public interest, I trace the emergence of a new political rationality. This economic political rationality is consolidated and dispersed with the rise of monistic interest.

Monistic interest joins a new mode of collective government to a new mode of self-government through economy. It might seem peculiar that I do not tell its story chronologically: that I present my alternative account of early interest after the studies of Shaftesbury and Bentham. But my project is complicated by the need to account for the emergence of something that is not generally recognized. Thus I must first establish the distinct identity of monistic interest:

of economy reconceptualized, or economy as government. Only then does it make sense to launch an inquiry into origins.

The Uses of Machiavelli

The concept of interest has been a basic constituent of empirical political science since its disciplinary origins, and many practitioners of this science view Machiavelli as a forerunner. This identification is primarily out of respect for Machiavelli's claim to study the world as he finds it, rather than draw conclusions from reflections on the qualities of religious or philosophical chimeras. The modern appropriation of Machiavelli is in many respects curious; in his discussions of Polybian cycles and the pre-eminence of virtue Machiavelli is closer to the ancients than he is to political science. We do, however, see ourselves in certain dimensions of his approach: Machiavelli is concerned with the collection, from historical and contemporary sources, of useful knowledge, useful toward the establishment of ordered places and their maintenance through time. And in his most influential work, *The Prince*, he reflects on what needs to be done by individuals to maintain and enhance the power manifest in control over such places. Here a connection with later reflections is apparent. But this connection obscures important discontinuities between Machiavelli's work and theories of interest. It makes sense that interest was not, for the most part, a category employed by Machiavelli. In its earliest uses as a specifically political term interest was tied to reason of state. And Machiavelli is a theorist of statecraft, but not of the state. The difference relies, in the case of *The Prince*, on whether the state (*lo stato*) is understood as a possibly mobile instrument of princely power or as a more fixed and permanent territorial apparatus that can itself be served.[2] That *lo stato* should be understood in the former sense only gains additional confirmation through its distinction from the republic and from politics in Machiavelli's work.[3]

To find in Machiavelli the origins of a theory of state interest is a commonplace, and yet one in need of re-examination. The reason for the finding is that interest of state is a basic constituent of the kind of *Realpolitik* thinking that demands the sacrifice of moral and religious considerations to political expediency. The effects of one's actions on an existing order take precedence because this order is among other things the very ground of possibility of religion and morality. This thought is basic to Machiavelli and is what has always scandalized many readers. But although Machiavelli might be lauded from a reason-of-state perspective, there is no such explicit doctrine in his own work. In fact, what makes the Machiavelli of *The Prince* especially scandalous to the modern reader is the lack of *any* requirement to either take for granted or formulate an end such as state interest for political action. Action is, in *The Prince*, preferably directed by the prince in the service of his power. That this end is likely to involve others, among them the commonweal of a principality, is a given; only a peculiar kind of individualism could suppose otherwise. And it is in this assumed connection or involvement between prince, territory, people, and their surroundings that we find the roots of the political theory of interest. There are, nevertheless, profound changes that occur in the movement from Machiavelli's statecraft to the modern idea of the state.

There can be little doubt about the influence of Machiavelli's work on subsequent students of statecraft and the state. Much of this later writing was ostensibly anti-Machiavellian. Machiavelli's name was then as now associated, however unjustly, with violence and despotism. In France alone, works on government, sovereignty, and reason of state, for all their differences, can each be read as responses to Machiavelli that theorize about structures prior to and situating the actions of princes.[4] That these structures—states—were altogether bound up with the person of the monarch during the age of absolutism did not make this development any less momentous. What tied the monarch to the state was *interest*. It might seem that interest simply legitimized princely actions that were formerly subject to prohibition by popes or estates through a variety of spiritual or juridical sanctions. But interest also constrained royal capriciousness by subjecting it to a new rational standard.[5] In the reason-of-state literature, this standard implied a new ethic and a new knowledge, both of which looked to the future.

Among humanist as well as Scholastic writers it was understood that life-threatening emergencies demanded and justified exceptional action. In chapter 5 I will discuss how this natural-law ethic, under the pressure of the Continental wars of religion, generated a special prudence for affairs of state to match their life-preserving importance. The heightened standing importance of matters of state allowed the natural-law ethic to justify a continuous course of preservation and augmentation, blurring the exceptional nature of the doctrine of necessity when it came to the actions of statesmen. What was preserved and augmented was an interest of state.

State interest entailed attention to an apparatus persisting through time, beyond the lives of its subjects and rulers. While the question of which course of action best served this interest was open, the debate was oriented toward discovering a best interest that could be known. The new interest-bearing entity (the state) and its environment (the state-system) acquired increasing fixity. One consequence of this mission and this fixity, in contrast to Machiavelli's doctrine, was the institutional ascent of the advisor, the transition from servant of prince to servant of state. Another was the possibility that anyone, regardless of status, might speak in the name of state interest and claim a minimal legitimacy. Both these consequences are of course implicit in aspects of Machiavelli's own peculiar advising performance. The most profound change from Machiavelli, however, concerned the adversaries against which the new state had to contend. The primary challenge to the prince's virtù in *The Prince* is *fortuna*, the contingency whose unpredictability makes time itself an enemy to order. By contrast, in the later work of writers on interest of state the prince's chief adversaries were foreign states in pursuit of their interests, and domestic factions and individuals who were said to place their private interests above those of the realm.[6] These enemies were knowable entities whose actions could in principle be predicted on the basis of a familiarity with their interests, and who could therefore be countered with a kind of calculus. Thus useful history was less the exemplary history of traditional humanism than it was the diplomat's or censor's report. Machiavellian virtù was not only narrowed and specified but actually transformed, changed from action into what we might call science, charged with the acquisition of a specific knowledge. What was already latent in Machiavelli's own project became increasingly manifest, but not without radically altering the doctrine: the importance of individual *savoir faire* was usurped by the power of the texts of theoreticians and reporters. Students of interest have to employ methods of deduction and observation, and can argue about the best mix of each. The key point is that they rely on methods. And methods are not only distinct from and supplemental to a ruler's virtù; a full reliance on method would supplant virtù altogether.[7]

Hobbes and Interest

Assuming that the contrasts between Machiavelli's work and any interest-based account of politics are clear, and the intellectual history is shown to be a good deal more complicated than the replacement of religious idealism by secular realism, then what about Hobbes? Do we not have in Hobbes the very model of an interest theorist? And again, doesn't he appear to be a quintessentially modern political theorist, replacing theological and collectivist grounds for political obligation by a secular and individualist philosophy based on the interest that everyone has in the avoidance of violent death? Rational-choice theorists of domestic and international politics, for whom self-interest and state interest are axiomatic assumptions of individual and state behavior, look to Hobbes as an early master of their craft. Interest-based analysis is assumed to be fundamentally Hobbesian. Hobbes, however, was not a philosopher of interest. If there was something of this orientation in his goals, there was little of it in his assumptions.

If I assume behavior in the pursuit of interest, it is safe to say that I assume a reflective practice of some sort. When we say that someone acts out of interest we also say that he or she acts in a calculating manner, not spontaneously or from impulse. It is precisely such calculating, however, that is not guaranteed in Hobbes's world. *Leviathan* can be read as a grand attempt to inspire calculation in its readers, to put reason in the service of a common passion so as to arrive at a common conclusion. But the elements of constancy and predictability that are characteristic of calculating behavior are not assumed by Hobbes; on the contrary, it is their absence that makes absolute sovereignty so necessary for any hope of a good life. A big problem, of which Hobbes is fully aware, is that the passion for security to which he appeals exists in widely varying degrees among individuals. Thus it is especially glory-seekers and religious martyrs—who have a frightening lack of regard for their own safety—who most endanger us all, and whose activities must be curtailed in any peaceful, stable regime. The self-interested self is not the problem for political order, but instead part of the solution.[8] At the very least, the lack of faith that his contemporaries are rational in this way separates Hobbes from interest theory.

There is a lot of controversy about the terms of Hobbes's assumptions and recommendations. Here we enter into the issues that have surrounded Hobbes's work, especially *Leviathan*, since its first printing: the politics of Hobbes interpretation. In the seventeenth century the controversy most often focused on whether Hobbes's writings were friendly or dangerous to English institutions—institutions that were for a time very dangerous, even fatal, to one another, making these alignments that much more complex. Today the issues are not wholly dissimilar, but they are couched in concerns about foundations, recommendations, and rhetoric in Hobbes's texts. Is Hobbes a positivist, or, to speak less anachronistically, what does Hobbes mean by "nature" and "natural law"? Does Hobbesian rhetoric frustrate or enable political dialogue? Are Hobbes's recommendations friendly or hostile to the liberty of subjects? These are not my questions; instead I raise a couple of difficulties in Hobbes in terpretation that further undermine attempts to read him as an interest theorist. At the same time, Hobbes's project will be shown to open the way for interest theory in significant respects. As with Machiavelli, it is primarily *responses* to challenges posed by Hobbes that advance monistic interest in particular.

Hobbes grounds his argument for absolute sovereignty in natural law. Preservation of life is fundamental.[9] It is a matter of necessity. This tenet of natural law is traditional.[10] That this natural law would systematically ground political authority in individuals' natural rights is, however, by no means traditional. Hobbes combines, among other things, natural law with extant consent theories and the reintegration of politics into a new (dis)order of nature that represents a clear break with Elizabethan cosmology.[11] In Hobbes's England, the natural law of preservation was still invoked largely as an exception. It was an emergency justification for violating *convention*, for violating rules and agreements made by people for their *convenience* in ordinary times. Hobbes abolishes this exception by making it foundational. Now severe crises, instead of provoking us to consider disregarding conventional rules for a prior need, are generally a reason for clinging to them that much more tightly.[12] And the natural law of preservation, which for Richard Hooker and others had no place in deciding matters of convenience, determines the character of Leviathan, possibly down to its details.[13]

Although it exaggerates to characterize any number of alternative developments at this time as responses to Hobbes, many writers labeled their real or imagined adversaries as "Hobbists." One vocabulary increasingly used by such writers in all camps was that of the "public interest," which potentially conflated matters of necessity and matters of convenience in a newly emerging scheme of evaluation. This scheme received its earliest and most energetic formulations before the appearance of *Leviathan*, from the very religious enthusiasts whom Hobbes opposed. Defending or advancing the public interest or interest of England was fused with serving God rather than Antichrist. Once preservation was understood, as it wasn't by Hobbes himself, as a matter of serving an interest, the exception was abolished and the distinction between action taken on behalf of life and action taken on behalf of the good life was destroyed. In chapter 6 I will examine how, in contrast to Continental writers on reason of state, English writers combined necessity and convenience in the name of a collective interest that focused inward, and that took precedence over a contested state. A similar collapsing of categories was achieved in the name of a new monistic self-interest, which initially emphasized, in response to Hobbists and enthusiasts alike, the transcendental self-interest of each soul in following the dictates of a natural theology.

The peculiar Hobbesian translation of natural law opened a space for interest, but did not fill it. Whatever one makes of his project, Hobbes's insistent voluntarism ultimately separates him from theorists of monistic interest. Two manifestations of this voluntarism are most important: a refusal of the notion that the will is bound by reason, and a reverence for the binding character of the commitments of voluntary agents.

For Hobbes, the will, or "last appetite," is not any more bound by reason than any other appetite. Hobbes is a theorist of passion rather than of interest. Hobbes constructed his theory of obligation as an incitement to calculation, saying in effect, "Before expressing your contempt for this regime, think about the consequences of civil war." He might have wished for rational utility-maximizing actors, but the "rationality assumption," as it is called today, was for Hobbes just another Scholastic absurdity. "The Definition of the *Will*, given commonly by the Schooles, that it is a *Rationall Appetite*, is not good. For if it were, then could there be no Voluntary Act against Reason."[14]

The voluntary act of promising, however irrational, is the form of authoring that is the very basis of Hobbesian authority. For modern interest theorists it makes good sense to enforce a system of promising that facilitates transactions, but it does not make much sense to attribute to the promise itself a binding character.[15] Hobbes looks like one of these theorists when he states that covenants without the sword are void. But the reason he gives for this position is, again, the natural law of preservation. For Hobbes, the keeping of covenants is the basis of all justice, but justice is only a possibility where peace has been established. He asks whether this justice could ever be in conflict with reason, as "the Fool hath sayd." What about all those times when it seems that there is much to gain and very little to lose from breaking faith? Although he makes reference to legal sanctions and the fear they inspire, Hobbes's solution to this conundrum does not rely on a utilitarian scheme of threats carefully measured to outweigh the advantages of all possible unjust actions. Instead, he again relies on the law of preservation. Just as the perception that preservation is at stake supplies the only justification for breaking faith in the state of nature, so preservation is ultimately why injustice must be eschewed by the subject of a commonwealth. The unjust man cannot rely on others to trust him; no one will continue to keep society with a cheat, and without society one has little assurance of survival.[16]

Hobbes's own materialist ontology and emotivist ethics are likely to distract us from the thoroughly juridical character of his project. He is, after all, a contract theorist of political obligation. One example should suffice to illustrate the gulf between Hobbes the jurist and any theorist of interest. Modern readers of Hobbes, perhaps already annoyed by his doctrine that consent under threat of death is no less consent, are likely to misread or discount his insistence that the sovereign can do no injury to the subject. But the sovereign can't do injury to the subject because the sovereign is authorized by the subject, and, understanding "injury" in its root juridical sense, "to do injury to ones selfe, is impossible."[17] It is impossible to be legally guilty of an offense against oneself. This clarification of the author and authority of the sovereign's acts is irrelevant to the modern utilitarian reader, who knows that people can make bad bargains, and who only holds people to them to facilitate bargaining. But the distinction between injury and harm is crucial for Hobbes and his contemporaries.

A tension in Hobbes's work, then, at least from our standpoint, is that the Hobbesian individual, who operates according to a mechanistic psychology of desire and aversion, is fundamentally a juridical subject. Covenants are the glue with which the artificial man, or Leviathan, is constructed out of natural man.[18] David Hume is among those later writers who threw this tension into relief, by taking up Hobbes's psychological project at the expense of the juridical.[19] And in doing so Hume relied on the language of interest. According to Hume, the governed do not submit to their governors out of any contractual obligation, but only because and so long as it is in their *interest* to do so.[20]

Hume and Interest

The example of Hume illustrates the opposition between interest theory and the contract theory of political jurisprudence—between, that is, the subject of interest and the juridical subject.[21] This opposition is blurred or even obscured by rationalist appropriations of contract theory, and by the ambiguities of the language of consent. And it is fundamentally obscured by monistic interest itself, which structures rights as relations while obscuring its own relational character. But for our purposes, it is enough to reiterate that the subject of interest is not bound by commitments per se—only by calculations of advantage or disadvantage.

Although Hume is consistent with interest theory on this point, he is not, however, a philosopher of monistic interest. "Interest" in Hume's writings is not a technical term used with any stipulated precision; insofar as it refers to something involving the interior of the self, it seems to refer to the "calm passions."[22] The "interest" that is opposed to contract as the basis of government is even more elusive. Hume suggests that government generally relies on the "natural" basis of the interests of the governed.[23] These interests typically refer to relations between governors and governed, rather than to self or public interests. The redefinition of nature to include civil interests is very significant, and is common to many writers of the Scottish Enlightenment.[24] It tends, as in Hume, to construct rights as artificial relations underpinned by natural relations of interest. But this naturalization of interest does not necessarily promote economy. For one thing, the conjectural history that is also prominent in this school historicizes naturalized civil society, thus proliferating schemes of evaluation. And interests for these theorists, whether resident in the self or in the situation of the self, extend beyond the reach of knowledge. They cannot be fully subjected to a science of society. Also, Hume and others remain theorists of the passions, no matter how domesticated these passions appear by comparison with Hobbes. And certainly for Hume himself passions, even calm ones, are by definition not themselves rational.

The gulf separating Hume from monistic interest is revealed by considering his understanding of reason. Reason for Hume is strictly instrumental; it might identify means for specific ends, but it does not perform the disciplining function of economic reason. It is instead the "slave of the passions." "Interest" can refer to some of these passions, or to a reflection on "remote" consequences that "in an improper sense we call *reason*,"[25] but interest is not a guaranteed director of the will or otherwise supreme. "Men often act knowingly against their interest: For which reason the view of the greatest possible good does not always influence them." To think otherwise is "the common error of metaphysicians."[26] The writers of the Scottish Enlightenment, including Hume, contributed in various ways to the consolidation of economic rationality: in their indebtedness to and refinement of the self-economy of Shaftesbury's *Inquiry*, their promiscuous use of the new abstraction "society," their working out of mechanics of articulation between these categories, and their promotion of political economy as an art-and-science of government. But as with Hobbes, it is primarily in appropriations of Hume and in responses to him (such as Bentham's) that we see a systematization of psyche and polity by monistic interest.

Despite profound differences, Hobbes and Hume are both theorists of passion rather than interest.[27] Each refuses the rationality assumption, and each deploys the language of interest itself sparingly or unsystematically. There is in Hume, however, the presence of interest as a "calm passion," and this raises the question of how passion and interest relate. In *The Passions and the Interests*, Hirschman sees in the notion of a revised passion the key to the meaning of "interest" in early modern Europe. Interest for Hume is a steady and benign passion; Hirschman argues that in earlier models it was any passion that was promoted for its potential to restrain other passions. Hirschman's account is notable for highlighting the regulatory function of interest. But it leaves obscure what it takes to be the intimate relations among interest, reason, and system. Hume sees no necessary relationship between interest and reason, or between reason and system. How then do we account for monistic interest, where interest supplies, in both self and society, the rationale of a system?

Passions, Interest, Imagination, and Economy

Hirschman asks how it is that economic activity came to be prized, and answers that the initial arguments on its behalf were conservative and political. Interest was a language of restraint. But because the language of interest is flexible, as are models of the passions, Hirschman notes a "semantic drift": "interest" came to refer more and more to the passions and practices that we call economic, when other passions can also serve a restraining purpose (for example, a passion for reputation might countervail incontinence as effectively as greed does).[28] He glosses the problem of this semantic drift by suggesting that the requirements of clarity, regularity of purpose, and reassuring constancy were better met in the emerging economic sphere than they were elsewhere: there was greater potential for peaceful competition or even harmony of interests.[29] And he supplements this functionalist hint by moving from an earlier literature about philosophical psychology (the dynamics of the passions) to a later one emphasizing the political benefits of commerce (commerce polishes manners and forges ties that bind and stabilize, rulers can be restrained by a plan of political economy that mustn't be disrupted). Here Hume as a theorist of the "calm passions" forms a kind of bridge: he took wealth-pursuing passions, proven as countervailers, and argued that they are themselves innocuous and that their satisfaction demands relatively harmless or even beneficial pursuits. Hirschman's story leads him to Adam Smith, whose placement in the narrative allows Hirschman to claim that Smith's legacy effectively buried the countervailing model and the political functions of interest. The psychic role of interest was lost in Smith's blurring of passion and interest, and his monumental emphasis on the material welfare of "society" eclipsed altogether the question of the political benefits of interest-pursuit.

Hirschman supports this conclusion with a quotation from *The Wealth of Nations* that aptly captures the most famous interest-theory of them all: Smith's intoxicating vision of a self-regulating market of producers.

It is thus that the private *interests and passions* of individuals naturally dispose them to turn their stock towards the employments which in ordinary cases are most advantageous to the society. But if from this natural preference they should turn too much of it towards those employments, the fall of profit in them and the rise of it in all others immediately dispose them to alter this faulty distribution. Without any intervention of law, therefore, *the private interests and passions* of men naturally lead them to divide and distribute the stock of every society, among all the different employments carried on in it, as nearly as possible in the proportion which is most agreeable to the interest of the whole society.[30]

Consistently with his narrative, Hirschman emphasizes what have typically been read as components of self-interest ("private interests and passions") but does not emphasize self-interest's monistic partner, "the interest of the whole society." He hasn't offered a historical account of this interest, just as he hasn't noted any functional difference between self-interest, which is another holistic interest, and interest as a countervailing or calm passion. "Society" is an abstraction that is not found with any regularity in English-language sources until the early eighteenth century; before that time "society" meant either a particular association—for example, the Society of Friends—or a condition of fellowship. We must not take this abstraction for granted. Similarly, we must not take its partner, a certain kind of self, for granted. What work do these abstractions do, and what is *their* history?

Hirschman's fascinating framing of the problem of interest and its solution obscures crucial features of monistic interest, features without which we might still ignore, misidentify, or take for granted its categories. Monistic interest invokes economies of aggregate commensurables to be maximized; it structures projects of self and collective government as projects of maximization. Hirschman's focus on the passions in his account of interest is problematic so far as the English and British documentary record is concerned. (And Britain is where he ends up, with what his subtitle implies are "arguments for capitalism.") What are we to make of the troubling incongruity that interest-talk is everywhere in the English seventeenth century, yet surprisingly little of it, especially early on, refers to passions, countervailing or otherwise? Perhaps the evidence demands that we ask a question different from Hirschman's about interest and economy: not what role did interest play in valorizing "economic" passions and practices, but what role did it play in making all passions and practices seem governed or governable by economic rationality?

The claim that individual interest begins as a particular passion does not hold for the English record. It seems more plausible with regard to Continental—especially Spanish, Italian, and French—vernaculars. In the title of a sixteenth-century Italian play, and throughout La Rochefoucauld's seventeenth-century *Maxims*, a "psychological" meaning of interest prevails.[31] Even in La Rochefoucauld, however, it appears that interest is not so much a version of the passion of self-love as it is the soul to self-love's body. Interest is what gives direction to self-love; without interest, passion would be blind.[32] That interest sees and is seen is verified by eighteenth-century Continental writers on aesthetics and morals: the imagination is identified as the organ of interest. This is because interest at the level of the self moves one by means of an image, for example a picture produced by and for the mind's eye.[33] It is the production of this picture that constitutes the reflective moment in this interest, and its pleasing or displeasing character is the force that stirs one in the manner of a passion. In the following chapter, I show how Shaftesbury's *Inquiry* anticipates much of this aesthetic self-interest, and does so in the service of an aestheticized public interest. Self-interest, then, is not so much Hirschman's countervailing or calm passion as it is a particular way in which the self relates to itself as an entire passionate economy, a way that is necessarily mediated by the imagination.[34]

What are we to make therefore of Smith's interest of society, and how do we understand the apparent self-interest that serves and is served by it? By no means did Smith think that everything was governable in accordance with economic rationality: if anything, just stock, as directed by the instrumentality of profit, and wealth (stock's aggregate). Profit is indeed a peculiar goal, in that its realization usually implies its conversion into means for another goal: more profit, and so on. But the prudence that governs profit-pursuit is for Smith one of several virtues. For example, one reason for me to observe economy is so that I can be liberal; liberality is itself a distinct virtue that cannot entirely be subject to prudential calculation, otherwise it wouldn't be liberality. Society's interest is the accumulation of wealth, moreover, not because wealth happens to be the aggregate of individual stock, but because of wealth's many uses. Like Hobbes and Hume, Smith thus opens a space filled by others. In Smith's case, however, we encounter the language of monistic interest, and we can make an argument for the presence of an economic rationality. Hirschman's account begs the question of the sources of this mode of government. But he does provide an enticing short treatment of texts and events that are crucial to answering the question. He identifies Continental reason of state as positing a kind of "rational will," and he notes the proliferation of the language of interest and its peculiar adaptation to describe domestic factionalism in seventeenth-century civil-war and Interregnum England. I argue that it is in the developing consensus around pursuit of the "public interest," and in the ways in which this consensus refigures kingdom and commonwealth, that we can see some of the first traces of the linked and governing economies of monistic interest.

Reading Hirschman on the passions, we might come to the conclusion that the problem of political order is primarily a problem of disciplining disruptive forces that spring from within unruly selves. And we might see interest as one solution to this problem, replacing *ancien régime* constraints that were losing their effectiveness. Interest on this account serves as the regulator of generic selves in the service of generic order. But monistic interest, unlike a countervailing passion, links the interior of the self directly to a particular conception of the whole, to society understood as an aggregate. Monistic interest promotes a type of self-relating practice that does much more than serve this order negatively, by keeping the self in check; it positively promotes the aggregate interest at the expense of alternative relations and alternative forms of association. Hirschman is well aware of this, of course; that is why he turns from the passions to eighteenth-century arguments about the political benefits of commerce, and why he subtitles his book "Arguments for Capitalism before Its Triumph." But because he approaches his material with the usual assumption that the meaning of economy resides in a distinct field of practices, his essay's treatment of interest-passions, commerce, and politics does not link introspection with a distinct mode of government. In the work of Shaftesbury and Bentham we can see a very different interest from the countervailing or calm passion investigated in Hirschman's intellectual history: we see instead an interest that organizes self and society as economies. The attention to countervailing passions preemptively limits interest to a particular function of the self, a function that is no more than a semblance of what we commonly understand by self-interest. Self-interest is much closer to the rational will that Hirschman identifies with interest of state, where the ends that one pursues are not the dictates of a particular passion but instead the demands of a consistent and durable aim or principle. This principle is not entirely divorced from virtue, as many critics of reason of state would insist; instead it incorporates and translates a virtue initially theorized as civil prudence. When eventually transplanted to and transformed in the social self, this prudence does not directly serve the state or state power. Instead it serves self and society structured as nested economies.

Hirschman is himself an accomplished economist. His essay works to uncover what both his colleagues and their critics tend not to see: the political foundations of modern economic thought, and specifically a governmental project embedded in its assumptions. He recognizes that this project and these assumptions go well beyond economics as a discipline and its applications. But his analysis of the governmental project is limited by the disciplinary assumptions of his question about interest, which views economy as a field of practice and not as a governing rationality. And so within economics itself, Hirschman's essay takes us only so far in appreciating the implications of the work of his most ambitious colleagues. Gary Becker, for example, is probably the most prominent and prolific contemporary developer of multidisciplinary applications of economic rationality. Becker is an economist, but he is also a political scientist, a sociologist, and an anthropologist. He is a self-styled economic imperialist; he argues that all human behavior might be better understood through basic assumptions of utility-maximization, stable preferences, and equilibrating markets.[35] This includes all kinds of activities that might not seem to have much to do with markets: from making and keeping friends to doing research to taking a walk in the park. Becker does not use the language of interest, and he theorizes within an insistently positivist framework. But his science suggests all kinds of possibilities for an aggregate interest-maximizing coordination of individual conduct. Becker has not only revolutionized modern economics; he is an important theorist of the transformation of contemporary government.

I have argued that we political theorists will continue to miss the significance of work like Becker's so long as we simply dismiss it or, alternatively, normalize it by casting it as a refinement of a continuous rationalist tradition. What Becker refines is a specific rationality: the rationality of monistic interest. The distance between Machiavelli, Hobbes, Hume, and Smith on the one side, and Becker on the other, is vast. Where then do we look for a fuller understanding of the latter's project? My treatment of Shaftesbury and Bentham investigates the intellectual foundations of Becker's economic rationality. To appreciate the ramifications of Becker's neoliberalism—that is, to understand transformations in contemporary government—we need to turn away from high-canon political thought, and away from theories of the passions. To better understand Becker we need to turn toward the history of monistic interest.

Hirschman presupposes a systematic spatial representation of the psyche in which "economic" drives become privileged elements. He does not call this representation an economy. But it is an economy in the sense which was current during the period under consideration. The economy, understood as a totality of practices of production, exchange, and consumption, did not exist as such in the seventeenth and eighteenth centuries.[36] Instead when "economy" named a site, it named a site governable much like a household. The patriarchal householder, unlike the sovereign, was in and of the household or governed space. And he was subject to a judgment of success or failure measurable by the rules of economy. Hirschman's presupposed psychic space has an ancient pedigree, as does its mirroring of government. But in Shaftesbury's *Inquiry* this psychic space, along with everything else, is a newly abstracted *economy*, and not just by analogy; everything is joined into one universal economic system. And every economy has its interest. Hirschman argues that interest *becomes* economic. What if, instead of becoming economic, interest already is economic? "Economic man"—the creature of self-interest—will remain a mystery so long as he is conceived as being driven by a kind of rational passion. Similarly, he is not simply the product of the privileging of a particular set of practices. The secret to this man is simply that he is economic. The multiple involvements of his interior and exterior lives, and the borders between them, have been resolved into a self-economy that opens toward the future and contributes to a global economy. And economic man is structured and guided by a monistic interest that is not an attribute of any kind, but is instead the very rule of his being.[37]

Monistic interest imposes economy on a self that has been and continues to be figured in a variety of ways. Monistic interest receives an early and comparatively static construction in Shaftesbury's *An Inquiry Concerning Virtue, or Merit*, first printed in 1699. What is beautiful in Shaftesbury's *Inquiry* is a well-ordered "oeconomy"; in the case of the self reflecting upon itself, it is the spectacle of a harmonious economy of affections that is pleasing to the mind's eye. Although inspired by Stoicism, the self-economy of the *Inquiry* doesn't operate in Stoic isolation from political order; instead it is integrated into a similarly economized polity. "Interest," "oeconomy," and "society" are key terms in the *Inquiry*, which links systems, or economies, of everything from parts of organisms to the economy of the universe. My consideration of Shaftesbury is limited and transitional. It is limited in that I only treat the somewhat anomalous *Inquiry*. It is transitional in that Shaftesbury's model is introspective, but not yet prospective, and his organ of introspection is no longer conscience, but not yet imagination. I explore Shaftesbury's text for its introduction of a full-blown interest monism, free for the most part from the ambiguities that beset the less systematic uses of interest found in the writings of contemporaries. A look at the *Inquiry* encourages us to reexamine certain favored dichotomies in the history of modern European thought, dichotomies that obscure the importance of the category of interest and that get in the way of a sound reading of

Bentham. The system presented in this text is very much like a system of natural theology, yet it is explicitly secular. It does not oppose virtue and interest. It is individualist *and* collectivist. Its metaphors are mechanistic *and* organic. It exhibits Enlightenment *and* Romantic tendencies. It is a treatise of morals *and* aesthetics. Its morality praises egoism *and* altruism; its aesthetic is rationalist *and* sentimentalist. It identifies the natural with the civil. And it does all of this quite coherently. Above all, the *Inquiry* shows us the link between interest and economy, and interest's reliance on the pains and pleasures produced by the exercise of an introspective faculty. Such a faculty is essential for the interested creature's relation to itself and, through this relation, to a newly construed society. The imagination becomes the medium for the government of the economic polity of monistic interest.

3   Virtuous Economies

Shaftesbury's *An Inquiry Concerning Virtue, or Merit* (1699, 1711) is commonly read as an inaugural contribution to the eighteenth-century British debate about the naturalness of egoism or altruism, a debate about what its participants would call the moral sense, sympathy, or benevolence.[1] Skeptical about either a transcendent good or the existence of an engaged deity, the British moralists, as they came to be known, were peculiar for their repeated attempts to ground ethical truths in a kind of map of the self.[2] When we explore the contours of the self, do we find a terrain like Hobbes's, where crude emotivism demands supplementation by the sovereign or God, or do we find something more hospitable to sociability? Shaftesbury has traditionally been placed on one side of this question, at the beginning of the century naturalizing altruism, and Jeremy Bentham on the other, at the end of the century naturalizing egoism. Closer readers have noted that a kind of hedonism is what is basic to each, but such moral-philosophy readings miss the significance of a common project. Rather than a mere contribution, the *Inquiry* is one site for the inauguration of the very terms in which many of the questions about it are raised. These terms, I argue, are those of monistic interest.

   The characterization of individual and collective can take and has taken many forms. The modern form that concerns me here is marked by two powerful features, both of which are on exaggerated display in Shaftesbury's *Inquiry*. One feature is a simultaneous retreat into the self and reach for the global at the expense of everything in between. Another is a particular homology and link between individual and collective: the structuring of both by a logic of commensurability and maximization that produces a distinct set of possibilities of antagonism or complementariness between them. In the introduction I argued that these features are powerfully present in contemporary theory and practice. In chapter 2 I argued against conflating monistic interest with canonical theories of statecraft, sovereignty, rights, passions, and civil society; and I reformulated Albert O. Hirschman's stimulating insight that interest-theory figures in the slow accretion of a mode of government that we no longer recognize as such. In this chapter I explore an early construction of the social self of liberal government. The *Inquiry* arranges terms in relations that eventually come to be basic to the presuppositions of a broad stream of liberalism and social science. Individual and social whole are elevated at the expense of individuality, plurality, and intermediate association; virtue, interest, pain, pleasure, and an introspective spectator-self are connected without recourse to natural law, and in a manner that anticipates but does not realize the economic government developed in the work of Bentham. Canonized in the history of moral philosophy as an argument supporting altruism against egoism, the *Inquiry* is one of the places where such an opposition is generated. If we read it as a work of political theory, we can see how it effects a reorientation in government, by displacing religious enthusiasm—what we would now call "fanaticism," or perhaps "fundamentalism"—with a noble enthusiasm for virtue. The *Inquiry* demonstrates how a monistic construal of interest plays a crucial role in the rise of the vision of a polity figured as and ruled by economy.

The meaning of "interest" and its prevalence had undergone significant change before Shaftesbury's writing. In the English seventeenth century, various constructions of interests were overshadowed by and assimilated to a new interest of the whole, relating this whole to itself and its parts. Before the civil wars, "interest" was used primarily in a rather restricted juridical sense, to refer to a particular right or claim in a world of overlapping and intertwined rights and claims. This juridical interest was overlaid with others, and overshadowed by the "public interest." The public interest was a battle cry in the wars; it appropriated and transformed Continental interest of state and its translation of natural law to fit a context of apocalypse. For the more enthusiastic soldiers of the public interest, preserving the nation was fused with preserving its souls, and with advancing the "interest" of God. The new interest of the whole was reoccupied in a variety of ways, but it continued and continues to suggest an interest prior to the state that implies a general rule of governance. "Self-interest" organizes the self as a whole, and as a component of the larger whole. Self-interest, like the public interest, is never plural; it reduces notions of private interests and multiple relations to a single economic—etymologically, a householding—relation of the self to itself. As the ruling principle of self or whole, singular interest overwhelms prior distinctions and limits. Nothing is *a priori* indifferent to interest. Rule by interest is neither rule by will nor rule of law; without resolving the paradox of a rational will, it breaks the bounds of this Scholastic theologico-political opposition. Interest challenges law with a kind of prerogative, and prerogative with a kind of law. As we will see in the work of Bentham, interest is the ideal language in which to express, justify, and direct the potentially infinite and ever-changing reach and requirements of society and its restless, forward-looking members.

The basics of a new scheme are on display in Shaftesbury's essay. The scheme is starkly at odds with Hobbes's state of nature, as it is with Hume's interest-plurality. Here the order is an economized natural society, a system fully organized under a ruling principle of interest. There is no civil society or economy in the modern sense; there are no levels with different logics between the whole and the economized selves that are its parts. And the parts illustrate the relationship of this economic scheme to a kind of sentimental introspection, a retreat into the self that under the rule of interest reduces all relations to an aesthetic experience of pleasure or pain. Pleasures and pains are the pleasures and pains of spectatorship, of a spectator self turned inward. This aestheticization of interest marks a final conquest of any remaining distinction between what is necessary and what is convenient: the necessary is absorbed into the fitting, good, or beautiful. And this is achieved by way of a theory that appears to celebrate plurality and sociability over religious monism and the fancies of the isolated self: the *Inquiry* praises fellowship and condemns theological self-interest. Versions of Shaftesbury's spectator can be found throughout the eighteenth century. Bentham's interest theory is based on this type of reflection, but in Bentham this self-relation is integrated into a theory of action and motivation that can serve as the basis for scientific government. In Shaftesbury's *Inquiry*, the link between the introspective pleasures and pains of the self and the harmony and felicity of the whole seems to be guaranteed by the rational design of the creation—by a species of deist providentialism. That which is good for society is pleasurably beautiful, and that which is bad is painfully ugly, for everyone including the most incorrigible evildoer. In Bentham's work the guarantee is issued by systems of training and incentive that target his designated faculty of spectatorship, the imagination, in a way that both establishes its dominance and assures its activity to be always already social. Bentham's theory of discourse and art-and-science closes the circle by establishing his political science itself as an instrument of government.

My emphasis here on a kind of solipsistic economy will seem peculiar to those familiar with Shaftesbury's role as an early theorist of the public sphere. Shaftesbury's political allegiances changed over his lifetime, but he was from beginning to end a partisan of *society*, an entity free from identification with either church or state. Thus he is associated with "polite Whiggism," with a movement to find in manners and the insulated sites for their exercise, and in deliberative norms and forums in particular, the means for promoting an independent public of polished social individuals.[3] This is a project with multiple and ambiguous consequences. By focusing exclusively on *An Inquiry Concerning Virtue, or Merit* I am privileging the moment of integration of individuals into a body, society, ruled by a single interest. This should not be taken as a reading of the life and work of Shaftesbury, a figure rightly associated with the cultivation and celebration of an emerging public sphere of performance and criticism. My treatment should be taken, however, to raise some questions about contemporary contrasts that are prevalent in public-sphere literature. What might it mean if this distant theorist of publicity and public reason is also a distant theorist of desire, managerialism, image politics, and the search for authenticity?[4]

Whatever its shifting status in Shaftesbury's other writings, the term "public" in the *Inquiry* has nothing to do with a condition of publicity, with a particular sphere, or with particular roles or aspects of people or things. Here it is used interchangeably with "social," "natural," and "species," and all these terms refer to the whole taken as a whole, and as an aggregate of everything within it. Thus the "public interest," which might seem a quintessentially political notion, is indistinguishable from the interest of the economy or system of the whole; it is the interest of natural society. The public interest of the *Inquiry* is an aestheticized version of the public interest of seventeenth-century political debate. That mode of imagining was initially stimulated by religious enthusiasm: enthusiasm Shaftesbury laments, that turns individuals' attention away from their worldly relations.[5] In *A Letter Concerning Enthusiasm* (1708, 1711), Shaftesbury presents a nuanced and irony-laden critique of enthusiasm suggesting that his *Inquiry* is itself inspired by enthusiasm, a "noble" enthusiasm of superior quality and effect.[6] But if to turn away from *inter esse*—from being between things— is to turn away from worldly relations, we will see that the monistic interest of Shaftesbury's *Inquiry* has something in common with the very rigorism he condemns.

Reading the *Inquiry*

The *Inquiry* has virtue as its object of inquiry and has several striking features:

—It is one of the earliest texts in English to use the term "society" in its modern sense. Even in the work of Shaftesbury's tutor, John Locke, society is still a particular association or a general condition of fellowship.

—It is riddled with the language of "oeconomy," and establishes multiple economies or systems in an exhaustive hierarchy that culminates in the economy of the universe.

—Each of these economies has an "interest" that it naturally pursues.

—Virtue is for the most part identified with the interest of that economy or systemic whole of which any virtuous entity is a part. Shaftesbury's essay explains how virtue is to the advantage and enjoyment of the virtuous creature.

That virtue is its own reward is an ancient and enduring ethical theme. What is distinctive here is what we might call Shaftesbury's ontology, and in particular how it is, on his account, that virtue rewards. Moral philosophy and natural philosophy—only recently distinguished from one another in more pious literature—are combined within a eudaemonic system that is explicitly secular.[7] This system provides a framework for, among other things, resolving the perceived conflict between virtue and commerce: excessive luxury does come in for condemnation, but luxury is naturalized as a passion, and the contribution that it and other "self-passions" make to society is recognized and affirmed. Shaftesbury provides categories for the scientific Whiggism of the Scottish Enlightenment, and in particular for the fuller overcoming of the conflict between virtue and commerce in the works of David Hume and Adam Smith.[8] He introduces the moral sense developed by Francis Hutcheson, the introspective pleasure of which is, in the *Inquiry*, the virtuous self's reward.[9] With his system, Shaftesbury opens the way to a more radical resolution of the tension between virtue and commerce than that accomplished by his Scottish successors. In this text we can see the groundwork laid for a strictly utilitarian conception of value and personality that transcends the paradigms of wealth and corruption altogether by finding a common source for what others would later distinguish as economic and aesthetic value.[10]

In the *Inquiry*, Shaftesbury describes the order of nature and its goodness, which consists in the way each part serves both itself and the system of which it is a part. Systems are made up of parts that are themselves systems, and all are folded into the universal system. What is truly good or ill in an individual creature is not the help or harm done by it to itself and the system of which it is a part, but the helpfulness or harmfulness of its affections or passions. These can be helpful or harmful to the creature itself, to its species, or to the entire "animal system" or oeconomy of which all species of creatures are parts.[11] The passions themselves make up an "inward anatomy," also an economy, that must be finely balanced to serve the well-being of the creature and its species.[12] Human beings only, and not other animals, are capable of virtue or merit; this is because of their ability to *reflect* on their passionate economies.[13]

In his discussion of human affections and their effects, Shaftesbury uses the term "species" in much the same way as he uses "natural," "social," and "public." The natural or social affections are those that serve the interest of the whole—of the species, of the public, of society. These include the clumsily named "natural affection," as well as "parental kindness," "zeal for posterity," "concern for propagation and nurture of the young," "love of fellowship and company," "compassion," and "mutual succour." They all relate the individual to the social whole in the same way that body parts relate to a bodily whole.[14]

Individuals have their separate "self-systems" (Shaftesbury's term)[15] that are served by the "self" or "private" or "home" affections. Examples of these affections are "love of life," "resentment of injury," "appetite for nourishment or means of generation," "emulation," and "indolence." Also present here is an affection called "interest." Interest is a passion that serves private interest. This is not redundant. It expresses the difference between interest understood as a particular passion and interest understood as the ruling principle of the self-system. This latter interest, which is not a passion so much as a relation, is a monistic interest that is perfectly homologous with the interest of society.[16]

It is crucial that there be neither too much nor too little of the self and natural affections. If these are not in balance it can easily lead to the individual's misery or ruin. Private affections are a necessary but not sufficient condition for the exercise of virtue; virtue demands the involvement of the social affections as well. Immoderation in the force of affections is vicious, and moderation must be judged with reference to the specific passionate economy of the individual concerned. These economies will especially vary by type—male and female, young and old, and so on—that is, each type will have a different mix of passions requiring different amounts of any particular affection.[17]

There are some passions, however, that serve neither the public interest of the species nor the private interest of the individual. These are the "unnatural affections," which are wholly vicious. They include "delight in beholding torments," "delight in what is injurious to others," ungrounded "ill-will," "envy" of the happiness of others when it does not affect our own, and simple misanthropy.[18]

Is there not a reward of pleasure, though, in the satisfaction of these and other wholly vicious affections? Shaftesbury maintains that this apparent pleasure is really the cessation of pain; anyone beset by such passions is in a state of torment, and the relief from gratifying them is only temporary.[19] And in any case, the pleasure that the reader may suppose comes from the gratification of a passion, no matter how noble that passion, is not the pleasure of virtue. Understanding the basis of real pleasure will give us insight into how it is that virtue is its own reward. Nine-tenths of pleasure is not physical but mental. And, it seems, all mental pleasures either result from or already are social affections.[20]

Contemplative delights, for example from doing geometry, are social in that they result from an appreciation of the ordered harmony of the whole.[21] But better still are the pleasures of "virtuous motion." The pleasure derived from virtue is not exactly from practicing it; rather, one first enjoys the sensation of being moved by a social affection, and then experiences pleasure in observing the beauty and proportion of the virtuous act.[22] Thus it is related but superior to the speculative pleasure of mathematics. Here, "together with the most delightful Affection of the Soul, there is join'd a pleasing Assent and Approbation of the Mind to what is acted in this good Disposition and honest Bent. For where is there on Earth a fairer Matter of Speculation, a goodlier View or Contemplation, than that of a *beautiful, proportion'd* and *becoming* Action? Or what is there relating to us, of which the Consciousness and Memory is more solidly and lastingly entertaining?"[23] The beauty of one's good acts will entertain one in one's memory long afterward. Most enjoyment is the aesthetic enjoyment of *spectatorship*, and in particular this distinctive spectatorship of the mind reflecting on itself.

At this point in his discussion of pleasure Shaftesbury actually introduces the figure of the theater. After an intervening paragraph on the superiority of the "kind" to the "vulgar" affections in the "passion of love between the sexes," he elaborates on the relationship between the social or natural affections of whatever stripe and mental enjoyment, a relationship that dissolves into identity:

> We may observe, withal, in favour of the natural Affections, that it is not only when Joy and Sprightliness are mix'd with them, that they carry a real Enjoyment above that of the sensual kind. . . . Where a Series or continu'd Succession of the tender and kind Affections can be carry'd on, even thro Fears, Horrours, Sorrows, Griefs; the Emotion of the Soul is still agreeable. . . . For thus, when by mere Illusion, as in *a Tragedy*, the Passions of this kind are skilfully excited in us; we prefer the Entertainment to any other of equal duration. We find by our-selves, that the moving our Passions in this mournful way, the engaging them in behalf of Merit and

Worth, and the exerting whatever we have of social Affection, and human Sympathy, is of the highest Delight, and affords a greater Enjoyment in the way of *Thought* and *Sentiment*, than any thing besides can do in a way of *Sense* and *Common Appetite*. And after this manner it appears, "How much *the mental Enjoyments are actually the very natural Affections themselves.*"[24]

Pleasure is predominantly mental, and mental pleasure is the pleasure of a spectator-self that is moved by what it sees. And it seems that the play in which this spectator is absorbed is the play of the self's own emotions.

Shaftesbury appears to mitigate this self-absorption in a subsequent passage that is ostensibly about the importance of fellowship. Yes, mental enjoyment and natural affection are identical, but pleasure is also a consequence of this affection. Thus by way of this social affection we can enjoy others' happy "gestures, voices and sounds." And we have in addition, as virtuous selves, "*A pleasing Consciousness of the actual Love, merited Esteem or Approbation of others.*"[25] The former seems to be a direct enjoyment of fellowship; the latter is reflective, but not necessarily introspective. Shaftesbury calls these the "two branches" of mental enjoyment, but the predominance of the latter and the ultimate inadequacy of both become clear as the discussion proceeds. True natural affection relates to the social whole, and any partial affection is inherently unnatural and vicious:

> As PARTIAL AFFECTION is fitted only to a short and slender Enjoyment of those Pleasures of *Sympathy* or *Participation with others*; so neither is it able to derive any considerable Enjoyment from that other principal Branch of Human Happiness, *viz. Consciousness of the actual or merited Esteem of others*. For whence shou'd this *Esteem* arise? The *Merit*, surely, must in it-self be mean, whilst the Affection is so precarious and uncertain. What Trust can there be to a mere *casual Inclination* or *capricious Liking?* Who can depend on such a Friendship as is founded on no moral Rule, but fantastically assign'd to some single Person, or small *Part* of Mankind exclusive of Society, and *the Whole?*[26]

Fellowship is important not as a condition but as a feeling, and it must be a feeling for and with the whole of society. And mental enjoyment is ultimately found in the easy temper and quiet mind—"*as can freely bear its own Inspection and Review*"—of the individual possessing the proper balance of affections.[27] In the final analysis, then, it is the imagined connection with mankind that matters; seeing this within oneself is what provides one with pleasure.

All creatures capable of virtue are forced by reason's reflective capacity to engage in a continual "self-inspection." Vanity, it seems, is an aid to virtue. "The vainer any Person is, the more he has his Eye inwardly fix'd upon himself; and is, after a certain manner, employ'd in this home-Survey."[28] In his discussion of this psychic housekeeping, Shaftesbury at last introduces "conscience"—a term that had been thoroughly politicized by many generations of Dissenters. There is a natural conscience that exists regardless of religious conscience, and the former is the foundation of the latter. This natural conscience appears to be equivalent to the natural moral sense introduced early in the essay, a sense tendentiously attributed even to atheists.[29] Conscience is not an active organ that searches for and receives divine communications. Nor is it an unreachable, private part of the self that must remain outside the scope of power. Conscience, for Shaftesbury, is affected in prudential as well as moral matters;[30] and though discussed directly as a disapprover of immoral and imprudent affections and acts, conscience not only despises deformity and ugliness and the unnatural, it enjoys proportion and beauty and the natural. Conscience is passive, a spectator—a spectator with an impeccable natural aesthetic. "In whatever manner we consider of this, we shall find still, that every reasoning or reflecting Creature is, by his Nature, forc'd to endure the *Review* of his own Mind, and Actions: and to have Representations of himself, and his inward Affairs, constantly passing before him, obvious to him, and revolving in his Mind. Now as nothing can be more grievous than this is to one who has thrown off *natural Affection*; so nothing can be more delightful to one who has preserv'd it with sincerity."[31] Whatever name we give to this spectator, we know that its eye is turned toward the interior of the self, and that it constitutes the link between virtue and its reward. Introspective virtuous enjoyment has manifold ancient sources, and the hostility of the *Inquiry* toward partiality and reduction to self and whole may seem to many readers like nothing more than Stoic excess. What concerns me here, though, is the deployment of this radically introspective model of the self as the foundation of a natural philosophy of society.

The Conclusion of the *Inquiry* shows just how peculiar is the philosophical foundation of this economic self in economic society. Here Shaftesbury claims for his results the demonstrative certainty of mathematical proofs. He has engaged in a "moral arithmetick" the results of which are indubitable:

> For let us carry *Scepticism* ever so far; let us doubt, if we can, of every thing about us; we cannot doubt of what passes *within ourselves*. Our Passions and Affections are known to us. *They* are certain, whatever the *Objects* may be, on which they are employ'd. Nor is it of any concern to our Argument,

how these exteriour Objects stand; whether they are Realitys, or mere Illusions; whether we wake or dream. For *ill Dreams* will be equally disturbing: and a good *Dream* (if Life be nothing else) will be easily and happily pass'd. In this Dream of Life, therefore, our Demonstrations have the same force; our *Ballance* and *Oeconomy* hold good, and our Obligation to VIRTUE is in every respect the same.[32]

Shaftesbury's other writings are liberally sprinkled with moments of skepticism, irony, and ambiguity that are for the most part missing in the *Inquiry*. In this text he suggests that Hobbesian introspection (refined by Lockean reflection) can produce results that answer Cartesian skepticism not with a theory of knowledge but with a eudaemonics anticipating Bentham's claim that the sensations of pain and pleasure are more real than anything else. This real pleasure and pain is aesthetic pleasure and pain, the purest forms of which may well be found in good and bad dreams. The things that pass "within" us need not grasp any "Realitys" to produce effects that count, effects that are as real as anything can be.

A Very Private Public

How is it that this theorist of natural sociability offers such a private, even solipsistic vision? And can he not see the problems that might arise from a reliance on this vision? For Shaftesbury, the affirmation of society and the retreat from it are part of one and the same movement. We have seen this already in the stipulation of society as a natural whole in the *Inquiry*. In his *Sensus Communis: An Essay on the Freedom of Wit and Humour* common sense is maintained in the "raillery" and opinion that are defended against zealotry and narrowness of spirit. Yet in his *Soliloquy, or Advice to an Author* public speech is treated with great suspicion, and self-examination is recommended as the only way to anchor the self against the fancies stirred up by others.[33] Although these positions are not necessarily contradictory, they betray a deep ambivalence in Shaftesbury's work about spectatorship and social life, and their relationship to a now fundamental, yet problematic, faculty of the imagination.[34] This ambivalence was evident in the comment on tragedy quoted above. The passions, however natural, can be manipulated by "skillful illusions."

Shaftesbury betrays a similar ambivalence about the imagination in relation to virtue and commerce in the *Inquiry*. Under the heading "interest,"[35] the compatibility of acquisitiveness and virtue is affirmed: "NOW AS to that Passion which is esteem'd peculiarly *interesting*; as having for its Aim the Possession of

Wealth, and what we call a *Settlement* or *Fortune* in the World: If the Regard towards this kind be moderate, and in a reasonable degree; if it occasion no passionate Pursuit, nor raises any ardent Desire or Appetite, there is nothing in this Case which is not compatible with Virtue, and even sutable and beneficial to Society. The publick as well as private System is advanc'd by the Industry, which this Affection excites."[36] Should industry give way to passionate pursuit, it will do more harm to the individual than to the public.[37] Here Shaftesbury's concerns about desire resemble many earlier and contemporary reactions to the corrupting effects of money; he holds on to a distinction that recalls the Aristotelian one between good and bad acquisition. "Who knows not how small a Portion of worldly Matters is sufficient for a Man's single Use and Convenience?"

> There is little need, on the other side, to mention any thing of the Miserys attending those covetous and eager Desires after things which have no Bounds or Rule; as being out of *Nature*, beyond which there can be no Limits to Desire. For where shall we once stop, when we are beyond this Boundary? How shall we fix or ascertain a thing wholly *unnatural* and *Unreasonable*? Or what Method, what Regulation shall we set to mere Imagination, or the Exorbitancy of Fancy, in adding Expence to Expence, or Possession to Possession?[38]

The new natural religion of Shaftesbury's virtuous economy of society prepares the way for a more complete overcoming of the opposition between virtue and commerce. Shaftesbury's moral sense as a spectator-self bringing universal standards into individual psychic economies is a frequent figure in the writings of, among others, leading figures in the Scottish Enlightenment; by the time we get to Smith's impartial spectator there is even less doubt that this new conscience is furnished by society. In much of this writing the space of appearance is theorized *within* the self;[39] the spaces between selves provide rich metaphors, but these are for the most part transplanted into the relationship of the self to itself. Whatever remains of irreducible plurality in Smith—and much does—is fully transformed in Bentham's work. There the unbounded imagination that so concerns Shaftesbury is harnessed by an administrative apparatus whose tools are direct and indirect legislation, and whose material is a collection of actively self-interested selves. Bentham's regime operates in the service of national felicity, a goal that in the relatively closed, timeless, and perfectible universe of Shaftesbury still has limits, limits that cease to exist for an infinite universe ever open to and driven by the future.[40] In Bentham's world each individual is turned inward toward an imagined future that is interest. In Bentham's ideal, techniques of government will succeed in harmonizing these images, will reinforce the orientation and set the limits of individual projections by both stimulating and regulating the imaginations of subjects. Shaftesbury's social system and divided home-inspecting selves provide the basic materials for Bentham's projections; Shaftesbury's fears about skillful illusions and the restless pursuit of the future become the basis for utilitarian hopes for the administration of a better and better world.

Unworldly Interest

Shaftesbury's *An Inquiry Concerning Virtue, or Merit* helps set the terms for the fitting of incommensurables to an order of aggregable interest. It links this new order directly to a particular construction of the self, a self whose standard is a kind of proto-authenticity, the self-possession of the feeling individual. My pleasure and pain, at least, are my own: I feel therefore I am. But are these feelings my own? The pleasure that is the measure of self and social interest is of a particular kind. It is, first of all, the aesthetic delight of spectatorship. For Shaftesbury, that we enjoy what is virtuous, that it is beautiful, seems to be guaranteed by the fundamental harmony of the original creation, a creation that has provided us with common organs of sense and the potential for virtuous passions to please them, and that has arranged matters so that the actions that result from these pleasing passions contribute to the good of the whole. The presumption of a prearranged correspondence guaranteeing the universal validity of subjective enjoyment seems to be broadly characteristic of early British aesthetics.[41] But what is not so common is the strict association of this enjoyment with introspective experience, where it is our own passion, and not anything external to us, that is beautiful. Shaftesbury's doctrine relies on providential correspondence, but this correspondence does more than guarantee the validity of aesthetic judgment. For Shaftesbury, enjoyment is predetermined by the interest of an economized social self. For Bentham a providential arrangement will no longer be necessary to secure this determination. Not a watchmaker God, but mechanisms of security provided by, among other sources, the market and the state, will guarantee the validity of expectation as interest.

In its purest form, then, monistic interest relates its subjects identically to separate aggregable worlds, whereas interests could be and have been represented to relate their bearers differently to a common world. To the extent that monistic interest drives us, our situation is analogous to—but possibly more put-upon than—the situation of anxious souls obsessed with their fate in the hereafter. Throughout his writings, Shaftesbury's polite Whiggism attacks religious enthusiasm, and does so as part of a concerted effort to replace prophetic by social identity.[42] I have suggested that this alternative, at least as displayed in the *Inquiry* read by itself, might in turn be charged with other-worldliness. Shaftesbury's own words against preoccupation with the afterlife are instructive: "Other Interests are hardly so much as computed, whilst the Mind is thus transported in the pursuit of a high Advantage and Self-Interest, so narrowly confined within our-selves. On this account, all other Affections towards Friends, Relations, or Mankind, are often slightly regarded, as being *worldly*, and of little moment, in respect of the Interest of *our Soul*."[43] This critique of transcendental self-interest applies to all interest monisms. Caught up in the rule of interest, we can remain blind to our interests. This might be the case whether the monistic interest we follow is that of the virtuous economy of society, the prudential economy of the self, or—as the author of the *Inquiry* and many others would have it—both at the same time.

4 Imagining Interest

How does monistic interest govern? The scheme of Shaftesbury's *Inquiry* was static and focused on the self's relationship to itself; his ethics were perhaps a negative, but not yet a positive political project. Jeremy Bentham, on the other hand, was a decidedly political theorist. From his attacks on Blackstone's legal theory in the 1770s to the constitutional work of the 1820s, Bentham's voluminous writings addressed the problem of government and contributed to a project of government. When we examine this project, we see that Bentham adapts Shaftesbury's radically economic premises to a framework that rescues them from their poles of solipsism and universalism. Bentham stabilizes and mobilizes the introspective dissolution of the divide between reality and fantasy in the *Inquiry* with a theory of law that relies on a distinctive antirhetorical rhetoric. "Interest" is a key term for this rhetoric, and its relentlessly monistic deployment is basic to Bentham's legal and political science. He presents interest as foundational: it is the origin, ground, and purpose of human action and good government. Interest is ostensibly pre-political, arising from a world of pain and pleasure flows among mobile sensitive creatures and between them and their environments. Thus it is commonly assumed that Bentham advances a materialist naturalism. But the problem with the pains and pleasures of interest, given this explicit presentation, is that they are visions of the future at least once removed from one's psychosomatic condition. We will see that the pleasures and pains that make up interest turn out to be specific products of the imagination. Law in Bentham's work functions to fix the specificity of the imagination's products—to fix expectations. I thus argue that interest is not pre-political; and it is not simply the goal of good government; it is, additionally, produced by and used as a tool of government. Ultimately, monistic interest not only describes and evaluates conduct but arranges it as well, and arranges it in and for a flexible program of economic government.

Defenders and critics alike have long recognized the central importance of the term "interest" in Bentham's writings. They can see that he is, following Hume, for better or worse offering interest as a substitute for natural rights or for some other test of political obligation and state legitimacy.[1] But in their attempts to get interest right—to fix its referents and establish its grounds—they persist in getting it wrong. Its centrality in his work explains the scramble to point to what Bentham's interest names, to confirm or disconfirm if what it names is correctly named, and to judge whether such a thing should serve as the foundation of government. This chapter will demonstrate that these lines of criticism seriously underestimate the scope of Bentham's achievement. In his work, interest is always already the construct of a regime: the utilitarian regime produces its own foundation. Diverse writers criticizing classical and neoclassical liberal approaches have long been making this very kind of point: one that does not accept the opposition between interest and value and the clean divide between the empirical and the normative that often goes with it. But they do so in a way suggesting that their opponents' arguments are confused. My argument is that Bentham's work makes use of what such writers pose as criticism. Bentham is not at all confused, just far more subtle than his critics suppose.

Friends and enemies take seriously Bentham's hedonic philosophical materialism, and on this basis his psychology and ethics of interest are either defended from, or attacked with, the charge of reductionism.[2] They take seriously his frequent resonances of their own constructions of the social, and on this basis the politics of interest is the politics of freedom for those who see natural harmony in Bentham's regime, and the politics of dictatorship for those who see artificial harmony there.[3] All these positions presuppose interests that either are or are not accurately represented, and are linked either malignantly through coercion or benignly through consent. Bentham does much to encourage these readings: he proffers interest as the focus of a hard-headed materialism and rigorous realism. He does this in part by way of contrast; he lampoons, for instance, natural-rights doctrine as mere discourse that appeals to imaginary figures, or "nonsense upon stilts."[4] But despite this foregrounding, Bentham's writings themselves grant to discourse a constitutive role in government, and do so precisely by defining interest as a product of the imagination. This of course does not mean that interest is merely imagined.

Hanna Pitkin takes Bentham criticism to task for assuming coherence where none is to be found. She finds in Bentham a fundamental "slipperiness": one that changes the meanings of key terms like "interest" depending on context. Bentham, she charges, often uses narrower meanings to distinguish utilitarianism from the doctrines it criticizes, and uses broader meanings to defend against possible rejoinders.[5] But despite her criticisms of them, Pitkin takes the path of other critics by trying to ground Bentham's vocabulary in the world of political experience. The difference is that she suggests this is a dead end, because there is too much "slippage" here to be conclusive. If we take another path, and read Bentham more closely, we see that Pitkin is wrong: there is slippage in Bentham's vocabulary, but this slippage is remarkably systematic. Bentham's vocabulary consistently gestures toward concrete experience, but his arguments identify the imagination as a crucial site for the production of materiality. When this move is recognized, and its relationship to his governmental project is clarified, Bentham's thinking is quite coherent. P. J. Kelly reads Bentham closely and identifies elements of this coherence. He gives expectations their due, and recognizes that interests are not pre-political. In his excellent reading of the civil law manuscripts, Kelly comes very near to the ultra-conventionalist account of Bentham forwarded here. He finds that law is constitutive of individual identity itself. But Kelly overlooks the details of the relationship between expectations and the imagination, and he assumes like others that experienced pleasures and pains are efficient causes of action for Bentham. My argument, however, is that any pleasures and pains that matter are themselves products of the imagination fixed by discourse.[6]

Bentham scholars have worked hard to change his image as a vulgar act-utilitarian calculator of pains and pleasures. This is especially true of the recent wave of revisionists who, benefiting from the editorial work of the Bentham Project, have explored the sophistication and contemporary relevance of Bentham on institutional and constitutional design, rights, and publicity.[7] The other Bentham persists despite their efforts, however; one reason for this is that the most widely circulated of his texts, *An Introduction to the Principles of Morals and Legislation* (1780, 1789), is full of reductive examples and arguments. Revisionists know that Bentham himself never repudiated his early work on pleasure, pain, and interest; on the contrary, interest grounds the late constitutional work as well, and is frequently defined in the same manner as before, in terms of an ostensibly crude materialist theory of human nature and human action. The other Bentham, then, is difficult to expunge. In what follows I will show how we can find the sophisticated Bentham in his supposedly most vulgar arguments. I do this not so much to embrace the new rather than the old Bentham, but instead to show how the two figures can be reconciled. The coherence that this chapter finds between the old and new Bentham illuminates his political science and the governmental functions of monistic interest.

If we attend closely to Bentham's theory of motivation, as laid out in *An Introduction to the Principles of Morals and Legislation* and *A Table of the Springs of Action* (1815, 1817), we see that in Bentham's own terms all material motives are imaginary. "Thus," he writes, "it is no otherwise than through the medium of the *imagination*, that any pleasure, or pain, is capable of operating in the character of a *motive*."[8] We see that suffered and enjoyed pains and pleasures ultimately don't matter: they are not part of interest. This passage, and others that define interest as motive and as the sum of expected pain and pleasure— that is, as "a *balance* on the side of good"[9]—are at the heart of my argument. Bentham's scheme requires the retreat from viscerality that actually determines Bentham's interest. What first looks like a plurality of interests grounded in present experience and relations is always a prospective singularity: a "balance" or sum of expectations and apprehensions of the future. I argue that this balance, according to Bentham, is always calculated in the context of a kind of common landscape. This landscape is constructed by law—or, to be more precise, by the forces of direct and indirect legislation that structure the belief essential to expectation.[10] Direct legislation aims at maximally coordinating the sanctions and rewards of law; indirect legislation coordinates the sanctions and rewards of social systems like the economy, culture, religion, and public opinion. The landscape offers prospects—prospective visions or points of view— from which in my mind's eye I can see hazards or benefits on the horizon.[11] There is no interest without these sanctions and rewards and their security; and new measures of government construct new interests that can tip the balance of expected good away from forbidden or toward subsidized activities.

Words and images are the primary materials of this landscape's construction—which, *qua* interest, is itself the ground and reference of all government of self and others. Bentham's deployment of interest as a foundation, however, requires a foregrounding of embodied experience that is accompanied by a rise to prominence of expectation and the imagination, and thus a retreat from his foregrounded viscerality. In the remainder of the chapter, I demonstrate the pervasiveness and functions of these movements in Bentham's work. This theoretical legerdemain disguises a lack of foundation: a lack that successfully supports a new theory of interest. Bentham's interest requires a related movement that alternately trivializes and elevates speech and writing—what he calls "discourse"—and the understanding. I examine the political import of this movement by investigating the relationship that it builds between the imagination and the landscaping that is for Bentham direct and indirect legislation. Bentham's interest emerges not only as purpose and product but as tool of government. We are mistaken, then, in trying to get to the bottom of interest, or in supposing that interest as a tool of analysis either aids *or* obfuscates political inquiry. Instead, interest helps to construct the political landscape itself, thereby transforming inquiry into another social system of indirect legislation.

Defining Interest I

Unlike a right, an interest is pre-juridical in Bentham's work: it exists regardless of the existence of a sovereign grant. Interests are what we identify and satisfy when applying the principle of utility, or greatest-happiness principle. But even in this seemingly straightforward role, we see the complexities of interest in Bentham's thinking. "By the principle of utility," he writes, "is meant that principle which approves or disapproves of every action whatsoever, according to the tendency which it appears to have to augment or diminish the happiness of the party whose interest is in question."[12] This is the normative standard for Bentham's lifelong project of rational jurisprudence: a law is a good law insofar as it serves interest. But interest guides legislation in a double sense. It is the basis also of the motives that drive all human action. Bentham states that the principle of utility is not only indicative of what ought to be (in the form of the greatest happiness principle), but also "indicative of what *is* . . ., it states as the sole actual *object* and *end* of every man's every action, his advancement of his own interest."[13] Thus while not all interest is self-regarding (it might make me happy to see you happy), all action is guided by interest. "In regard to *interest*, in the most extended, which is the original and only strictly proper sense of the word 'disinterested'," he maintains, "no human act ever has been or ever can be *disinterested*."[14] The axiom that all action is in the service of interest is fundamental to what Bentham calls the "logic of the will": those rules of operations of the will that must be heeded by all successful governors.[15] As the sole "end" of all action, the moralist and legislator must work with interest to serve interest: the end of all good government.

This curious relationship between means and ends—that actors' interests should be served, and that the only way to enhance their interests is to appeal to their interests—is foreshadowed in the arresting image that opens *An Introduction to the Principles of Morals and Legislation*: "Nature has placed mankind under the governance of two sovereign masters, *pain* and *pleasure*. It is for them alone to point out what we ought to do, as well as to determine what we shall do. On the one hand the standard of right and wrong, on the other the chain of causes and effects, are fastened to their throne."[16] The passage leads the reader to believe that what Bentham means by happiness is grounded in natural pleasures and pains; such talk of nature directs us to bodily experience. But the governance of pleasure and pain requires that they be understood in terms of interest. And only when translated into interest will they literally add up to happiness or its opposite.

Whose interests are we talking about? Interests belong to individuals. As Bentham explains, "the community is a fictitious *body*, composed of the individual persons who are considered as constituting as it were its *members*. The interest of the community then is, what?—the sum of the interests of the several members who compose it." "It is in vain," he continues, "to talk of the interest of the community, without understanding what is the interest of the individual. A thing is said to promote the interest, or to be *for* the interest, of an individual, when it tends to add to the sum total of his pleasures: or, what comes to the same thing, to diminish the sum total of his pains."[17] Likewise, "an individual's happiness is increased in only one of two ways—1. by increasing the sum of his pleasures; or 2. by diminishing the sum of his pains."[18]

There have been countless debates about the terms of these aggregations. And many commentators have found the reductionism implicit in the possibility of such aggregation objectionable.[19] Too little has been said, however, about just what it is that is being aggregated on Bentham's own account. His rhetoric works on even doubtful readers to recall visceral pleasures and pains—a pain in the side, a pleasurably full belly, and so on. And such pleasures and pains can, certainly, be more or less intense or enduring—as can even the enjoyments taken in, say, the experience of a piece of music. But we understandably balk at a calculus of these. And we especially balk at the suggestion that one person's pleasures and pains are interchangeable with another's. Pains and pleasures are not ultimately, however, the stuff of Bentham's system. His material turns out to be far less visceral than this, and not exactly exclusively mental either—not in the sense, at least, of mental enjoyments and sufferings. The charge of reductionism is misplaced, because the possibilities for commensurability and aggregation here go well beyond anything allowed by immediate pain and pleasure.

Bentham's pleasures and pains are expectations—mental projections of the future—and interest is the sum of these. Understanding this is crucial to understanding the consequences of Bentham's prescriptions for interests. There is no natural dynamic, much less harmony, of interest. And it is misleading to suggest an artificial dynamic or harmony without adding that its very elements are themselves constituted in and by the field of interest that is the legislative domain. Achieving a harmonious order of interest is the challenge that faces the sovereign or constitution maker. Order must be constructed according to the "junction-of-interests prescribing principle." This principle demands that one be given the interest to do what contributes to the aggregate interest, and to not do what diminishes it.[20] Whatever their pedigree, those interests that are not optimal in light of this principle must be changed; mechanisms must be deployed so that doing what is in the aggregate interest is in one's own interest. Laws and their attendant penalties and rewards are simply motives provided by the legislator[21] who, since every motive has its corresponding interest, constructs interests. For example, an interest in not stealing is produced only when the costs of the punishment would outweigh any benefits. And theft would have no meaning without property itself—which is "an established expectation," established entirely by law.[22] Punishments may come from popular or religious sanctions in addition to the "political" sanctions of the penal law; these will ideally be coordinated by indirect legislation. And thus direct and indirect legislation together go into the makeup of interests: interests that must be constructed to maximize the interest of the community.[23] These measures are grounded on and apply Bentham's logic of the will. The only reason to make people do anything is to augment their own and others' expected sum of pain and pleasure; at the same time, the only way to make people do anything is through the operation of an expected sum of pain and pleasure upon their wills.[24]

Bentham persistently writes as if there is a connection between his project and the physical and emotional ups and downs of everyday living. But when we look closely at these references, we find that this is never a living in the present or the past: it is always a living in the future. We can trace Bentham's foregrounding of, and retreat from, viscerality by examining how pain, pleasure, and interest function as efficient causes of acts: how they function as motives or "springs of action." Pain as motive, for example, recalls to me yanking my scorched hand out of reach of a flame. But we will see that Bentham's spring is much more like the spring of a watch; its energy is not expended in one burst but is instead always regulated. With the metaphor of the spring, Bentham invokes the cause and effect of bodily pains and pleasures—of, that is, a reflex and thus nervous response. Yet the regulation of the spring as watch-spring, and thus the regulation of the individual who acts, depends on the retreat from viscerality. Ultimately it is not pains or pleasures but the provision and coordination of motivating images—of imaginable, believable futures—that are the means and goal of regulation.

Defining Interest II

The idea of the spring of action is most fully developed in *A Table of the Springs of Action*, but pleasure and pain as determinants of action are discussed at length in *An Introduction to the Principles of Morals and Legislation*. The account in the *Introduction* begins with sanctions, the "sources" of pain and pleasure, and culminates with motives.[25] The sanctions are four sources of motives[26] that will be expanded to five and more in later accounts.[27] In the *Introduction* these sanctions are physical, political, moral or popular, and religious.[28] The *Introduction*, with a disproportionately large chapter entitled "The Division of Offences," is the beginning of a never-completed, voluminous program for deployment of the political sanction.[29] Through the codification of distinct commands and punishments, it aims to reorganize the law so that the motives it provides—the behaviors it prevents—correspond to the dictates of utility. Moral and religious sanctions sometimes supplement, sometimes antagonize the program of the legislator.[30] The essay on "Indirect Legislation" begins a project even more potentially voluminous than the legal program: it recommends ways for the legislator to enlist these other sanctions and more generally modify conditions through means that include but go beyond the issuing of laws.[31] Ideally all available sanctions would work toward the same purpose: the rearing of a harmonious "fabric of felicity."[32]

Again foregrounding a materialist naturalism, Bentham writes the following about the relations among the sanctions: "Of these four sanctions the physical is altogether, we may observe, the ground-work of the [other three]. . . . None of *them* can operate but by means of this. In a word, the powers of nature may operate of themselves; but neither the magistrate, nor men at large, *can* operate, nor is God in the case in question *supposed* to operate, but through the powers of nature."[33] Sensitive beings experience physical pleasures and pains; it is by these means only that sanctions other than the physical can function. It thus seems that again, for Bentham, physical pleasures and pains are what lie at the bottom of the logic of the will; they are what constitutes interest. We all seek pleasure and avoid pain. Utilitarianism is merely systematizing and applying this simple truth. Feeling is universal to sensitive beings, and is more proximately real than the worlds of things and ideas. "For sensations alone are the immediate subjects or objects of experience. It is from them that we infer the existence of this or that other real entity in the character of a productive instrument or cause."[34]

As pat as this may sound, it raises a number of problems. Bentham grounds his doctrine in the pain of a blow versus the pleasure of a caress, covering also the pain of bitter versus the pleasure of sweet, as well as the pain of humiliation versus the pleasure of pride. And he emphasizes the immediacy of feeling: the first two measures of pain and pleasure are intensity and duration.[35] The relationship of interest to these immediate sensations is introduced in the general chapter on pleasures and pains. "Pains and pleasures may be called by one general word, interesting perceptions. Interesting perceptions are either simple or complex."[36] Note the shift to perception. An interesting perception is complex when it involves a combination of pains and pleasures. Interest itself is what Bentham calls a fictitious entity, but one firmly rooted in what he calls the real entities of pleasure and pain.[37] On estimating the value, or motive force, of pleasures and pains, Bentham writes: "In all this there is nothing but what the practice of mankind, wheresoever they have a clear view of their own interest, is perfectly conformable to."[38] The possibility is now raised that perception could be faulty: one might not have "a clear view" of one's interest;[39] and utilitarian prudence requires the proper weighing of near and distant pleasures and pains.[40] Any interest itself, however, is supposed to be constituted strictly by what Bentham calls material relations. In describing consequences of acts, he notes that those "can be said to be material, as either consist of pain or pleasure, or have an influence in the production of pain or pleasure."[41] And hence, again, what is in my material interest is what will give me pleasure, or take away my pain. That materiality itself, however, might be a matter of consequences is noteworthy, especially since the consequences determining it—namely, pleasure and pain—have been defined as interesting perceptions. What kind of ground is interest?

Interest directs action with regard to things outside the individual, but this outside is mediated in a peculiar fashion. The things that make up interest are of almost limitless variety, and seem to be as much temporally as spatially removed from psychosomatic immediacy. All this is very confusing for Bentham's readers. We might suppose that Bentham's "interest" has something to do with more familiar practical and plural senses of the term: that the connections to one's interests are more durable and institutional than phenomenological; and that these connections, even if viewed phenomenologically, are thought to be of the past and present, and not necessarily of the future. Bentham seems both to expand and to reduce our interests: for him, it seems, I am interested in anything so long as it can make me feel pain or pleasure. But the interest that counts—the one, if I view it clearly, that both should and does guide my practice—is not many things but one. The interest that counts is also, as we will see, always something that I view prospectively. The monistic and prospective character of Bentham's interest raises serious questions. What is the connection between interest and the materiality posited by Bentham as the priority of the physical sanction?

The definition of "interest" offered in *A Table of the Springs of Action* allows us to trace what I have called Bentham's retreat from viscerality:

> 1. A man is said *to have an interest in any subject* in so far as that *subject* is considered as more or less likely to be to him a source of pleasure or exemption: subject, viz. *thing* or *person*; *thing*, in virtue of this or that *use*, which it may happen to him to derive from that thing; *person*, in virtue of this or that *service*, which it may happen to him to receive at the hands of that person.

I have an interest in my doughnut and I have an interest in my lover. Furthermore,

> 2. A man is said *to have an interest in the performance* of this or that *act*, by himself or any other—or in *the taking place* of this or that *event* or *state of things*,—in so far as, upon and in consequence of its having place, this or that *good* (i.e. *pleasure* or *exemption*) is considered as being more or less likely to be possessed by him.

I have an interest in eating my doughnut and I have an interest in making love with my lover. Moreover,

> 3. It is said *to be a man's interest that* the act, the event, or the state of things in question should have place, in so far as it is supposed to be that—upon, and in consequence of, its having place—*good*, to a greater *value*, will be possessed by him than in the contrary case. In the former case, *interest* corresponds to a *single item* in the account of *good and evil*; in the latter case, it corresponds to *a balance* on the side of *good*.[42]

This "balance" is the crux of the matter. The particular persons and things of (1) dissolve into the particular actions and events of (2). The particular actions and events of (2) dissolve into the comparable possibilities of (3). The balance struck in (3) assesses the relative value of two possibilities; interest corresponds to the value of something happening rather than not happening. This opens the way to assessing a universe of possibilities: to a calculation that takes into account the probability of possible futures, relations of causation and mutual exclusivity, and so on. It is, by implication, interest as a balance of balances, or best possible outcome, that motivates action. And thus interest is resolutely future-directed and singular. It is because interest can always be aggregated from distinct interests that Bentham rarely employs the plural.

Interest—insofar as I have a "clear view" of it, and insofar as my actions or the actions of those I can influence will realize it—will direct my practice.[43] Laws, as noted, are nothing more or less than motives provided by the sovereign. What laws and other sanctions do is make up the elements of our calculations, and thus our interests, by ideally bringing them into harmony with one another so as to maximize the interest of the community. Bentham wants lawmaking to be like landscaping. At one point he describes his project in the *Introduction* as "striving to cut a new road through the wilds of jurisprudence."[44] Landscaping is not about making paradise on earth: "If this be paradise, paradise is but at best what the Asiatics meant by it, a garden: it is still however a very pleasant garden to look to in comparison of the wilderness of evils and abuses in which we have as yet been wandering."[45] If lawmaking properly landscapes, people will no more want to commit crimes than they would want to walk into rather than around a pond or tree. But the obverse is true: without these new motives, committing what should be a crime may mean nothing more to an individual than taking a shortcut.[46] Thus, the first rule for determining punishments is that the "*value of the punishment must not be less in any case than what is sufficient to outweigh that of the profit of the offence.*"[47] Should the adjustment of the punishment to the offence not be adequate, we should not be surprised at the consequences.

Bentham acknowledges that codification of the law could require a great deal of expository writing.[48] The recurrent difficulties of legal philosophy—for instance, ambiguity, incompleteness, the relationship between law and case—are exacerbated by the irony that Bentham's version of command theory undermines authority. For Bentham, the law's legitimacy resides not in its source (whether it is thought to be legislature, executive, judge, procedure, or custom), but exclusively in its beneficial effectiveness; this effectiveness, on his terms, requires completion, the reduction of ambiguity, and a great deal of publicity.[49] He is not unaware of how challenging codification is—but he does seem to think the project a finite one.[50] Although Bentham remains throughout his writings somewhat doubtful about realizing his jurisprudence, he always declares its firm ground: pain and pleasure are real. He continues foregrounding a materialist naturalism. He acknowledges that interest is a compound phenomenon, but its components—pain and pleasure—are presented as the simple stuff of experience. Let us now examine his retreat from this position.

"Pleasures and Pains, Their Kinds"

According to Bentham, the grounding of interest in pain and pleasure is unproblematic because the items to be aggregated are perfectly knowable and commensurable: "pain" and "pleasure" name "homogeneous real entities."[51] What are these real entities? We have seen that Bentham's argument relies on the visceral undeniability of the experience of pain and pleasure. But in his urge to classify, homogeneity and viscerality are compromised. In the chapter of the *Introduction* entitled "Pleasures and Pains, Their Kinds" Bentham lists fourteen "simple" pleasures and twelve "simple" pains of which all complex pleasures and pains are composed:

> 1. The pleasures of sense. 2. The pleasures of wealth. 3. The pleasures of skill. 4. The pleasures of amity. 5. The pleasures of a good name. 6. The pleasures of power. 7. The pleasures of piety. 8. The pleasures of benevolence. 9. The pleasures of malevolence. 10. The pleasures of memory. 11. The pleasures of imagination. 12. The pleasures of expectation. 13. The pleasures dependent on association. 14. The pleasures of relief. . . . 1. The pains of privation. 2. The pains of the senses. 3. The pains of awkwardness. 4. The pains of enmity. 5. The pains of an ill name. 6. The pains of piety. 7. The pains of benevolence. 8. The pains of malevolence. 9. The pains of the memory. 10. The pains of the imagination. 11. The pains of expectation. 12. The pains dependent on association.[52]

These lists are odd for a number of reasons. I want to focus again on the slippage here: Bentham's move from a material to an imaginary account of interest. This move only confirms—in the *Introduction*'s sense of "material"— that the imagination is material.[53]

Recall Bentham's statement that immediate feeling delivered by the powers of nature is what is really real.[54] But surely not everything listed above can qualify as equally real in this way. Many of the pleasures and pains listed are social and comparative, and mediated in a way that makes them problematic goods or evils in themselves. Bentham's own analysis shows many of them to be pleasure or pain from the possession of potential for enjoyment or suffering.[55] Such potentials can't exactly be equated with their actualizations; instead they constitute a kind of story about pains and pleasures and their sources. This already suggests a retreat from reality as Bentham ostensibly defines it. Indeed, Bentham's foregrounded world of visceral experience collapses. If pain or pleasure can be induced by bringing to mind pleasurable or painful objects absent in time or space, the possibilities are infinite. Stranger still than the social pleasures and pains are the pleasures and pains of the imagination that raise the specter of a surplus of feeling generated solely from within: a kind of mental self-stimulation that Bentham's scheme cannot easily accommodate. This surplus could disrupt the primacy of material motive-relations that require dependable connections between the environment and the feeling subject. The imagination is, as Bentham defines it, a faculty freely combining bits of memory with bits of circumstance to provide new pleasures and pains that can resemble any of the others. "The pleasures of the imagination," he writes, "are the pleasures which may be derived from the contemplation of any such pleasures as may happen to be suggested by the memory, but in a different order, and accompanied by different groups of circumstances. These may accordingly be referred to any one of the three cardinal points of time, present, past, or future."[56] The pleasures of the imagination, which are posited among the fourteen simple pleasures, are thus potentially a multiplier of the other thirteen pleasures. "The pains of the imagination," Bentham similarly concludes, could potentially multiply the other eleven simple pains, and "in other respects they correspond exactly to the pleasures of the imagination."[57]

It could be argued that Bentham is insulated from these problems by the doctrine of associationism. He is, after all, avowedly influenced by David Hartley's work.[58] The autonomy of the imagination could thus conceivably be limited through the imposition of a scheme of causal necessity of mental associations, ultimately derived from experience.[59] In a footnote in the *Introduction* the analysis of the complex pleasures of a country scene combines association and imagination in an attempt to reduce the products of the latter to the workings of the former.[60] Curiously, though, the pleasures and pains of association and imagination do enjoy the separate listings quoted above. Bentham designates an independent faculty of the imagination with its own pleasures and pains.

How do we distinguish the pleasures of the imagination from the pleasures upon which they are parasitical—especially when most of those pleasures are already once removed from the visceral? Memories are "referred" to the cardinal point of the past, but reveries may be referred to past, present, or future. The non-sensuous pleasures of wealth, power, and the like involve pleasure from the potential for pleasure, at any time in the future. How is the pleasure of imagination any less real—or, for that matter, any different? The faculty of the imagination is crucial to Bentham's system, but it is also a source of danger. It is capable of mimicking all possible pains and pleasures, perhaps to the point of actually assuming their identity. (Remember: the pleasures and pains of the imagination are on the list of simple pleasures and pains—the things that add up to happiness and interest.)

Why, then, must the imagination be involved? And how is it to be restricted? It raises the specter of chaos and rampant self-stimulation, of complete detachment from the consequential scheme on which Bentham insists. Yet this same insistence demands the imagination for its power to contemplate the future.[61] Not all contemplations of the future can be equal, however. Otherwise an appraisal of interest would be impossible. It is not the case that the grounding of interest in the imagination means that anything goes. Thus Bentham introduces, as pleasures and pains wholly separate from those of the imagination, the pleasures and pains of expectation. "The pleasures of expectation," he writes, "are the pleasures that result from the contemplation of any sort of pleasure, referred to time *future*, and accompanied with the sentiment of *belief*. These also may admit of the same distinctions [as those of memory and imagination]." Similarly, "the pains of expectation may be grounded on each one of the above kinds, as well of pains of privation as of positive pains. These may be also termed pains of apprehension."[62] Footnotes in the *Introduction* confirm that these pains and pleasures can be made up of any of the others, and are distinguished by their futurity alone. All pains and pleasures that are not expectations or apprehensions, Bentham writes, are pains of "sufferance" and pleasures of "enjoyment."[63]

Expectations and apprehensions, I argue, are the "pleasures" and "pains" of Bentham's logic of the will, and this is the stuff of which interest is composed. Expectations and apprehensions are projections, "referred to time future, and accompanied with the sentiment of belief." Belief, presumably, is what distinguishes expectation from mere imagining, and from ungrounded fantasizing about the future. But what does the role of expectations imply for enjoyment and sufferance? "Pleasures of expectation" are listed as one of the pleasures, but aren't other non-sensuous pleasures—such as the pleasures of wealth—strictly speaking pleasures of expectation? Isn't their enjoyment merely enjoyment of, at best, security of expectation? Could even sensuous enjoyment itself be a pleasure of expectation for Bentham: one of continued enjoyment? What does it mean to enjoy or suffer in a Benthamic world? We will see that according to Bentham's account of action and motivation, we are always acting and thus always expecting and apprehending. This suggests that the apparently large remainder of pleasures and pains of enjoyment and sufferance reduces to nothing; these can't have any role in the accounting that constitutes interest. Thus concrete experience, which appeared to precede the work of the imagination, is in fact subordinate to it. Through a closer inspection of the theory of action in both the *Introduction* and the *Table* we can better comprehend the crucial role of expectation in Bentham's system. Action and inaction are based in motive, and motive consists of interest composed entirely of expectations and apprehensions, or believed imaginings. We can follow through to the end here the movement away from the world of feeling bodies implied by Bentham's rhetoric of pain and pleasure. This will reveal just how ideal and discursive the foundation of interest can ultimately be.

Motive and Action

If we look at Bentham's treatment of interest from the perspective of what we call agency, the course I have identified through the imagination can be interpreted as an anticipatory parody of contemporary methodological disputes: biological, behavioral, choice-oriented, and linguistic explanations all have their turns. Bentham's concern is ultimately not with any one of these foundations of inquiry, however, but with what we would call "policy outcomes." Political science for Bentham is an art-and-science of government; like medicine, its study of its subject-matter—namely, conduct—is inseparable from the reform of its subject.[64] To appreciate how Bentham's ambiguities can be mobilized for a particular project of government—government of, by, and for imagined interest or what we might call rational expectations—we need to attend to his study of action. Here we see how what Bentham calls "discourse" can be manifestly dismissed and at the same time latently empowered.

Bentham's definition of what it is to act is very broad. Everybody acts all the time: "By positive [acts] are meant such as consist in motion or exertion: by negative, such as consist in keeping at rest."[65] Few acts are completely unintentional. "This is the case with those acts which alone are properly termed *involuntary*: acts, in the performance of which the will has no sort of share: such as the contraction of the heart and arteries."[66] An act plus its consequences equals an action.[67] A consequence is intentional when it was contemplated beforehand, and directly so "when the prospect of producing it constituted one of the links in the chain of causes by which the person was determined to do the act."[68] This chain stretches from motives—which, as we have seen, are known as springs of action—to consequences. Circumstances and consciousness of them are important in determining the intendedness of consequences: "advisedness, with respect to the circumstances . . . extends the intentionality from the act to the consequences."[69] Whether advised or not, the intention of an act is not less of a link in the causal chain: "the effects of an intention to do such or such an act, are the same objects which we have been speaking of under the appellation of its *consequences*: and the causes of intention are called *motives*."[70] Motives "give birth to" actions.[71]

What are motives, and where do they come from? In a discussion of physical versus mental acts, Bentham divides the latter into acts of the will and acts of the understanding. Here again he limits the possibilities of independently generated pleasure and pain, and more generally strikes a materialist pose. Acts of the understanding, by themselves, do not "produce either pain or pleasure." Thus they are not "material," and motives that give rise to them are "purely *speculative*."[72] They are *practical* only if they alter the estimation of the circumstances of action. The problem of belief, which I treat below, will greatly expand the latter category and complicate this picture. At the beginning of the chapter on motives in the *Introduction*, however, Bentham demotes the understanding by insisting that those "motives with which alone we have any concern, are such as are of a nature to act upon the will."[73]

With these motives Bentham links an environment to the animate being within it; this being can change or reinforce circumstance by means of motivated action. The connection here is ostensibly narrowly material; "motive" here refers to something that can be directly charged to exchanges between a painful or pleasant environment and the will of a feeling individual. According to Bentham, our current view of motives is clouded by ghosts produced from the pens of traditional moralists and from other unscientific sources. These spirits will vanish as soon as we deploy the matter-of-fact naturalism he recommends. A close reading of his theory of motivation, however, shows how the real entities, the natural masters—pain and pleasure—appear at this point only to disappear. In this manner the imagination and the discourse that stimulates and regulates it are not demoted; they are instead reconfigured and redirected so that they serve rather than thwart good government.

Contrasting literal and figurative senses of "motive," Bentham reiterates the realism and parsimony of his account of the logic of the will: "The word *motive* is employed indiscriminately to denote two kinds of objects. . . . On some occasions it is employed to denote any of those really existing incidents from whence the act in question is supposed to take its rise. [This is] its literal or *unfigurative* sense. On other occasions it is employed to denote a certain fictitious entity, a passion, an affection of the mind. . . . This latter may be styled the *figurative* sense of the term *motive.*"[74] Thus imaginary characters—for example "Avarice, Indolence, Benevolence"—haunt us as a result of the "dyslogistic" and "eulogistic" terms that bring disapprobation or approbation to motives that cannot themselves be either good or bad. Terms that refer to the same motive will carry conflicting sentiments (such as "thriftiness" and "niggardliness").[75] We must not be misled by these when analyzing the real incidents that they ultimately refer to, which can be divided along two axes: "internal" versus "external," and motive "in prospect" versus motive "in *esse.*"[76]

Bentham's discussion of these real motives is confusing and worth quoting at some length. It illustrates the logic of the will in action, and the operations of the pleasures and pains of which interest is composed. What is crucial here is the rise to prominence of expectation over enjoyment or sufferance:

> The real incidents . . . may be either, 1. The *internal* perception of any individual lot of pleasure or pain, the expectation of which is looked upon as calculated to determine you to act in such or such a manner . . . : Or, 2. Any *external* event, the happening whereof is regarded as having a tendency to bring about the perception of such pleasure or such pain. . . . Two other senses of the term *motive* need also to be distinguished. . . . Motive . . . must be previous to [action]. But, for a man to be governed by any motive, he must in every case look beyond that event which is called his action; he must look to the consequences of it: and it is only in this way that the idea of pleasure, of pain, or of any other event, can give birth to it. He must look . . . to . . . an event which as yet exists not, but stands only in prospect. . . . The posterior possible object which is thus looked forward to . . . may be termed a motive in *prospect*, the [event of looking forward to it an example of] a motive in *esse*: and under each of these denominations will come as well exterior as internal motives.

Roughly, relevant things happen in you or outside of you, and they'll happen later or they're happening now. Bentham's phrase for what will happen—that it is "in prospect"—is appropriate to something seen from a landscaped point of view: a view of the future that always matters in a present. He provides the following example:

> A fire breaks out in your neighbour's house: you are under apprehension of its extending to your own: you are apprehensive, that if you stay in it, you will be burnt: you accordingly run out of it. This then is the act: the others are all motives to it.

Motives can be put into the above two-by-two matrix (prospect or esse, exterior or internal) in the following fashion:

> The event of the fire's breaking out in your neighbour's house is an external motive, and that in *esse*: the idea or belief of the probability of the fire's extending to your own house, that of your being burnt if you continue, and the pain you feel at the thought of such a catastrophe, are all so many internal events, but still in *esse*: the event of the fire's actually extending to your own house, and that of your being actually burnt by it, external motives in prospect: the pain you would feel at seeing your house a burning, and the pain you would feel while your yourself were burning, internal motives in prospect: which events, according as the matter turns out, may come to be in *esse*: but then of course they will cease to act as motives.[77]

Presumably they will cease to act as motives because you will be dead. But why assume this? Why couldn't the real incident of the immediate pain from burning flesh work at some point as a spring to action? Because such a motive could not be taken up into a theory of *interest*. Interest dissolves as soon as pain or pleasure is in a proximity that keeps it from being imaginary. Instead, interest requires a kind of internal motive in *esse* different from the experience of pain or pleasure. Such a motive is given in what Bentham takes to be the ultimate motive at work in the above example: "that internal motive in *esse* which consists in the expectation of the internal motive in prospect: the pain or uneasiness you feel at the thoughts of being burnt."[78]

Bentham's remarkable assertion implies that external events are important insofar as they promote expectations. Many of these "external" events are themselves expectations: they are in prospect. Relevant internal events are also expectations, and it is precisely the event of these interior prospective views that most proximally provokes action.

For Bentham, everything that has happened until now—everything in *esse*— is just so much material for the updating of expectation that is ultimately what matters now. Of course, expectations of feelings are themselves accompanied by feelings in the present: pleasure for expectations of pleasure, pain for expectations of pain. Is this tingle of expectation the immediate motive to action?

Bentham tells us it doesn't matter: "Whether it be the expectation of being burnt, or the pain that accompanies that expectation, that is the immediate internal motive spoken of, may be difficult to determine. It may even be questioned, perhaps, whether they are distinct entities. Both questions, however, seem to be mere questions of words, and the solution of them altogether immaterial."[79] Note where this leaves us: a distinction diligently fought for and painstakingly enumerated throughout the *Introduction*—often by means of neologisms—between real pains and pleasures and the fictions that are dependent on them is a mere question of words. It is indeed a question of words, and Bentham's trivialization of it is another decoy signaling a move away from the hedonic naturalism toward which he so consistently gestures. Already there is some question as to the status of pains and pleasures of expectation; if these in turn become mere expectations of pain or pleasure, then a central link in the chain of action dissolves. If, as we shall confirm, expectations are products of the imagination, then real motives—the generators of action—are themselves generated by the imaginations of actors. Ultimately, the same independence of Bentham's human organism that frees it from organic determination is what opens it to inorganic constitution and regulation by the words and images that make up the arsenals of political forces.

Belief

The fundamental role of the imagination's expectations in the construction of motivation and action is confirmed by *A Table of the Springs of Action*. A comparison of the *Table* and the *Introduction* clarifies Bentham's confusing account of belief and "acts of discourse," and clarifies the link between these and expectations. When we turn to the *Table*, we find in the "Explanations" an explicit acknowledgment of the centrality of the imagination. Here Bentham writes that pleasures and pains motivate action only insofar as action "is regarded" as a means of obtaining pleasure or avoiding pain. If it does not affect action, a pleasure or pain is "inert." "Mere imagination" is inert, as is memory: if I go someplace on the basis of a pleasant recollection of it, it is the expectation of a new and equally pleasant experience that motivates me. Expectations are "pictures" of the future composed by the imagination that are "accompanied with a *judgment* more or less *decided*—a *persuasion* more or less *intense*—of . . . future realization." Bentham retains the name "expectations" for expectations of pleasure, and gives to expectations of pain the name "apprehensions." And here he follows through his argument to its logical conclusion: imagined and believed pictures relevant to potential actions are the true springs of all actions. "Thus," he concludes, "it is no otherwise than through the medium of the *imagination*, that any pleasure, or pain, is capable of operating in the character of a *motive*."[80]

Pleasures and pains that are not projected by the imagination—namely, pleasures and pains that are enjoyed or suffered—are inert. They thus do not function as motives or to ground interest. And in the same way, any product of the imagination is inert if not accompanied by the "persuasion" of "future realization"—if not accompanied, that is, by what Bentham calls belief. Although all motives are said to be derived from "original" pains and pleasures ("the immediate and simultaneous accompaniments of *perception*"),[81] it is unclear how their experience, appropriation, reorganization, and projection can work. We have seen how broadly Bentham defines action; even when at rest, his individuals are acting. At this point, the economy of feeling, memory, and imagination cannot withstand much scrutiny. How does all of this work? Where do these "pictures" and their accompanying "persuasions" come from? What is it that transforms past and present experiences into pictures of the future—into pictures accompanied by a soothsayer's confidence?

To some degree, according to Bentham, people have to be taught to expect: to look out for tomorrow. And teaching them to expect is inseparable from the work of structuring what it is that they should expect: from the work of structuring prospects. Everyone, including the madman, calculates.[82] But one problem is the difficulty that many individuals have in giving sufficient weight to distant pains or pleasures compared with near ones: they don't have what Bentham calls "a clear view."[83] Pointing out distant penalties and rewards is the function of the moralist or "deontologist," but moral or prudential training cannot be separated from the question of how vision corresponds to reality, and the related quest for mutuality of expectation among subjects. The deontologist's political role as an indirect legislator is apparent from the following: "The legislator *creates*, of himself, new interests. To the deontologist it belongs, of himself, to bring to view existing interest, and even, in proportion to the influence of his authority, to apply the force of the moral or popular sanction to the creation of new interests."[84] Laws create interests by changing the mix of expectations and apprehensions, but the landscape is always better known by some—for example, deontologists—than by others, and their role is to sketch out the landscape's prospects and explain to different people how they fit in. They can also reinforce existing prospects or create new ones by directing praise or opprobrium in constructive ways. But how are these things done? What finally are the methods and mechanisms of direct and indirect legislation, and how are they supposed to work?

If we turn back to the *Introduction*, we see that immediately after discussing the most proximate motive to action, "that internal motive in *esse* which consists in the expectation," Bentham returns to the understanding: many "acts" of which have been declared not "material." It turns out that the understanding is not at all immaterial, but instead may provide a crucial link in the chain of action. "Any objects," he writes, "by tending to induce a belief concerning the existence, actual, or probable, of a practical motive . . . may exercise an influence on the will, and rank with those other motives that have been placed under the name of practical.[85] Belief, we should recall, is what distinguishes an expectation from something merely imagined. Where belief is wanting, and then supplied, belief is the cause of an act.

The importance of belief as motive is what compels Bentham to acknowledge the power of words. But this is done in the course of discussions that consistently belittle discourse. The double movement is evident from the cataloguing in the *Table* of dyslogistic and eulogistic terms for identical motives. These terms make no difference (they produce figments—the motive they identify is the same) and yet make all the difference (they produce figments—these must be identified and neutralized). In the *Introduction* Bentham denigrates discourse as subordinate to real physical and mental states and acts:

> Acts may be distinguished into *external* and *internal*. By external, are meant corporal acts; acts of the body: by internal, mental acts; acts of the mind. Thus, to strike is an external or exterior act: to intend to strike, an internal or interior one. Acts of *discourse* are a sort of mixture of the two: external acts, which are no ways material, nor attended with any consequences, any farther than as they serve to express the existence of internal ones. To speak to another to strike, to write to him to strike, to make signs to him to strike, are all so many acts of discourse.[86]

Speech and writing—even as exhortation—are apparently merely descriptive. But the inconsequentiality of discourse is belied by a later passage on understanding, belief, and motive that takes up again the example of your neighbor's burning house.

> The pointing out of motives such as these, is what we frequently mean when we talk of giving *reasons*. . . . I observe to you, that at the lower part of your neighbour's house is some wood-work, which joins on to your's . . . in order to dispose you to believe as I believe, that if you stay in

your house much longer you will be burnt. In doing this, then, I suggest motives to your understanding; which motives, by the tendency they have to give birth to or strengthen a pain, which operates upon you in the character of an internal motive in *esse*, join their force, and act as motives upon the will.[87]

"I suggest motives to your understanding." It is not clear that suggestion can only work by way of the understanding, or that the understanding is the site of, and not merely a contributor to, belief. What is clear is that acts of discourse are not merely descriptive but potentially most consequential. Discourse can motivate, because it supplies belief, and belief is what distinguishes expectations from inert imaginings. The "I" of the above example is a deontologist—a role we all play—who brings to view an unseen prospect. But speech and writing are of course the tools with which legislators and deontologists construct and maintain the common landscape of motivating prospects, and thus construct interest itself.

Discourse

In the opening of the *Introduction* Bentham sharply distinguishes rhetoric from philosophy in writing as well as speech. After the colorful introductory passage on the "two sovereign masters," he inserts a one-sentence paragraph: "But enough of metaphor and declamation: it is not by such means that moral science is to be improved."[88] Using antirhetorical rhetoric Bentham often attributes ill effects to rhetoric, and indicates that what he calls discourse should be limited to description: speech and writing should simply supply images that correspond to the world of inner and outer acts. But the images that are crucial in Bentham's theory of motivation are images of the *future*, and this seriously complicates the problem of correspondence. Images of the future are verified in the present by the flimsy endorsement of belief. Where does belief come from? Influencing belief, it turns out, is the proper "use of discourse."[89] And it is the awareness that people will be swayed by words when they should coolly evaluate their source that prompts Bentham to by turns deny, inveigh against, and enlist the power of rhetoric.

Bentham is concerned about a wide range of rhetoric—poetry comes in for severe criticism—but he is especially hostile to explicitly political falsehoods and embellishments. Most of the sophisticated and plain nonsense that goes by the names of philosophy and common sense succeeds, he maintains, because it is literally music to the ears.[90] By contrast, utilitarian teachings may be tinny or otherwise painful to absorb, and will have to stand on their ultimate usefulness to the reader and humanity at large. As early as 1776, in *A Fragment on Government*, Bentham recommends replacing the cacophony of political rhetoric with a discourse of utility. Instead of falling out over emotional appeals and lurid symbols, political actors would conduct their disputes clearly and constructively in the language of interest.[91] Early in his career, Bentham attributed the irrationality of political discourse to the ignorance and confusion of the participants. Later he would see "sinister interest"—the interest of a ruling part opposed to the whole—behind every embellishment. And this contributed to a greater emphasis on constitutionalism and democratic publicity as crucial indirect means to more effectively govern governors and secure expectations.[92]

I have argued thus far that much rests on the reliance on expectation as the stuff for the calculation of interest. We act on the basis of a balance sheet whose entries are expectations; these are projections accompanied by the sentiment of belief. Discourse plays a fundamental role in the formation of belief. But what should we believe and not believe, and how are we to distinguish discourse that properly influences belief from discourse that improperly influences it? Bentham works with a correspondence theory, of sorts, that distinguishes truth from falsehood, and this distinction is somehow directly related to that between good and bad government. The grounding of interest in the imagination opens up difficulties that are thus for Bentham necessarily governmental.[93]

There is, first, the danger of an entrancement with images and idle beliefs of all sorts. The work of the imagination is always needed to guide interested action, but if not regulated it may contribute to unpredictable action of any sort whatever. Second, there is the danger that the prudential calculus will cause some individuals to pursue relatively predictable projects hostile to the interest of the community. They will get it into their heads that they stand to gain from antisocial or criminal activity, because they have certain expectations that are too high, or apprehensions that are too low. Ultimately, poorly regulated imaginations and the threat of insidious projects are part of the same problem for Bentham: a problem of inefficient plurality. Bentham's account of motivation is such that action must take its bearings from a very particular type of representation. Core propositions for the logic of the will are conditionals: "if I do x, then y will follow." It is these conditionals, always counterfactual ones from the point of view of the individual actor, that anchor Bentham's correspondence theory. And structuring a clear landscape of conditionals is the work of direct and indirect legislation. These conditionals are fundamentally what I should believe, and discourse from any source that supplies or reinforces them is properly used. Ideally these conditionals will constitute a whole whose singularity, coherence, and completeness will bound, conjoin, or replace all other representations of the social. This system of representation will generate—for each of its targets individually—a secure and uncontradicted set of images and accompanying beliefs. This system will ideally produce the clear view that interest requires: it will produce a clear set of expectations.

Legislation and Punishment

It is law, then, that is real. Direct and indirect legislation structures and supports belief. The purpose of the laws is to structure games of interest. The clearest example of this is the complex of games structured by the laws undergirding what we call the "free market." For Bentham, market competition is a prime example of indirect legislation. It is the kind of efficient plurality the refinement of which is the province of political economy, an art-and-science of government that supplements his political science.[94] "Extortion [of exorbitant prices for commodities or for labour] . . . can be combated in the way of indirect legislation or not at all. Happily it is that sort of offence the mischief of which is lessened instead of being augmented by the multitude of offenders. What then is there for the law to do? there needs no more than to encrease that multitude as much as possible. Such or such an article bears a high price: a great profit is to be made by it, very well, let this be known, sellers multiply (competition takes place) and the price is lowered."[95] Note the importance of publicity. Laws of publicity are key to projects of indirect legislation, where agents police one another more effectively than they could be policed from a central point. Bentham writes in this vein about commercial standards that once designated become a means for traders to check one another. Such indirect governance is furthered by authenticating stamps or marks,[96] as well as by publication of "instructions relative to false weights and measures, false standards and tests of quality: and the deceitful methods that may be taken in the application of such that are true. . . . Instructions such as these every trader should be obliged to keep hung up . . . where it may be sure to meet the eye of every customer as he comes in."[97] Publicity is generally the guarantee that allows the moral or popular sanction to do its work. This work turns on "two great hinges, the *liberty of the press*, and the *publicity of the proceedings in courts of justice*. The bar of the public is in many cases the only tribunal before which the offence can be brought in the first instance: and as a court of appeal it is a powerful and almost necessary check upon the proceedings of every other."[98] Thus publicity is the tool of indirect legislation that polices state misconduct: it is central to the final chapter of Bentham's essay on indirect legislation, "Expedients against Misrule," which contains the germ of his constitutional thought.[99] Publicity is a fundamental instrument of security that fixes expectations; the sanctions that flow from public opinion do not have to be experienced, but can simply be anticipated, to effect the order and economy that they promote in every sphere.

Law and policy must create a clear set of expectations and secure them with publicity and punishment, and multiple subsidiary expectations will flow from these. Expectations will inevitably be generated in additional unpredictable ways, but these must not conflict with the horizon established by law. All expectations must be as compatible with one another as possible; these will of course include compatibilities that secure and promote productive incompatibilities, as with market competition. It is core expectations that must above all be secure—that is, apparent and credible. Bentham's goals do not imply extreme policy measures so much as a general shift in orientation. From much of his discussion of penal law it would appear that the utilitarian ideal is a kind of landscape architecture that blends "natural" and "artificial" elements of motive. David Lyons provides a good example of direct and indirect methods working together in rules of the road: the law establishes the direction of each lane of traffic, but what makes each driver obey this rule is primarily the fear of oncoming traffic in the other lane, not a fear of the police.[100]

The primacy of imagination and its security of expectation are apparent from Bentham's zeal to curb "alarm" and promote "example." Alarm displays the risks that publicity carries alongside its benefits. It is the widespread apprehension produced by offences; it is a great secondary mischief of most crimes against property and person.[101] Alarm is evil both in its extent—it spreads throughout the population—and because of the particular kind of apprehension that it is. Alarm is the apprehension that pain could strike without reason or warning. In a regime where individuals are governed through their expectations, and of which the governmental mission is the harmonious coordination and maximization of aggregate expectations, there can be no greater threat. In such a regime, crimes that cause widespread alarm might cause secondary evils well in excess of their primary mischief; these merit the most serious attention from authorities. "Security depends on the care taken to save from disturbance the current of Expectation."[102]

Example can use publicity in order both to promote and to economize on punishment: "example is the most important end of all, in proportion as the *number* of the persons under temptation to offend is to *one*."[103] The sanctions of direct legislation are effective only if they are known and remembered, and thus to be expected, as widely as possible. Publicity is crucial; the punished convict is relatively unimportant, and ideally would not even be necessary. "Again: It is the idea only of the punishment . . . that really acts upon the mind; the punishment itself . . . acts not any farther than as giving rise to that idea."[104] If punishment is necessary to give rise to the idea, we should get as much as possible out of the convict's costly pain. One way of increasing the value of punishment as example without inflicting more pain on the punished is "in a particular set of *solemnities* distinct from the punishment itself, and accompanying the execution of it."[105] This idea is also developed in the material on indirect legislation, in a chapter entitled "Problem VI: To strengthen the Impression of Punishments upon the Imagination." Here Bentham asserts the primacy of the visual image: "speak to the eyes, if you would move the heart." And again, as with the crucial role of persuasion in the construction of expectations, he smuggles in while refusing to acknowledge the discursive element in securing the validity of projections: those who have throughout the ages "endeavoured to profit" by the adage "speak to the eyes" include "the orator." History is rich with exemplary punishments, especially the history of the church, and these examples should be studied for good technique. The more pomp and ceremony the better. Ritual punishments should ideally be "among the first objects which strike the eyes of childhood."[106]

In rituals such as these, there is a felicitous blending of direct and indirect methods. Artificial motives are "naturalized," or, more precisely, political sanctions are grafted onto moral or popular ones through the training of young imaginations. Instead of doing battle with other sanctions, the sovereign punishment of examples can enlist their aid. After illustrating some of the horrors of past punishments which he considers for their exemplary value, Bentham raises directly the problem of creating extra apprehension by embellishing punishment:

> But it may be said, that every question has two sides—that these real representations, these terrible scenes of penal justice, will spread dismay among the people, and make dangerous impressions. I do not believe it. If they present to dishonest persons the idea of danger, they offer only an idea of security to those who are honest. The threat of terrible and eternal punishment for undefined and indefinite crimes, working upon an active imagination, may have sometimes produced madness. But here no undefined threatenings are supposed: on the contrary, here is a manifest crime proved—a crime which no one need commit.

Bentham seems to acknowledge here, sympathetically, the resemblance that this bears to the problematic assurances given to non-sinners when the torments of hell are described. This sovereign, by contrast, will not work in mysterious ways.[107]

The chapter on "strengthening impressions" ends with a proposal that further hints at a desire to replicate, through a kind of narcissism, the intimacy and power of the relationship between God and believer. Bentham considers the use of printed illustrations of punishments to aid in publicizing offences and their penalties: "If an abridgement of the penal code were accompanied with prints representing the characteristic punishments set apart for each crime, it would form an imposing commentary—a sensible and speaking image of the law. Each one might say, That is what I shall suffer, if I become guilty."[108] This "speaking image of the law" is, for Bentham, the essence of rule by law; it is less copy than original. In this regime of belief, such images are the opposite of idols; they are insurance *against* the political equivalents of idolatry and blasphemy. Mere reading cannot compete with a strong "afflictive idea"—one produced by grief, for example.[109] The illustrated text, mass-produced by the government (or better, by a low-bidding contractor), is an improvement on the absent presence achieved by unadulterated writing. The reproduced images guarantee that this absent presence will remain present. This is not because they are awful images of the sovereign. On the contrary, what serves as a motive is my image of my potential criminal self, constructed by projecting myself onto a copy of the illustration funded by the sovereign. The speaking images "speak" a text directly and intimately to the mind's eye of the subject ("speak to the eyes"). These publications reinforce a mental landscape by speaking directly to the imagination, ideally and finally in an inner voice that is in each case one's own.

Reality, in Bentham's work, is the coherent system of representation provided by the law and supplementary measures and effects of indirect rule: it is the system to which all accurate images and all true discourse must correspond. This system is to be continuously produced and refined by a science based strictly on the principle of utility. In his production of this science, the Benthamic experiment is already under way. Most of Bentham's work is one vast incomplete representation only apparently dependent on a connection to bodily experience—just as penal law, as he deploys it, only apparently depends on the pain of punishment. Punishment is simply an essential part of the representation. The governors' power of representation generates a "fabric of felicity." Sweet-sounding rhetoric abuses discourse by encouraging false belief;

but what is false is what is in competition with direct and indirect legislation.[110] This appearance is reality. According to Pitkin, we live in "a Benthamic world," a world recognizable "in its substituting of administration for politics, its oscillating between laissez-faire liberalism and the welfare state, its bureaucratization, the many large public and private organizations that manage, regulate, and channel our lives." As she concludes, "some of Bentham's ideas have become our commonplace assumptions."[111] My argument, however, is that we and Pitkin are not fully articulating these assumptions.

Appearance, Reality, Government

I have identified a systematic movement in Bentham's work, and suggested moreover that this persistent foregrounding of viscerality and retreat from it is a requirement of his project. Interest has no pre-political status in these texts, but it is important that it seem to, so that subjects will own their interests. My enjoyment and my suffering ostensibly belong to no one else. At the same time, though, it is crucial that my interest be the product of the ongoing engineering that links aggregate interest and incentive. What is potentially threatening to Bentham's project is not any drive within the self—he is profoundly liberal toward even the most widely condemned desires—but the relation that the self takes to its exterior, to things and to other people. The disruptive potential of plural involvements in concrete experience must be controlled. Some ties to others are important to good government. Thus the civil law that erects and protects the family association and the powers of fathers has crucial indirect functions.[112] Other ties, however, are suspect; some, like the ties that knit together the ruling class of Bentham's England, produce sinister interest, or an interest opposed to aggregate interest.[113] Controlling the prospects of such parts of society in the Benthamic landscape is a special challenge. But the disruptive potential of plural involvements, enjoyments, and sufferings in all parts of society is contained by the primacy of the imagination—by converting interest first into a relationship with oneself, into a balance of expectations.[114] Similarly, danger from the potential chaos of the imagination is contained by the foregrounding of a materiality that focuses and limits it.[115] We see how Bentham's theory itself serves as indirect legislation: with his foregrounding and retreat he landscapes a distinction between appearance and reality and uses each to guide the other.

I might seem to be arguing that interests are really social constructions, and to be contributing to a constructivist critique of interest-based analyses. Because interests refer to connections that are said to be more fundamental and palpable than values or ideals, it may seem that my argument—by exposing Bentham's interest as a product of the discursively landscaped imagination—sits firmly on the constructivist side of a methodological divide. But if the supposedly reductionist Bentham can be read as a constructivist, this raises further questions. Theoretically, the two moments of his foregrounding and retreat could proceed in reverse order.[116] Bentham's texts show that both sides of any divide between apparent and real are potentially disruptive; and they exploit the usefulness of the systematic divide itself. After all, theorizing the motives provided by various sanctions as imaginary does absolutely nothing to lessen their force. If leading with materiality helped persuade subjects to endorse their landscaped interests two hundred years ago, perhaps foregrounding the imagination would be, and is, similarly effective today. From Bentham we learn that our imaginations are subject to a very public and political constitution and coordination: one that ultimately regulates the conduct of self-regulating, self-interested individuals. His work deploys interest, the imagination, and political science as tools of government.

When I introduced indirect legislation, I used an anachronistic vocabulary in a phrase that isn't Bentham's: I wrote of the coordination of the social systems of economy, culture, religion, and public opinion. "Social system" implies a pre-harmonization in governance that Bentham himself doesn't presume.[117] For Bentham, one project of the researcher is to investigate the practices of subjects so as to aid in the production of such systems. Thus his economic government is open to a certain range of appropriations, depending on the state of the disciplines and of the practices that they study and police. Theoretical and empirical researchers are, according to him, engaged in indirect legislation. We might think, then, about our investigations in relation to particular landscaping projects, and about the relationship between these and specific perspectives on and prospects of the lay of the land. If the lay of that land is increasingly neoliberal, my reading of Bentham suggests the need to rethink contemporary normative and positive theory's common emphasis on the choosing subject—to understand this emphasis not as right or wrong, accurate or inaccurate, but as symptomatic and facilitative of a particular project of economic government.

5 State Rationality

From Bentham we have learned that monistic interest is a grammar of economic government. With it we are organized, and organize ourselves, in schemes of maximally productive freedom. Monistic interest reframes our experience, and thus our conduct, by focusing our attention on ourselves in a way that raises the plausibility of a commensurability among our multiple relations to the world of things and other people. This reframing is a basic presupposition of economic rationality. We have explored an early example in Shaftesbury's *Inquiry*, which directs that one see oneself as an interest-economy constituent within a larger interest-economy. Bentham mobilizes this introspective framework for a project of government. His work shows us how the imagination can serve as the basis for a practical reason that comprehends and guides individual conduct in the proliferation of technologies that produce and maximize *society*—the powerful new abstraction glimpsed by Shaftesbury. That Bentham figures this as an abstraction—he can agree with Margaret Thatcher that "there is no such thing as society"—only enhances the governing power of aggregate interest in its endless battle against uneconomical, and therefore sinister, relations. This is not to say that Benthamic rule is neoliberal—the type of welfarism that was attacked by Thatcher has of course itself been justified in Benthamic terms—but only that neoliberal rule can be understood as a renewal of Benthamic monistic interest and its economic rationality.

Within modern liberal and democratic traditions, the free pursuit of interest conjoins and sometimes competes with another more prominent model of freedom and justification, that of sovereignty. Monistic interest is a type of rule, but it is not like sovereignty—the concept of rule with which we are most familiar. We like to tell the political history of the present in terms of sovereignty, often progressively, in terms of a long march in the West from absolute monarchies to liberal democracies: to increasingly inclusive popular sovereignties constitutionally limited to recognize the sovereignty of individuals over themselves. And so neoliberalism looks like an extension, for better or worse, of individual over against collective rights. But neoliberalism is a renewal of monistic interest, the logic of which has always been distinct from, and in tension with, the logic of sovereignty. Monistic interest resembles instead another doctrine of rule associated with the modern state: reason of state. Sovereignty is a juridical doctrine, but reason of state has an anti-juridical cast. Bentham was nothing if not a writer of jurisprudence, but his jurisprudence was, in a way, anti-juridical. Bentham's project aimed at converting laws into tactics of government. In Bentham's texts, sovereignty is subordinated to interest; it is subjected to an economic rationality. Any sovereign will or wills should obey the dictates of utility: it should maximize aggregate interest. Thus there is nothing good in and of itself about democracy or any other sovereign arrangement: democracy is simply the most effective way to subordinate sovereignty to utility in our complex societies.

What is the difference, at the most general level, between the logics of sovereignty and utility? The logic of sovereignty is essentially circular: sovereignty serves itself.[1] The rule of the sovereign serves the rule of the sovereign. And this is a good thing that we can evaluate as good independently of any specific sovereign act. Thus there is good reason to obey the command of the sovereign in the mere fact that it is the sovereign's command. If we doubt this, we need only reflect on today's sanctioned sovereignties. For example, if we are asked "Why are you doing this?" we answer, from the perspective of sovereignty, that it is what the people want, or that it is what our constitution requires. Similarly, if I am asked "Why are you doing this?" I answer, from the perspective of sovereignty, that this is what I desire, or that this is my duty. By contrast, consider the logic of utility. I obey the rule of interest because it recommends what is best. And we aim to realize aggregate interest because it is what is best. Thus, if I am asked "Why are you doing this?" I answer, from the perspective of utility, that this is the choice that cuts down most on interference among my expectations, so as to maximize my interest; and if I am a Benthamic deontologist I observe additionally how it conforms with what is required by and for society, because interest and duty are one.[2] Similarly, if we are asked "Why are you doing this?" we answer, from the perspective of utility, that this is the measure that cuts down most on interference among individuals' expectations; it establishes or conforms with the arrangement that maximizes interest across society. Bentham has been criticized for not acknowledging the presumptive authority of law;[3] according to him laws and policies, no matter how enacted, can always be judged to fall short in their service to interest. Laws are fundamental as constructors of expectations and instruments of security, but only as such; they have no independent status and are continuously open to assessment and revision. For Bentham, all sovereignty is ideally subordinated to government by monistic interest. It will not do to object here that my contrast between sovereignty and utility merely reflects an ancient conflict between voluntarism and rationalism, or that Bentham merely updated an ancient prudence that always demands our consideration of what is best for us before we act.[4] As I demonstrated in chapter 4, the rule of utility as monistic interest is the rule of a distinct rationality that stimulates and regulates the imagination, and it ties its individual prudence not to an ethos or a pragmatics or a universal morality but to an economized polity.

In chapter 2, I argued that neither a canonical narrative nor Albert O. Hirschman's competing story could account for the rise of monistic interest in political theorizing. In this chapter, reason of state is offered as an alternative line—as a more plausible site of entry for a history of the politics of economic rationality. Reason of state, broadly speaking, was the doctrine that directed statesmen to pay less attention to law, honor, religion, custom, or personal service in their practice, and more to the consequences of their conduct for the preservation and augmentation of the state. Reason of state, I maintain, was an early and limited manifestation of monistic interest. The present chapter will argue this point by explicating and supporting the following claims:

(1) Reason of state was primarily a Renaissance humanist discourse, but it was not exactly Machiavellian. As Hirschman following Meinecke writes, it constructed a kind of rational will that was finally at odds with Machiavelli's statecraft.[5] This rational will was a special prudence for rulers that did scandalize many contemporaries who associated it with the reputation of Machiavelli. But if we focus on the scandal, on reason of state's supposed immorality and instrumentality, we miss what is most important about reason of state. So what is most important for our purposes?

a) Reason of state is often called a "realist" doctrine, and there is good reason for this. Earlier and contemporary writings about political association were likely to focus on the question of foundations—to tell a story about how government came into being, which is also a story of why it is necessary and good, and perhaps why this or that particular government is not good. Reason of state was relatively unconcerned with foundations. It pretty much accepted states as it found them, and focused instead on their preservation and augmentation. And in so doing, it developed a kind of history (in the early modern sense) that evolved from humanist exemplarity and the experience of the ancients into a type of knowledge focusing more exclusively on the present. We might characterize this knowledge as both empirical and practical, as realist. Realism is never of course the whole story. Just as economic realism is a way of seeing that can function as a rhetoric of governance and thus provide its own confirmation, so too this political realism effectively repositioned princes and statesmen—proscribing certain common types of conduct, elevating the status and proliferating the number of new knowledge producers, and imposing a regular discipline. This repositioning was both cause and effect of the emergence and reproduction of the institutions that make up what we call "the state."

b) In matters of state, reason of state blurred and finally obliterated a key distinction that is absent also in Benthamic interest: the qualitative distinction between preservation and augmentation. A related distinction is that between life and the good life. Roughly put, early Christian natural law reversed the pagan priority of the good life over life, but it maintained the distinction between them. (One's happiness might be one's own, but one's life belonged to God.) This was evident in the natural-law distinction between matters of convenience and matters of necessity. Something resembling reason of state was present before the modern state as an occasional doctrine of necessity: to suspend existing rules when acting to preserve life was justified by natural law. But when reason of state developed as a standing prudence for a permanent state, it undermined the distinction between preservation and augmentation. We see this in the monistic language of interest that came out of reason of state. Both preservation and augmentation are subsumed into *interest*. Just as it doesn't make sense for us to maximize Benthamic interest at one time and not at another, it doesn't make sense for the state to act now according to its interest, and at another time not.

c) And so reason of state was a new knowledge and a new ethic. But the literature itself consisted of a hodgepodge of older and contemporary themes. It first followed some of the stylistic conventions of the traditional advice-to-princes genre (as did Machiavelli's notorious manual), but it became less and less a collection of general precepts and more and more concerned with the description of particular conditions, recognizing that actions must respond to circumstances. Already in Giovanni Botero's *Della Ragion di Stato* of 1589 we see how important it will be not only to estimate one's own and others' military strength and discipline, but to know other measurable things that are determined by what we would call geographic, demographic, and economic research. We see the importance put on the need for good information, reliable counsel, and secrecy. And we see how reason of state took up the police discourse of cities—the preoccupation with regulating for their improvement any number of things from mores to hygiene to childrearing—and applied it on a new statewide scale. All this was for the sake of the future, and would make use, in some texts, of a kind of primitive probability. Reason of state prospected the future on the basis of knowledge of the present. It demanded continuous stock taking and the production of aggregate figures. And its counsel bound the newly legitimated absolutism of the prince to the interest of state. (Even in reason of state's more Machiavellian moments—when the prince's own people and foreigners seem almost to be equated as potential enemies—the ruin of the people is theorized as the ruin of rule and hence the ruin of the prince, and the people's good is his good.) Thus reason of state combined some of the scope of Bentham's concerns with his emphasis on calculation. It even developed a critique of what Bentham would call sinister interest—a critique of interests opposed to the public interest or interest of state.

(2) Reason of state has important affinities with Benthamic monistic interest and its economic rationality, but ultimately is strongly incompatible with it. Interest of state, even in its republican variants, is a "top-down" discourse; Bentham's aggregate interest is "bottom-up," and the whole for Bentham is a "fictitious body"—nothing more than its individual parts. There is a striking absence of reason of state in Bentham's work. (For example, he declares it a "dangerous" application of the principle of utility, but an application nonetheless, to sacrifice your own state if at war with a more populous enemy.)[6] Also, reason of state's state interest is monistic with regard to subjects, but not with regard to the other states with which it is in an often zero-sum game—whereas Benthamic interest is strictly monistic, and any important zero-sum practice would probably involve at least one sinister player, and so require reform. Finally and most importantly, state interest is contained by the state. This means that it is limited in the extent to which it can attack the institutions that are its basis, whereas Bentham was not. Bentham subjected state institutions to more relentless critique than any others, because of their greater potential to generate sinister interest. (His response to secrecy was publicity.) At the same

time, interest of state's containment by the state means that it directly governs only certain individuals and only in their capacity as statesmen, whereas Benthamic interest governs potentially all calculating agents in their every activity. Perhaps then we might fancifully see Bentham's individuals as mini-states—each one's sovereignty thoroughly captured by its reason of state, neither bound together by a superstate nor living in an unstable anarchy, but instead acting within a regulated cosmopolitan order purged of the political dynamics of alliance and counter-alliance.

(3) For a fuller understanding of monistic interest, we need to move from the Continent to England, where reason of state mutated in the context of a war-torn island nation with peculiar traditions of government. Here we see how a distinct notion of the public interest preceded state formation, linked with the imagination, and replaced private interest by self-interest. But this is the subject of the next chapter.

Neo-Stoicism

Reason of state (*ragion di stato*, *raison d'état*, *Staatsräson*) emerged alongside the new institutions of the modern state in Continental Europe in the sixteenth and seventeenth centuries. Europe remained throughout this period in key respects medieval, still divided among those who fight, those who pray, and those who work. But at least by the peace of Westphalia of 1648 the region was for the most part newly organized into recognizable states, with a weaker church and empire above and weaker estates below. Nobility and clergy were formerly both local and cosmopolitan, and many of their possessions were scattered. By the mid-seventeeth century nobility and clergy were more likely to be tied to increasingly compact states. The sixteenth and seventeenth centuries were of course quite bloody. The new proliferation of printed texts—especially the Bible—played a huge part in the confessional conflicts of the Reformation. Print was also crucial to the spread of a cross-confessional humanism: the second-most printed text, after the Bible, was Cicero's *De Officiis* (*On Duties*).[7] *On Duties* and other Roman texts offered among other things a certain solace, reminding their readers that others had found ways to make sense of and cope with similarly troubled times. Early reason of state was predominantly but not exclusively a humanist or at least Roman-citing literature; some writers associated with it quoted Cicero less often than Tacitus, whose bleaker vision and more staccato style they shared.[8] Reason of state was a common Continental project, not limited to any particular type of regime or to either side of the Reformation divide.

Much of the ethical and political writing from this time and place has a strong neo-Stoical flavor. (*On Duties* was itself a revision and popularization of Stoic doctrines.) This is important to our story of monistic interest, because Stoicism emphasizes the primacy and unity of the self and the universal, and it recommends a kind of consistent rationality. (Shaftesbury's *Inquiry* is called neo-Stoic, as is much eighteenth-century British moral philosophy.) Especially in its more rigorous forms Stoicism insists on an impartiality that has certain egalitarian implications; these qualities are resonant in Bentham's work. We can see elements of neo-Stoicism in two strikingly different sixteenth-century writers, Jean Calvin, the zealous Reformer (1509–64), and Michel de Montaigne, the skeptical Catholic (1533–92). Calvin, who quotes Scripture extensively but also relies on classical sources, begins the first paragraph of book 1 of *Institutes of the Christian Religion* with the following Augustinian heading: "*Without knowledge of self there is no knowledge of God.*"[9] Montaigne, who cites Cicero more than any other author, begins his *Essays* with a warning to the reader—"I am myself the matter of my book"—and his final essay praises living "'according to nature'" and states that "it is an absolute perfection and virtually divine to know how to enjoy our being rightfully."[10] Both writers have a conventionalist understanding of much inequality. And both respond to the clashing, inconstant, and frequently oppressive civil authorities of their time by recommending obedient service, but service marked by constancy and not at the expense of what we might call a kind of integrity.

Calvin and Montaigne also of course demonstrate powerful discontinuities among neo-Stoic possibilities. Some of these discontinuities are masked by the ambiguities of our vague and inadequate "integrity." A quick comparison with the much later Shaftesbury is instructive. Calvin's and Montaigne's conceptions of virtue clash strongly with one another and both clash with that of Shaftesbury's *Inquiry*. If Calvin's *Institutes* and the *Inquiry* are both focused on the interior of the self and emphasize the quality of what Shaftesbury calls the affections, still Calvin's emphasis on the worthlessness of all that is human and Shaftesbury's emphasis on conformity to a species-economy are strictly abhorrent to one another. And Montaigne's *Essays* differ from both the *Institutes* and the *Inquiry* in their attention to virtue as a matter of action and comportment—their attention to an ancient ethical tradition, developed by Cicero among others, that is more concerned with the exterior than it is with the interior of the self. Calvin's preoccupation with purity of heart and hidden motives vehemently rejects this tradition. Shaftesbury, on the other hand, is schizophrenic, but emblematically so. His "polite" writings contribute to a discourse of manners that extends, though in domesticated form, the concern with the exterior, while the *Inquiry* develops the self-inspecting preoccupations of much modern moral philosophy. This practice of self-inspection, with Calvin's conscience displaced by the imagination, is crucial to government by monistic interest.

Justus Lipsius (1547–1606) was a Netherlandish neo-Stoic who lived and taught on both sides of the confessional divide. He was associated by contemporaries with reason of state (though he himself didn't use this phrase).[11] The association stems from his popularization of a neo-pagan civil prudence that cautiously justified princely deceit. But Lipsius's prudence is of more lasting importance for assembling some of the elements of an emerging state rationality. The producer of definitive modern editions of Seneca and Tacitus, he was perhaps the most famous European philosopher of his time, and wrote a widely translated and read book of ethics, *De Constantia* (*Of Constancy*).[12] Civil prudence is the subject of *Politicorum Libri Sex* (*Six Books of Politics*), a cento, or patchwork, of ancient political wisdom that relies heavily on Tacitus and Cicero.[13] A treatise of this sort would normally begin with a dedication to a high personage and perhaps an additional note to the anonymous reader. Lipsius begins instead with a letter addressed to "Emperour. Kings. Princes."—that is, addressed to a varied collection of contemporary sovereigns. The opening is followed by a first book that is unusual in a manual aimed at princes; like the final book, it contains material useful not only for sovereigns but for "public" and "private" men as well. The first book deals with virtue and prudence, which should govern all in their dealings with one another. The last book treats civil war and tyranny and how individuals should respond to them; private men should respond with withdrawal and constancy. Virtuous prudence is the main subject of the work as a whole; the intervening books treat the specifically political prudence that elaborates a kind of neo-Stoic statecraft.

The subject of the *Six Books of Politics* is conduct, but the work is distinguishable from the ubiquitous conduct books of this and earlier periods (the medieval mirror-of-princes tracts can reasonably be called conduct books for rulers). For Lipsius's contemporaries, the important difference was in the last two chapters of the fourth book, where he defends "mixed prudence" in the conduct of princes. This prudence is allowable against domestic as well as foreign adversaries. Here Lipsius includes a brief apology for Machiavelli, "who poore soule is layde at of all hands," and justifies the use of "light" and "middle," but not "great" deceit. Light deceit is *"a subtile counsell, which swarveth from vertue or the lawes for the good of the Prince and the estate."*[14] Deceit requires secrecy.[15] Middle deceit, which goes beyond dissimulation to involve the purchasing of favor through bribery or fraud, must be tolerated under the conditions obtaining in Europe at this time. These methods, offensive to God and condemned in Scripture, are acceptable if "referred to the profit of the common wealth, which easilie draweth and draineth to it selfe, all the venime of vice that is therein. . . . *These things* do seeme *profitable as it were a medicine*."[16] Great deceits—treachery and injustice that involve, for example, the breaking of oaths, or the violation of one's own laws and subjects' privileges—are rejected with one exception: "except it be for his own conservation, but never to inlarge his estate. For *necessitie which is the true defender of the weakenesse of man, doth break all lawes*."[17] This exception seems to be the traditional one; it cleaves to the distinction between preservation and augmentation.

In ancient and medieval classical and Christian traditions law was understood to vary in its details, but to be commonly based on the law of nature. Natural law included a doctrine of exception, a doctrine that justified breaking civil laws and elements of natural law itself if necessary—for preservation. The law of preservation or law of necessity was a powerful justification of extra-constitutional sovereign prerogative. Cicero's *salus populi suprema lex esto* (the safety of the people is the supreme law) could be cited for this purpose.[18] Necessity played an important role in the early modern enhancement of the juridical status of sovereigns, as did their expanding role as religious leaders. Their new status was reflected in formal theories of sovereignty, which turned formerly exceptional powers into standing and superintending highest powers. The popularity of Cicero's slogan and the argument from necessity was only heightened by its capacity to underwrite the consolidation of authority in both monarchies and republics, and by its capacity to justify resistance as well.

Although Lipsius's great deceit is only permitted when facing a threat to preservation itself, his middle deceit is justified by "profit to the commonwealth." Lipsius's first defense of middle deceit cites *On Duties*; thus he marries his conception of public utility to that invoked by Cicero in the latter's discussion of the relationship between *utilitas* (the useful or beneficial) and *honestum* (the honorable).[19] Cicero's discussion was a common touchstone for the questions raised in and by Reformation statecraft, because the public utility was Cicero's highest justification for any action. In actions taken in behalf of the public good, the ultimate identity of the beneficial and the honorable is clear. In *On Duties* it is also clear that it would never be honorable to break faith or even defraud for one's own preservation or benefit; this does not mean, however, that there is a tension between *utilitas* and *honestum*, because the consequences of some dishonorable actions only *appear* beneficial—it can never be beneficial to dishonor oneself, even to save one's life.[20] This sheds light on the robustly political character of Cicero's understanding of the *salus populi* in the doctrine of necessity; it is for preservation of the *res publica*, not for the preservation of life, that one might engage in extra-legal measures. And preserving the republic is not itself about preserving life, but about preserving a way of life. The "public utility" of *On Duties* is a public benefit, possibly something well short of the republic's preservation, but the stakes are high and similarly political. To act for the good of the republic could only seem dishonorable; its honor would shine through in the end. (*On Duties* was composed in the wake of the assassination of Julius Caesar.)

Lipsius's public utility appropriated a Ciceronian standard that was inspirational for Renaissance republicanism and its philosophy of citizenship. One way to understand the modification wrought by civil prudence is that it gave Cicero's standard a more consequentialist and therefore proto-utilitarian reading; the dramatic extraordinariness of its application was converted into a strategic and even secretive regular practice. In the process the Ciceronian political distinctions that were so dear to early republicans were increasingly buried, as politics, including republican politics, became tied to emerging institutions of state. The historical irony here is that this was done, in part, in a Ciceronian idiom. Public utility, the contested good for the sake of which all those who are citizens act, became a measurable good pursued by a specialized class, who acted not so much for its sake but in order to safeguard and augment it.[21] And this modified Ciceronian ideal would in turn eventually erode the distinction crucial to extant conceptions of natural law—that between what is necessary and what is convenient. The conflation was manifest in the seventeenth-century translation of *utilitas* as "interest." Interest includes what is necessary as well as what is simply beneficial, and what is necessary is life, which the state preserves. Reason of state's interest of state would make life-preserving state preservation and augmentation fully commensurable with one another, endangering even Lipsius's doctrine of necessity.[22]

In their updating by denizens of early modern Christendom, Ciceronian ethico-political concerns were often translated into a moral idiom; his exteriorized language of honor was often translated into the more interiorized language of conscience. We see this even with Montaigne, whom I contrasted above with Calvin on this score, and who, even though he makes good fun of Cicero's obsession with his reputation, does not share Calvin's animus toward pagan virtue. Montaigne devotes one of his essays to *utilitas* and *honestum*, and applies the theme to statecraft. But the essay absorbs public utility into necessity rather than necessity into public utility, and it is ambivalent even about this doctrine of necessity. Montaigne writes the following about princely faith breaking: "No private utility is worthy of our doing this violence to our conscience; the public utility yes, when it is very apparent and very important." This would involve "some urgent circumstance or sudden and unexpected accident of state necessity." But "if there should be a prince with so tender a conscience that no cure seemed to him worth so onerous a remedy, I would not esteem him the less. He could not ruin himself more excusably or becomingly."[23] What looks to Montaigne like an honorable act of omission would be for later writers a dereliction of duty. Consider Cardinal Richelieu, for whose *raison d'état* this ruin of the prince would be the ruin of the state, and for whom the ruin of the state is the ruin not only of subjects' bodies but also of their souls, as the steady pressure of Reformation and counter-Reformation fused political and religious practice on both sides of the confessional divide. Advising Louis XIII, Richelieu wrote that "devotion . . . ought to be devoid of all overscrupulousness. I say this, Sire, because the sensitiveness of Your Majesty's conscience has often made you fear to offend God in reaching even those decisions which you cannot abstain from making without sin."[24] Note that both Montaigne and Richelieu oppose conscience to statecraft. We musn't, however, anachronistically attribute secularism to reason of state; Richelieu describes the consequences of indulging conscience here as "sinful." The theological charge of Reformation-era politics played a huge role in states' emerging independence and justification and in their subordination of their officers. It also contributed, ironically, to the separation of theological questions from questions of reason of state, and not only because some theorists, such as Lipsius, stressed the need for a public religious uniformity that left private belief alone. Precisely *because* of the state's increased religious importance it is perfectly consistent with a continuing theistic orientation that Richelieu would, as he notoriously did, invoke *raison d'état* to make alliances across the confessional divide—for example with Protestant Sweden against Catholic Spain.

The quotation from Richelieu effectively demonstrates how the political "realism" of *raison d'état* was not a matter of simply dropping one's illusions about the conduct of rulers and describing them and the world as it was. Richelieu, after all, worries that his own prince is overscrupulous. In other places he warns Louis about his emotional outbursts and loose tongue, the dangers of pity, and favoritism.[25] The picture we get from reading Richelieu is that of a prince far less likely to act according to his own interest and the interest of state than to act otherwise, and only protected from himself by the tireless activity of faithful advisors. It makes sense that what Richelieu called the "public interest" should be the charge of a collective of statesmen, because the reason that should govern public administration must never sleep. In remarks on foresight and on negotiation, Richelieu makes it clear that *raison d'état* is not only a difficult discipline but one that must be kept at all times and for all matters.[26] And when he writes about the public interest as the "first objective," it is clear that this is understood as a calculable objective pursued with unwavering focus.[27] Here the danger is the private interests that buffet public policy hither and thither—eventually, if left unchecked, to the ruin of the state now understood as the ruin of all.

Civil Prudence and Reason of State

How do we get from Montaigne's exceptional act to Richelieu's regular discipline, and from Montaigne's consequences of self-ruin to Richelieu's concerns about the destruction of the whole? One answer lies in the rich French intellectual history of the intervening half-century, which includes remarkable instances of rationalist skepticism and theistic Machiavellianism. This history has been well told by others.[28] I want to step back, however, from the questions that were most important to contemporaries and that have therefore most concerned historians of political thought. If we focus too much on the morality of politics we remain in danger of slipping back into the framework that I have criticized throughout this study, the framework that takes for granted categories like self-interest and public interest, and that explores the dilemmas their relations produce. Instead, we need to attend to the formation of these interests of self and whole which, as we have seen from readings of Shaftesbury and Bentham, are themselves already a complex of relations. And so we need to attend to a shifting terrain of background assumptions and practices.

If we return to Lipsius we can see that there is a troubling ambiguity from our perspective in his argument from necessity. Whereas other offensive means are justified by the profit of the commonwealth, great deceit is justified only by the priority of the prince's preservation, "but never to inlarge his estate." What are the connections here among prince, state, and commonwealth, and their respective preservation and profit? Lipsius is well aware that what is to a prince's benefit might not be to his commonwealth's. This is clear from the second book, where he writes about the prince that "*all his actions . . . ought to be for the good of his subjects, for which he ought to sed aside his owne privat benefit.*"[29] Such an orientation is what distinguishes a king from a tyrant, and a true principality from a false one. Our confusion results from the fact that Lipsius, like many of his contemporaries, assumes here that the state is not so much its own person as it is the prince's status or estate; at the same time, he shares our assumption that a tyrannical prince is not necessarily ruining himself in ruining this estate, but might somehow derive a "private benefit," if certainly not honor, from harming his subjects. In using this language—that there really is a private benefit to set aside here—Lipsius shows some (not uncommon) distance from classical and Christian ethics. These would hold that what seems like a benefit to the tyrant is in fact not one. Reason of state effectively repaired this ancient connection between the goods of realm and prince, but it did so on new and redefined terms. Some of these terms were the terms of a nascent political oeconomy, organized around the prince's pressing need to secure dependable sources of tribute. The problem of tying down a potentially Machiavellian prince is more generally solved, however, by the emergence of the state as a distinct personality with its own interest. This confirms a new absolutism through the strong identification of prince and state, but it also plants the seeds of that absolutism's eventual destruction.

We can track the emergence of a distinct state personality if we leap forward again to Richelieu's period and beyond. In 1637, long into the Thirty Years War, Louis XIII was faced with a resistance to taxation that was increasingly common in the stressed regimes of the period. His response was: "the money that I ask is not for gambling or foolish expenditure. It is not I who speaks; it is my state. It is the need that all have of it. Those who contradict my orders do me more harm than the Spanish."[30] What Louis was saying here is quite peculiar. Perhaps it is a kind of mix of past and future sovereignty—something, in effect, like the following: I am speaking not as Louis de Bourbon, but as Louis XIII. Thus my purpose is not only not frivolous, it is not exactly my purpose but our purpose. But our purpose is my purpose when I speak as Louis XIII; it is the purpose of "my state." The Spanish harm it, that is to say me, that is to say us, and so do you when you disobey me—that is to say, when you disobey my state. This is a more complicated package than the traditional distinction between the private and public persons of the king: between Louis de Bourbon and Louis XIII. It could be that the state here merely suggests the king in his royal person, but if so, it is one that is quite dynamic and existential. Or maybe it is merely Louis XIII's status or estate, which comprises all his territories and subjects, but then the collapse of identity is somewhat peculiar. Something new seems to be emerging, something confirmed by Louis XIV's notorious if apocryphal "L'état, c'est moi." This attributed assertion of identity implies a more complete alienation than what is expressed in the phrase of his predecessor.

We now speak not of "my state" but of "the state," and its priority is taken for granted.

Of course this new state—this something that seems to reoccupy the territory of republic and realm and that is more than anyone's estate or status—can be and has been seen and understood entirely within the framework of sovereignty. Jean Bodin, in his *Six Livres de la République*, had made a juridical argument that recognized an absolute and perpetual power, located in either a prince, aristocracy, or people, and bound only by the laws of God and nature. Bodin also developed themes that are of greater relevance to us here: he wrote about various existential needs of the republic rather than simply about its legitimacy, and his juridical argument was tied in complex ways to these requirements, sometimes specifically in the language of "interest."[31] Thus Bodin, like Hobbes after him, can be considered a theorist of the state as well as a theorist of sovereignty. Like reason of state, the new absolutist theories of sovereignty contributed to the construction of a state personality, both legitimating the increasing absolutism of monarchs and overshadowing them with the states in whose names they acted. But specifically juridical supports, critiques, and reconfigurations of absolute sovereignty differed from the dynamics of reason of state and state interest. They revolved around obligation and consent, and their most prominent issue was in seventeenth- and eighteenth-century social contract theory and in eighteenth- and nineteenth-century rule of law and popular sovereignty. But from seventeenth-century Dutch republicanism to nineteenth-century British Radicalism, another tradition of argument would see monarchs as presumptively unfit because of the tension between their personal interests and the public interest or interest of state.[32]

Toward the conclusion of this chapter I will turn to a treatise by Henri, Duc de Rohan, a Huguenot associate and sometime enemy of Richelieu's, to illustrate how princes were explicitly subordinated in an advice-to-princes piece that marked the emergence of distinct state personalities with continuous interests. State interest subordinated princes, but not within a dialectic of sovereignty and public law. With Rohan we can see that a non-juridical discourse was governing princes with a distinct and existential political rationality: a reason of state that did not care about origins or obligation, only about present and future interest. Interest of state regulated princely behavior, but not in the language of law. Rohan's piece is remarkably free of general precepts; its focus is the identification of an interest based on worldly observations. These observations constituted a kind of new knowledge of state—a primitive statistics—that took on a significant governmental role. General precepts cannot govern one as fully and continuously as particulars can. Reason of state, like economic rationality, is more exacting than many alternatives. If we go back to Lipsius and his contemporary Giovanni Botero, we can see how in this respect also reason of state differed from both juridical rule and from Machiavellian statecraft.

Lipsius was recognized by contemporaries as a theorist of "the new-found politicke" because of his "Machiavellism": his justification of "mixed prudence." But Lipsius himself attacked the widespread cynicism associated with courtiers: cynicism that was tied by others, but not by Lipsius, to Machiavelli, who celebrated the dissimulation that Lipsius cautiously defends. Machiavelli's celebration of dissimulation in *The Prince* is a celebration of the prince's potential to master *fortuna* with his *virtù* in the pursuit of glory for himself and his possessions. And although Machiavelli's book was of course itself advice—its scandalous content took the form of an established advice-to-princes genre—it advised the prince to beware of counsel and to rely as much as possible on his own wits. Lipsian prudence had a very different orientation from Machiavellian *virtù*; this difference was clearest concerning the pursuit of glory and the reliance on counsel. His prudence also differed from the contemporary cynicism (rightly or wrongly) associated with Machiavelli: a cynicism that saw politics as the simple and simply immoral pursuit of profit by rulers. Attention to these differences can help us to see the emergence of a reason of state that serves the state by preserving and augmenting it. On the matter of sinfulness that so concerned contemporaries we can see how Lipsian prudence acted as a bridge between Montaigne's and Richelieu's orientations. But if we pay too much attention to the (im)morality of reason of state we will lose sight of some of the shifts that may have been less noticed by contemporaries, shifts that register a new logic of rule. What is interesting for our purposes is not only this difference between Montaigne and Richelieu: that a prince's ruinous conscientiousness would be admired by the former and condemned as sinful by the latter. In addition, we should attend closely to the kinds of knowledge that governed action directed by a mature reason of state. This knowledge fills the other gap between Montaigne and Richelieu: the movement from *a* reason of state to *the* reason of state, from exceptional doctrine of necessity to regular discipline. Here we can see some elements of a new concatenation through which statesmen would govern and be governed.

In other words, what is important is less the relationship between the special prudence of rulers and the moral valences of classical and Christian ethics, and more the baggage that came with civil prudence. This baggage itself imposes a kind of virtue that explains some of reason of state's distance from Machiavellian *virtù*; it imposes the virtue of a knowledge and method of state, the virtue of a primitive statistics. We see some of this baggage if we look more closely at Lipsius's prudence. The advice-to-princes genre—and this includes Machiavelli's own entry—consisted of a series of precepts to be absorbed as part of the education of the prince. The newer humanist versions of this genre—again including *The Prince*—were likely to illustrate and support such precepts with examples, with what the period called histories. In telling and retelling histories one was not at all preoccupied with chronology—their pastness or presentness was not what was at issue—but with this illustrativeness, and ancient writers' accounts of great Roman deeds and events provided the richest source of examples. This is not to say that the rhetorical work of histories overwhelmed or could even be separated from their evidentiary status, or that their exemplariness rendered them somehow secondary to other literatures or stated purposes. Histories were worth telling and retelling in and of themselves, even without additional textual apparatus. The *Six Books of Politics* is itself filled with precepts from histories; nevertheless, Lipsius argues early on that prudence cannot rely on these. Thus his work is filled with general tips on the need to get specific.

> *Prudence* hath two parents, *Use, and Memory of things.* . . . Use is more sure then the other. . . . For it instructeth us, by our own not by other mens harmes, by examples neere at hand not farre distant. . . . *Use surpasseth the rules and precepts of all teachers.* And who so hath much experience may wel brag, *that he hath particular knowledge of good and evil.* This is profitable, (or rather necessarie) for everie art . . . : and principally it conduceth unto Civill pollicie. . . . In which neverthelesse this evil happeneth, that it is not learned by precepts, but *taught by time.*[33]

Prudence has just been defined in the previous chapter as "*an understanding & discretion of those things which we ought either to desire or refuse, in publike, & in privat.*"[34] And of its power, Lipsius wrote that "*all things yeeld obedience unto Prudence*, even Fortune her selfe: neither is it said without cause, *A wise man frameth his owne fortune.*"[35]

Prudence, which has the power to master fortune, comes most assuredly from experience and cannot be reduced to precepts. Lipsius immediately follows these claims, however, with a chapter endorsing memory and histories, and with one of many statements of the importance of counsel and doctrine.[36] Government requires prudence because "*force that is not assisted with advise, of it owne selfe destroyeth it selfe*"; the prince requires assistance because "*it is seldome, or never seene, that a Prince is of himselfe endued with competent wisedome.*"[37] Of the prudence proper to the prince, Lipsius writes that it is "a verie *diffused* thing, *confused, & obscure.*" It is diffuse because it concerns particulars, and "particulars are infinite." It is confused because it is "the election of those things, which never remaine after one and same manner." And it is obscure because "the affaires and successe of worldly matters, are covered with a thicke mist."[38] Governmental prudence, then, is knowledge of particulars—but of which particulars? Lipsius distinguishes civil from military prudence, devoting a book to each. The discussion of civil prudence includes much that would seem, according to the doctrine, to be of limited use. For example, Lipsius points out the need for rulers to know the specific characteristics of their own subjects and of neighboring peoples, but the discussion quickly lapses into a long and unflattering description of common people in general.[39] More care is taken when he goes on to some of the specifics of maintaining authority. Consider, for example, the problem of revenue. The surest route to authority is power, and power consists first and foremost in wealth understood as treasure: "*All things are sould for money.*"[40] But the extraction of tribute is one of those sensitive areas that can, if imprudently handled, endanger authority by generating hatred. General precepts here include the need for restraint on the part of the prince, and wariness and cautious oversight of the generally scurrilous race of tax collectors. But some precepts insist on the acquisition of more specific knowledge. For example, accounts should be made of expenditures and given to the people to supplement instruction in the necessity of taxation.[41] Dissension can be reduced by respecting equity in taxation, which can only be done by "*the assuring of every man his substaunce, a most profitable thing to advance a kingdome to greatnesse.*" And this in turn requires powerful censors—ideally chosen by the people—to "*value the ages, races, families, and revenues of thy people*" and "*set downe the uttermost estimation of their substance.*"[42]

The need for specific knowledge and reliance on it is even clearer in the case of military prudence, the subject of the fifth book. But first, we should note that the text's incorporation of military discipline and organization into a treatise on politics and civil doctrine is itself significant. It betrays the thorough merging of issues that might otherwise be thought fit for separate treatment, and suggests the normalization of a regime of continuous military endeavor and, if not standing armies, at least a standing system of tribute and ready stores of arms and victuals so that armies can be quickly raised and deployed when needed. That these are features of a generalizable state apparatus is confirmed by Lipsius's scrupulous if unclear reference, in a treatise addressed to monarchs, to others—perhaps not only regents but also republican councils. He writes that "*the authority, and advise of enterprising a warre, doth remaine in the power of the Prince*: Or else with those in every common wealth, who supply the place of the Prince."[43] For Lipsius, the concerns of all rulers, whether monarchs or not, were similar. The important distinction for him was that between "public men" and "private men"; he emphatically insisted on it because it was a distinction so difficult to maintain (and so necessary, for the peace of private men) in a world of warlords and rampant civil war.

It is in the discussion of war consultations and reports that we see most clearly the features of a prudence of particulars. "All things are to be enquired after: *thou oughtest not to be ignorant of thine owne armie, and the enemies: likewise, the scituation of places, the nature of countries*." And, "if it be manifest, that thy side is the strongest, which thou must looke into seriouslie, and without flattering thy selfe, . . . then do not *differre the battaile, when oportunitie is offered*." Moderate attention to divine signs and dreams is appropriate.[44] But the rationalism of Lipsius's approach to all information is apparent from his care to distinguish report from rumor, and by his insistence that consideration of the quality of consultations be separated from the question of success or failure:

> the *Carthaginiens did execute those Captaines who enterprised any warre, led thereto by bad counsell, though good & prosperous fortune did follow . . .* : which they did not unconsideratelie. For although *fortune prevaileth much in all things, but especiallie in martiall affaires*, . . . yet surely counsell hath therin a great & forcible part: and it is by good advise, for the most part that she is good unto us. Whereupon *Attius* said, *that every man was the framer of his owne Fortune*: and *Fabius* was of this minde, *that Fortune had no great power over a good and vertuous Emperour but the minde and reason did rule over him.*[45]

Acquisition of vetted reports on all relevant factors followed by sober calculation of the chances of success or failure: Lipsius's prudent ruler is closer to a modern student of probability taming chance than he is to a Machiavellian prince subduing *Fortuna* with *virtù*.[46]

The movement away from precepts and toward particulars is also evident in a text published earlier in the same year (1589) as Lipsius's *Six Books of Politics*: Giovanni Botero's *Della Ragion di Stato* (*The Reason of State*). Botero (1544–1617) was from Piedmont, a teacher and papal diplomat who was close to, but never accepted into, the Jesuit order. His book, like Lipsius's, attacked what he saw as the cynical politics of courtiers; it was posed, like many others from the sixteenth through eighteenth centuries, directly against the specter of Machiavelli. The book was the first to use "reason of state" in its title; its dedicatory letter begins as follows:

> In recent years I have been obliged by various circumstances . . . to frequent, more than I should have wished, the courts of kings and great princes, in Italy and beyond the Alps. Among the things that I have observed, I have been greatly astonished to find Reason of State a constant subject of discussion and to hear the opinions of Niccolò Machiavelli and Cornelius Tacitus frequently quoted. . . . I was amazed that so impious an author [Machiavelli] and so wicked a tyrant [Emperor Tiberius, who was praised by Tacitus] should be held in such esteem that they are thought to provide ideal examples of the methods by which states should be governed and administered; and I was moved to indignation rather than amazement to find that this barbarous mode of government had won such acceptance that it was brazenly opposed to Divine Law, so that men even spoke of some things being permissible by Reason of State and others by conscience.[47]

Despite this opening, what follows relies heavily on Tacitus for support; it also joins *The Prince* in endorsing dissimulation and in moving away from traditional juridical and governmental themes and toward the simple, unadorned question of how to preserve and extend one's state, where "state" is defined in the opening of the first book as "a stable rule over a people."[48] Very important to this rule is prudence and the "forms of knowledge" which increase prudence; it is again in the particulars of the determination, content, and application of this knowledge, and not in Botero's commitments or equivocations regarding conscience and traditional virtues, that we can see what was most important to an emerging logic of rule.[49]

Much of *The Reason of State* consists in the usual collection of precepts and their illustration with exemplary histories. Botero's illustrating histories seamlessly blend, in a method common to other, especially Italian texts, textually supported ancient and unsupported contemporary examples. What is particularly interesting for our purposes is the range and depth of Botero's illustrations, characteristics of a part of the knowledge specific to his reason of state. Reason of state is "knowledge of the means by which . . . dominion may be founded, preserved and extended. . . . It is concerned most nearly with preservation, and more nearly with extension than with foundation."[50] Some of what follows is abstract and general as with Lipsius; but one immediate difference can be seen in Botero's provision of knowledge about the people. Instead of a list of characteristics of common people everywhere, Botero engages in a comparative geography, stressing the differences that climate and other factors make in the dispositions of peoples. Botero writes more fully than Lipsius in the historical mode—he relies less on his citations for their maxims and more for detailed illustrations of his maxims. And in a text that makes a typical appeal for Christian unity against Turks and other "infidels," he uses often favorable examples from Ottoman and even Chinese practices interchangeably with European ones. And he combines this range with a penchant for numerical measurement, thus beginning to fill in the "disinterested" content by which state interest would come to be defined. "Admit to your counsels no one who owes allegiance to another ruler, for he whose interest lies elsewhere cannot give you an unbiassed opinion, and interest enters in many and subtle ways into the consultations of princes."[51] Reason of state requires disinterested information, often acquired or at least held in secrecy, and following its recommendations might require disciplining by secreting away one's passions: "There is nothing more fatal to dissimulation than the impetuousity of wrath, and the prince must so control this passion that he never betrays himself by words or other signs of anger or emotion."[52]

Botero, like Lipsius, advised the prince about what knowledge he needed and, again like Lipsius, gave special emphasis to the problem of wealth.[53] Because of wealth's relationship to preserving and extending the state, knowledge of the sources of wealth was an important part of the reason of state. Botero did not give Lipsius's advice to measure the wealth of one's state, but he expanded the scope of matters that concern wealth, and deployed numbers to illustrate their connection to it. All this was necessary because of wealth's relationship to ready money and the things that could be done with it. The prince must not think that he can raise money in times of need only: "it is essential to have money ready for such emergencies."[54] There is no set formula of how much to have; the situation of a country with regard to commerce and neighboring states is relevant. Certainly one standard is only to tax so much that "the trade and commerce of the country continues its normal course": anything more will ruin people, state, and prince. Here Botero offers both reported and hypothetical numbers, and in describing the results of overtaxation deploys the loaded and ambiguous pastoral image of a prince "unable to shear his subjects, let alone fleece them."[55] Population is crucial—"the ruler who has many subjects will also have plenty of money"—and here again Botero deploys numbers to illustrate.[56] But "nothing is of greater importance for increasing the power of a state and gaining for it more inhabitants and wealth of every kind than the industry of its people and the number of crafts they exercise." A "conflux of money and people" is the inevitable effect of a plurality of occupations, which is much more important to wealth than the fertility of the soil. Contemporary numbers are provided to illustrate this, as they are to illustrate the importance of attention to "marriage and the upbringing of the young."[57] Supervision of not only fertility but also care is crucial. Consider the problems of Cairo and Constantinople: "Plague and disease arise . . . from the closeness and discomfort of the dwellings, the filth and dirt of living conditions and lack of care on the part of the government to keep the cities clean and the air purified, and other similar causes. All these things make it difficult to rear children, and although great numbers are born, comparatively few survive or grow to be men of any value."[58]

We see that Botero's reason of state incorporated the contemporary project of "policing." Policing was an urban practice and the subject of an urban literature, and it is fitting that the section on industry was transplanted from Botero's earlier treatise on *The Greatness of Cities*, and that he further made his points about lack of care with population numbers from contemporary Europe that illustrated the limits of urban growth.[59] Police ordinances, which dated from the late Middle Ages, were aimed at regulating a fantastic range of activities in the towns. The new humanist civil prudence, which circulated in the universities, trained contemporary bureaucrats, Calvinist and Jesuit alike, to carry this rage for order beyond the cities and into provincial and state administration. Thus this prudence—whose greatest and most circulated theorist would be Lipsius himself—implemented policing on a new national scale.[60] Botero's *Ragioni di Stato* was first translated into German not as *Staatsräson* but by a title that included "*guter Polizeien*."[61] Reason of state's incorporation and extension of policing was highly significant, because the literature on policing was about governing inhabitants more than it was about governing territory. And police governed them very much in the name of their own good; it fostered, among other things, health and life, as in the example above from Botero.[62] The regulations of urban police presupposed that the discipline also emphasized by both Lipsius and Botero did not apply exclusively to soldiers, but could be generalized to others. The Genevan Calvin, for example, took it for granted when discussing a specific discipline—church discipline—that "no society, indeed, no house which has even a small family, can be kept in proper condition without discipline."[63]

The *étatisation* of police was marked by the appearance of something called "political economy." Political economy, for the Aristotelian tradition, is a category mistake: a conflation of the principles that govern city-states with those of household management (*oikonomia*). The first title to use this phrase—Antoine de Montchrétien's *Traicté de l'Oeconomie Politique* (*Treatise of Political Economy*, 1615)—confronted this tradition head-on:

> In the State as in the family it is of good fortune and great profit to manage each man according to his own particular inclination. And considering this relationship with regard to the advantages [*l'utilité*], . . . one can quite rightly maintain, against Aristotle and Xenophon, that economy [*l'oeconomie*] cannot be separated from politics [*la police*] without dismembering the principal part from its Whole, and that the science of acquiring goods, as they call it, is common to republics as well as to families. For my part, I cannot but be astonished that in their political treatises, which have otherwise been so diligently written, they have forgotten this public administration [*ceste mesnagerie publique*], which the necessities and duties of the State require having as one's principal concern.[64]

What is remarkable is the clarity with which economy is identified as a mode of government, and one that connects with the "particular inclination" of each man.[65] Here a complex of concerns and methods of interior administration, central to which was the "science of acquiring goods," joins with the application of civil prudence in matters of war and peace, as reason of state dictated the superintendence of wealth creation that the eighteenth century would call "mercantilism." But economy came to regulate the actions of princes themselves as its requirements became properly political. When the state was figured as a household writ large, rule was a matter of management and the ruler was brought within the managed space. This incorporation of the sovereign is suggested by Montchrétien's attention to the example and responsibilities of the prince in the last part of his treatise.[66] But in early political economy the sovereign, like the patriarch, was still at the center: to serve economy was to serve him. Political economy also helped forge, however, an entity that overshadowed the majesty of the king. Public administration on a national scale brought a new uniformity to the space of the state's domestic rule, which was increasingly figured *as* domestic —and so it was "oeconomic" in the contemporary sense.

Again, the significance of this for our purposes is the development of a particular logic of rule and an orientation that comes with that logic. The rationales, applications, and methods of reason of state, police, and political economy do not by any means seamlessly cohere, but political economy is another site where we can see pressure put on a distinction upon which contemporaries would continue to insist: the distinction between the preservation and the augmentation of the state. The increasingly common phrase "preservation and augmentation"—characteristic, for example, of Spanish reason of state—spoke to both the importance of the distinction and its erosion.[67] Lipsius's special prudence, and reason of state generally, of course relied for their justification on the state's fundamental role as a preserver of life; this is the justification that would also produce the "new natural law" of Grotius and Hobbes and ground modern social contract theory.[68] But reason of state, although it relied on the exceptional importance of preserving life, undermined survival's exceptionalism by articulating a standing prudence. Exception became foundation as in modern natural law, but here for a distinctly nonjuridical political rationality. The purpose of preservation and the needs of its guarantor were now seen to require a continuous administration, and were becoming blurred as goals with the prince's pursuit of "*the happie life of his citisens.*"[69] Reason of state provided a new standard linking pursuits that had been linked in importantly different ways: a standard that blurred the distinctions among pursuits by rendering them increasingly commensurable with one another. Thus the doctrine constructed the outlines of an aggregate that could be imagined as a kind of grand economy, improvable according to a single metric, that would be developed in the work of Shaftesbury and Bentham. The language of a singular "interest" combined various state pursuits, and would join in a common and continuous project life and the good life, ruler and subjects, present and future.

Interest of State and Monistic Interest

The notion of a state interest contributed to the rise of the peculiar abstraction that is the modern state. Many literatures, some of them not the least bit "Machiavellian," contributed to a notion of state interest. Interest of state helped to normalize a regime that at least in its outlines is a permanent apparatus of rule characterized by Quentin Skinner as doubly impersonal: it can be abstracted from both rulers and ruled.[70] The abstraction was implied in the personifications of states present in the later reason of state literature. Reason of state had fully arrived when it performed this abstraction and personification. Again, we might think of the transformation as more a matter of sovereignty, in relation to emerging schemes of international and public law. But states were personified as bearers of interest well before they were personified as juridical actors.

And so the Treaty of Westphalia (1648), for example, is of great significance for ending the Thirty Years War and establishing what would appear to some contemporaries as a state system, but it and subsequent treaties into the next century and beyond were agreements not between states but between possessors of states.[71] States were, however, personified as interest bearers already during the Thirty Years War. Various discourses that emphasized the existential requirements of the new orders and their denizens gave content to their emerging legal forms, and did so in part through the abstraction posited by the language of interest of state.

This abstraction is most apparent in the reason of state literature itself. To illustrate the personification of states and other work done by interest of state I want to turn to one of the more famous passages in the reason of state literature: the opening to the Duke of Rohan's *De l'Interest des Princes et des Etats de la Chrestienté*. First printed in 1634, this text was much reprinted, imitated, and translated (into English in 1640). Its proliferation indicates the success enjoyed by a new logic of interest in seventeenth-century Europe. The passage below illustrates not only that interest can govern, but that its government—unlike any stable sovereignty—is the dynamic government of a distinct rationality unconcerned with the past. It also illustrates how this precursor to monistic interest naturalized civil prudence and reason of state. Note how in this respect Rohan's *raison d'état* was different from Richelieu's, in a way that brings it closer to Bentham's government by monistic interest. In this passage, interest is not a difficult duty against which rulers chafe.[72] Instead, interest itself rules, and the problem is to get a clear view:

> THE PRINCES commaund the *People*, and the *Interest* commaunds The *Princes*. The knowledge of this *Interest* is as much more raised above that of *Princes* actions, as they themselves are above the *People*. The *Prince* may deceive himselfe, his *Counsell* may be corrupted, but the interest alone can never faile. According as it is well or ill understood, it maketh *States* to live or die. And as it allwaies aimeth at the *augmentation*, or at leastwise the *conservation* of a *State*, so likewise to get thither, it ought to varie according to the times. So that to consider well the interest of the Princes of this time, wee need not remount very high, but only take the standing of present affaires.[73]

Take the standing of present affaires he does, as the text goes on to engage in a kind of consummate political analysis. Rohan considers the situation and aims of major and some minor powers of Europe one by one, generating maxims for them, and proceeds to a longer account of recent events, narrated in terms of parties either following, or not following, their interest. And if the passage above makes us doubt that Rohan's states were impersonal and personified, we need only look to the commencement of each state's chapter, where Rohan begins with geography, for example: "France being seated betweene the *Alpes* and the *Pyrenean mountaines*, and flanked by two *seas*, seemes to be invited by *nature* to oppose it selfe against the proceeding of this puissant Neighbourhood." And "England which is as a little world apart, had not any thing to doe with other *Princes*, but onely so far as the necessitie of commerce did oblige her, which was then her true interest."[74]

In Rohan's treatise we can see the culmination of some of the trends I have discussed: the development of an ethic that conflates preservation and augmentation and is always oriented toward a future, its production of a governing knowledge, and its thorough subjection of sovereigns. We see in these trends some of the features of the monistic interest of Benthamic rule. Most importantly, we see in Rohan the continuousness of the subjection to interest: he implies that there is always a best thing for the sovereign and those in service to the sovereign to do, just as Bentham's maximizing logic implies this for all of us. Thus the diverse goals and bodies of knowledge that go into interest's definition are by implication calculable commensurables. But the differences with Bentham are striking. Rohan's text is almost entirely concerned with relative positioning. His is precisely the kind of pluralist and political orientation that is carefully circumscribed by a rigorous economic rationality: it is too likely to be, in the language of modern economics, inefficient.

Rohan's relative pluralism is a consequence of his focus on the dynamics of interstate affairs; his is largely a treatise on foreign policies. He was not completely inattentive to domestic affairs, however. Divide-and-conquer stratagems are occasionally aimed not only outward but at potentially restive subjects, and Rohan notes the particularly strong interest that some of the states of Europe, for example England, have in unity.[75] But Rohan's domestic reason of state is still quite distant from government by monistic interest. For Bentham, almost any recognizable domestic interest of state is likely to be a sinister interest: an interest opposed to that of the "interest of the community." Bentham's aggregate interest is an economic abstraction that sums the separate economized interests of several individuals. And these interests—products of individual imaginations—are absent from the discourse of interest of state, which need not take any heed of individuals per se or their self-interest.[76] This contrast is most dramatically illustrated by comparing the stress on secrecy that runs throughout the reason of state literature, including Rohan's work, with Bentham's constitutional reliance on publicity. Publicity is the tool guaranteeing that governors themselves are properly governed: otherwise they will develop the sinister interest of a domestic reason of state that is really, properly exposed, the interest of the ruling part of society.[77]

Furthermore, as I have already noted, state rationality as a monistic interest is in general highly limited in the scope of its government by comparison with the monistic interest of economic rationality. Reason of state primarily directs the conduct of statesmen, and not private individuals, and primarily statesmen only insofar as they are acting as statesmen (as opposed to proprietors, penitents, friends, and so forth).[78] Because of our formulaically liberal assumptions about government, this seems quite counterintuitive. And of course, twentieth-century state socialism's failed experiments with the command state, and more notoriously the disastrous mid-century experience of the total state, give convincing support to these assumptions. But even in the command state, state interest will not direct that which is held back from the state; should the state destroy the private, the personal escapes it. Economic rationality, on the other hand, directs anyone at anytime whose multiple affairs are imagined as a single economy. Economic reason shapes all kinds of activities that have no association with what we define as "the economy." This shaping—involving, as it does, one's relation to oneself—is often not experienced as an intervention or infringement; it may even bring with it a sense of liberation, a heightened sense of control. Economy thus has a remarkable capacity to enframe anything that might be held back from it.

The puzzle, then, is how to account for these similarities and differences. How did the monistic interest of state rationality break free of its containment by state institutions and become a logic of rule for individuals? How did it transform into an object of potentially universal aspiration that could serve as a critique of the state? How did the public utility or "public interest"—a republican category reoccupied by reason of state—become in turn reoccupied by economic reason? To answer these questions, we need to leave the Continent and travel to seventeenth-century England, especially to the civil wars of mid-century, where we can spot the appearance of a powerful bottom-up alternative to the top-down rule of the state. I will not characterize what we find there as a story of republican revivalism, or bourgeois revolution, or the origins of popular sovereignty, liberal individualism, or civil society—although much of the same supporting evidence can be and has been interpreted in one or more of these terms. Instead my story recounts how an economic conception of individual and collective government arose, along with the possibility of the mode of rule articulated by Bentham and his successors. Here the focus will be explicitly on some of the dynamics of the language of interest—and in particular, on the development of pluralist and monistic usages and the productive contrast between them. When we attend to the language of interest we can see seventeenth-century English politics in a new light. We can understand English exceptionalism in a new way—as crucial not only to the rise of a distinctive political rationality and the institutions appropriate to it (such as political parties) but to the rise of the economic rationality and economic government that displace this politics and shape its institutions, and do so not in the name of an aggrandizing state but eventually in the names of choice and efficiency.

In one sense, state rationality already was economic. At least in its domestic orientation, we have seen that state rationality was and is a monistic interest that surveys and aggregates commensurable resources calculated to be of more or less benefit to the state. But this monistic interest is limited by the requirements of state that are attached to and confine it (thus, from the standpoint of classical economics, reason of state is "mercantilist"). One way to highlight the inadequacy of state reason as a ruling monistic interest in opposition to Benthamic government is to point to its opposition to conscience, to its construction of a public morality that potentially conflicts with the private moralities of its agents (think of Louis XIII's sensitivity) and of subjects. And one way to demonstrate how monistic interest could come to possess and be possessed by individuals is to contrast English revolutionary pursuits and the pursuits of reason of state. The new public interest and self-interest were not opposed to conscience; on the contrary, they were its very expression—constructed from and fueled by it. They paved the way for the rise of a more fully economic social morality that could triumph over public and private—and for the domestication of conscience in Shaftesbury and the mobilization of the imagination in Bentham. In the varieties of monistic interest from the English seventeenth century we see a conflation of matters of necessity and convenience, present and future, and self and whole similar to that demanded by reason of state. But here the rationality that dictated this conflation did not descend, for the most part, from princes and ruling councils. Instead it sprang from the anarchy of civil war, from individual consciences inspired by God and nation.

6 The Public Interest

In the previous chapter, I demonstrated a curious continuity between reason of state and economic rationality. Reason of state, I argued, imposed a continuous forward-looking discipline on statesmen. This discipline involved the calculation of a best interest from the weighing of implicitly measurable and commensurable means and goals. Reason of state, however, pursued a very limited monistic interest. Its interest of state remained attached to the state and proceeded down from it. Thus it could form the basis for a critique of statesmen, but not of the ruling apparatus or state as a whole. Reason of state was not broadly dispersed. To the extent that it incorporated and nationalized a police, it still conducted its public administration from central points; reason of state's main concerns in this administration were those, such as the management of wealth, that were thought to have a significant impact on military power. And this matter of power itself necessarily focused the state on its external enemies; reason of state looked outward to a strategic context. Unlike economic rationality, its calculations involved the assessment of interests that it could potentially predict and affect, but not govern—the interests of other states.[1]

The economic rationality of monistic interest has multiple origins. Reason of state is perhaps the most important of these. But the seventeenth-century English public interest sheds reason of state's pluralism and parochialism, and so represents a closer antecedent to monistic interest. Some commentators have seen in the rise of the public interest the emergence of a politics that has little or nothing to do with reason of state. More recently these concepts have been much more closely linked.[2] I will argue that the public interest is linked to and even derived from reason of state, but that it marks a significant mutation of it, one peculiar to the English context. In this complex mutation we find much of what closes the gap between interest of state and monistic interest. Arguments made in the name of the public interest, the interest of the nation, the interest of England, and so on were legion from the 1640s on. Although the terms are different, these singular interests could be invoked interchangeably for the "domestic" interest of the whole that the public interest names. What did these arguments have in common with, and how were they different from, the logic of reason of state? Although the public interest was and is a heavily contested category, we can safely make a few generalizations that distinguish it from reason of state's interest of state.

The public interest and reason of state share much. They both represent new rationalities that reoccupied and transformed the natural-law doctrine of necessity, demanding a specific type of knowledge and a new orientation, the pursuit of the future.

(1) Like interest of state, the public interest took its inspiration from natural-law necessity, deriving initially from a vernacular rendering of Cicero's *salus populi*. The doctrine of *salus populi suprema lex esto*—the safety of the people is the highest law—could be invoked both in support of and in opposition to princely prerogative, and so it was in early Stuart England. The English "public interest" seems to have been a Parliamentary rather than a Royalist phrase in the conflict over the exercise of prerogative by Charles I. In any case, the fear and accusation from both sides of this struggle was that the doctrine of necessity could justify any action by its claimant, who might begin to see necessity everywhere. And indeed, when it came to acting for the public interest this fear was well grounded, because the public interest, like interest of state, would blur the line between necessity and convenience. Whereas the *salus populi* could be threatened but not really diminished or advanced, the public interest could be both threatened and advanced, and so it could be both preserved and augmented.

(2) Because of this similar link to necessity—a doctrine, we should remember, that was not only humanist but common to all traditional natural law—the public interest, like interest of state, justified the overruling of existing law and ethics to do what was best according to the new standard. In the case of reason of state, we saw that the state's relationship to the preservation of life justified a kind of standing ethic for rulers that was no longer exceptional. In its valoriza-

tion of life itself and in its service to the Reformation state, a mostly Christian humanist civil prudence appropriated and transformed Ciceronian doctrine. Nothing was more important than the state, and so it made no sense to act at one time for state interest, and at another not. But might there not be all kinds of things more important than the public interest in those cases where only its diminution or augmentation was concerned, and not the safety of the people? As it turns out, there wasn't anything more important than the public interest, because in its early formulations it was often fused with the "interest of God." In the anti-Catholic and millennial fervor that gripped England in the 1640s and 1650s this interest of God might be continuously engaged against the popish interest or Antichrist, and so serving this interest amounted for many of its followers to a full-time commitment.

(3) The theological connection points to another similarity between reason of state and the public interest. Both anticipated and encouraged, and would come to require, the development of a kind of knowledge that we might characterize as empirical and practical. Richard Hooker, a highly regarded apologist for Elizabeth I's settlement of the government of the Church of England, had chided Dissenters for their exclusive reliance on the Bible and their insistence on conclusions that were probable rather than demonstratively certain.[3] The later partisans of the public interest not only read preceptual certainties out of Scripture, they read events themselves out of Scripture, scrutinizing its histories for actual correspondence with their own. Contemporary and later configurations of the public interest that were less fused with the interest of God would also rely on historical or probable knowledge. These connections between the public interest and an orientation toward facts (Biblical facts were facts) were confirmed by the rise of the doctrine of moral certainty in association with the scientific revolution, when probable knowledge would dethrone demonstrative certainty as the standard of science.[4] In chapter 5 we saw how important factual reports and a primitive statistics were to the determination of state interest. To the extent that a concept of the public interest was stabilized in the late seventeenth century, determining it involved the production of similar knowledge.

(4) Reason of state and the public interest both imply a new temporality. As with state interest, knowledge of the public interest is knowledge of the present for service to the future. The dominant conception of the public interest was from the beginning doggedly prospective. For its earliest adherents, this orientation toward the future was an orientation in eschatological time; for us, interest is a goal that resides in the ever-receding open horizon of horizontal time.[5] There were of course various formulations of the public interest in the

seventeenth century, and those that were more Ciceronian, for example, were likely to be less prospective. But the commonest formulations, from those of the 1640s to many of the more secular conceptions of the 1660s and beyond, looked to present and future only. After the Restoration of 1660, there was a powerful backlash against the religious enthusiasm that in the minds of many contemporaries had fueled the conflict. One of the responses to enthusiasm, which was simultaneously a response to "atheism" or "mechanism," was the modeling of a transcendentally self-interested individual. J. G. A. Pocock warns against the "oversimplification . . . that an intensely religious consciousness of individuality was secularized into bourgeois rationalism overnight."[6] The less intensely religious consciousness of rational theology served as an important bridge between the conscience-driven saint of the seventeenth-century wars and the economized self of eighteenth-century self-interest.

The public interest's relationship to self-interest brings us to crucial differences between it and reason of state. The public interest's insistent monism, and its dispersal throughout the polity and diffusion among inhabitants, mark significant steps toward the economic rationality of monistic interest.

(1) Reason of state, I have noted, must always look partly or even mostly outward, toward a strategic context of a plurality of states whose actions can be anticipated and perhaps even shaped, but definitely not governed. The public interest, on the other hand, looks exclusively inward, toward interior interests that it can potentially govern. Thus the public interest is more consistently monistic; when figured as an aggregate interest it implies the economization of its field of concern.

(2) Reason of state remains territorial. Even its incorporation and extension of the police regulation of cities is assimilated to a project of territorial defense and control. The public interest, on the other hand, is not territorial. The public interest concerns itself immediately and directly with a population. This is clearest, again, when the dominant conceptions of the public interest become aggregate ones.

(3) Reason of state, as we have seen, can discipline statesmen—but it does so on behalf of a reifying state and its sovereignty. The public interest, on the other hand, can discipline the state itself. State interest is nothing without the state; the public interest is something without the state. The public interest is a decentered standard of rule.

(4) Reason of state stood against conscience. Even when reason of state is understood as Richelieu's regular discipline that must be followed to avoid sin, it is likely to offend tender consciences. The public interest as a regular disci-

pline was initially a standard *generated* by conscience. It was through listening to the voice of conscience, often listening together in prayer, that the rebellious saints might discover the public interest.[7] Thus the sensitive conscience, a disadvantage for service to reason of state, is an advantage for service to the public interest.

(5) The public interest not only involved a far more intimate and encompassing connection with individuals than did the interest of state; ultimately it presupposed a specific kind of individual. Whether pious or not, this individual was one whose relationship to his own affairs could mirror the public interest's relationship to its interior, and could do so in a way that might promote both private and public economy in a context of seemingly universal commensurability.

While not equivalent to Shaftesburean or Benthamic economy, articulations of the public interest did set the theoretical preconditions for intimately linked economies of self and society. In this way they expanded, diffused, and developed the rationality that was incipient in the governing logic of Continental reason of state's pursuit of state interest. We can best see this development by tracking the proliferation and mutation of the language of "interest" in mid-seventeenth-century England. Reason of state itself played a role in this proliferation and mutation; the popularization of interest of state doctrine in England coincided with the crisis of the 1640s. Although this chapter will engage only a small number of the relevant sources, I hope to give readers a sense of the twists and turns of the interest-talk of this time and place. My approach in this chapter is to give neither a political history nor the history of a concept: "interest," after all, does not name a single concept, nor does it name a collection of neatly distinguishable concepts. What I will track, though, is the rise of new uses of interest that share a kind of family resemblance, and that were reproduced through their service as a common language in which fierce battles of religious and political settlement were fought. My shorthand for this family of uses is the "public interest"; the traits shared by this class are those enumerated above under that name. The public interest put pressure on less monistic uses of "interest," and was itself transformed through its multiple iterations.

In the 1640s the conflict between king and Parliament could be accommodated, and in some respects contained, through narratives that described it in terms of a conflict over interests. This way of describing the grounds and goals of struggles was new outside of courtrooms, and was in some respects a transposition of juridical language. In other respects it was a transposition of the language in which Continental reason of state theorists described the activities of states. It might come as some surprise to learn how relatively unimportant interest was to early discussions of trade and wealth, except as money interest, and how relatively important it was in sermons. In England, it is in the most theologically charged settings that one sees the earliest emergence of a guiding singular interest, and so one finds it mostly coming from the pens of the "Puritan" opposition. The public interest justified executing Charles I in 1649, but by the late 1650s it was common across the entire political spectrum, from the most enthusiastic revolutionaries to the most determined Royalists. The public interest justified restoring Charles II to the throne in 1660, and in the aftermath of the Restoration many arguments about trade and toleration were made in the name of the public interest or interest of England. At this time more millennial constructions of the national interest were not only censored but actively combated with a theory of transcendental self-interest benefiting self and whole and anchored in a governable as opposed to antinomian conscience. By the early eighteenth century even republican arguments, which ostensibly invoked a classical virtue relatively unconcerned with the interior of the self, could mutate into arguments for a more economic construction of public and private in the emerging pair of self and society.[8]

The seventeenth century is better known as the century when a particular kind of sanctioned pluralism in politics developed, in which the language of interest also played a significant role.[9] Once Restoration "faction" was legitimized as "party" after the Glorious Revolution of 1688, a new scheme of politics, describable in terms of interest-opposition, would emerge. This development is not my focus.[10] And in any case this interest-pluralism developed in a context domesticated by an incipient monistic interest. It developed alongside, and often in tandem with, the appearance of a particular scheme of self- and collective government that joined the introspective subject to a new abstraction, society. The rise of interest-pluralism was coincident, that is, with the emergence and proliferation of economy as government.

Baseline: Hooker's Laws

A look at Richard Hooker will show us how necessity was conceived before reason of state and its knowledge and ethic enjoyed any significant presence in English argument. In the 1580s and 1590s, Hooker wrote what remains perhaps the most powerful and complete work of Anglican doctrine, *Of The Laws of Ecclesiasticall Polity*. His was the learned voice of the original Establishment, justifying Elizabethan church-government in moderate tones that expressed many of the fundamentals of English Renaissance political thought. Hooker targeted the original Dissenters: various other Protestants, many of them Calvinists, who urged the reformation of the English church away from the rule of bishops and other "Romish" trappings. In his preface, Hooker both acknowledges and qualifies the primacy of conscience, pointing to the fallibility of dissenting judgments: "Not that I judge it a thing allowable for men to observe those laws which in their hearts they are steadfastly persuaded to be against the law of God: but your persuasion in this case ye are all bound for the time to suspend, and in otherwise doing, ye offend against God by troubling his Church without any just or necessary cause." Hooker challenges his readers to provide arguments that are "demonstrative" and "necessary" when they call for a new church discipline. He argues that their claims to be following divine law are based on "mere probabilities."[11]

What can we be certain of? In Hooker's view, we can be certain of nature, because nature belongs to God: "Those things which nature is said to do, are by divine art performed, using nature as an instrument."[12] And so nature, no less than Scripture, is revelatory. Scripture reinforces the message of nature, which is often obscured by "iniquitous custom" or weakness or laziness of the understanding.[13] Scripture often requires interpretation, and interpretation is subject to dispute. But anything plain in Scripture, such as fundamental articles of divine law, can also be known from nature. The means by which the laws of nature are made known to all earthly voluntary agents is reason. Of the demonstrative as opposed to probable conclusions of reason we can be certain, and this reason is itself inoculated against skepticism: "The main principles of reason are in themselves apparent." Hooker defends reason against itself by quoting the ancient wisdom of Theophrastus: "They that seek a reason of all things do utterly overthrow reason."[14] According to Hooker, there are axioms in no need of proof that are "drawn from out of the very bowels of heaven and earth."[15] These principles and those deduced from them make up "the sentence of reason" that is the "natural measure whereby to judge our doings, . . . determining and setting down what is good to be done."[16]

Hooker's sentence of reason binds everyone, but the scope of its determinations is actually quite limited. Reason does not tell us with certainty how to arrange our political affairs. Just as there is nothing necessary about the reforms demanded by Dissenters, there is nothing necessary about the Elizabethan settlement that Hooker defends. In a statement about the limits of the laws of reason, Hooker again distinguishes between necessary and probable conclusions. Probable judgments are appropriate to matters of *convenience*, and the line between the obligatory and the convenient marks the threshold from the pre-political to the political: "Within the compass of [the laws of reason] we do not only comprehend whatsoever may be easily known to belong to the duty of all men, but even whatsoever may possibly be known to be of that quality, so that the same be by *necessary* consequence deduced out of clear and manifest principles. For if once we descend unto probable collections what is convenient for men, we are then in the territory where free and arbitrary determinations, the territory where human laws take place."[17] Natural law establishes limits, but it does not descend to the details of large areas of human conduct, including political affairs.

Hooker's understanding of the purposes of government is a traditional one; it echoes Aristotle in spirit and is not at all foreign to our ears. According to Hooker, people form political associations because they are basically flawed; government frames our actions so that we can live more virtuously and thus more happily. Government promotes virtue, but the means by which it does so should depend on the specific people concerned and the conditions under which they live. Natural law does not mandate any particular set of political arrangements: "all public regiment of what kind soever seemeth evidently to have risen from deliberate advice, consultation, and composition between men, judging it convenient and behoveful."[18] Political association makes the good life possible by removing impediments to it, but the conveniences promoted by it presume that basic needs have been met: "But inasmuch as righteous life presupposeth life, inasmuch as to live virtuously it is impossible except we live, therefore the first impediment, which naturally we endeavor to remove, is penury and want of things without which we cannot live."[19] Survival itself is not a matter of convenience, but of necessity.

Hooker's political philosophy was thus fully compatible with the *salus populi* justification of prerogative, but not with the standing superintendence of reason of state. In political affairs, natural law mandated the exception, but not the rule. The idea of the emergency exception was taken for granted by Hooker; it even has place in what we would call his natural as opposed to his moral or political philosophy. For Hooker and his contemporaries, natural law was both physical and moral law, and the earth itself was not necessarily marked by regularity in movement and purpose. Exceptional events in nature—such as volcanoes and earthquakes—were in obedience to a more basic natural law than the one that normally governed; they served collective rather than private goals at points of crisis. At such times a natural agent (say, a mountain) behaved "as if it did hear itself commanded to let go the good it privately wisheth, and to relieve the present distress of nature in common."[20] This doctrine, as peculiar and voluntarist as it might seem to our standards of reason, was couched in an insistent theological rationalism. Although, according to Hooker, God works his own will and pleasure and we understand his purposes about as well as dogs understand ours, "thus much is discerned, that the natural generation and process of all things receiveth order of proceeding from the settled stability of divine understanding."[21]

Hooker's arguments were consistent with an Elizabethan worldview that linked natural and political hierarchies in a great chain of being, marked by numerous correspondences that look as bizarre to us as his exceptional mountains. His arguments were also compatible with traditional and more lasting theories of English constitutionalism. Hooker's natural-law doctrine fit with the traditions of a monarchical rule located within a distinct form of government including Lords and Commons, grounded somehow in consent and peculiarly adapted to the "liberties of England." Such matters of convenience were most important. They were not, however, determined by natural law. Instead their specifics were freely developed by a people over time through the exercise of their probable reasoning in pursuit of the good life: "As for laws which are *merely* human, the matter of them is anything which reason doth but probably teach to be fit and convenient, so that till such time as law hath passed amongst men about it, of itself it bindeth no man."[22] Therefore Hooker's doctrine was also consistent with the theory of law, custom, and reason that would be developed by the common lawyers of the early seventeenth century.

In 1615, during the reign of James I, his attorney general for Ireland, John Davies, wrote that the common law of England, which "is nothing else but the common custom of the realm," was "most perfect and most excellent" and superior to written law. We know this because unlike imposed statute, civil, or canon law, "a custom does never become a law to bind the people until it has been tried and approved time out of mind, during all which time there did thereby arise no inconvenience: for if it had been found inconvenient at any time, it had been used no longer, but had been interrupted, and consequently it had lost the virtue and force of a law."[23] This endorsement of customary law could support a generous and deferential view of both statutory authority and sovereign prerogative. Prerogative was rooted in that other unwritten law, natural law, which justified prerogative's power to transgress existing law in times of necessity. But the endorsement of princely prerogative did not justify a Continental reason of state or theory of sovereignty. Even the developing absolutist theory of divine right, which looked to opponents like a foreign threat to English constitutionalism, recognized the presumptive authority of settled law and the monarch's subservience to natural law. None of these doctrines supposed that monarchs were bound to frame their actions in continuous pursuit of the preservation and augmentation of their states. For these doctrines, as for Hooker, there was a concern as to what was "fit" or "unfit," but there was no logic that dictated a particular course of action when it came to matters of convenience. And there was a common juridical language—a language of right, authority, obligation, and obedience—in which conflict and agreement were expressed.

At this time, the English word "interest" was grounded in this common juridical language. An interest was the stake of a party to a judicial proceeding, or if not, it was metaphorically linked to that context. Few people had interests, and interests decidedly concerned matters of convenience. "Interest" did not yet refer to a goal or a passion, as some of its Continental cognates did; its only other use referred to interest on money, masking and legitimating usury with a juridical category. In older uses of interest, the king as sovereign seemed to be outside of relations of interest. For example, a response by James in 1606 to parliamentary grievances suggests that the Crown is not "interested" in either their dismissal or redress: "In case the complainants might be permitted to try the right in course of justice, his Majesty, for satisfaction of all parties interested therein, hath remitted the determination thereof to such proceedings in law as is usual in like cases and standeth with the common justice of the realm."[24] Similarly, in Parliament in 1610 Francis Bacon reportedly objected to a free debate, distinguishing questions of the king's prerogative from matters concerning "the right or interest of any subject or the Commonwealth."[25] Before too long, however, the king *qua* king would be characterizable as an interested party, and discussing the decidedly necessary "public interest" would entail discussing the royal prerogative and the king's interest.

Background and Beginnings I:
Necessity, Convenience, and Trade

Before we turn to mutations of "interest," however, we need to attend to the early-seventeenth-century writing on "trade." Writings that we are now tempted to call "economic" because of their field of concern and their discursive regularity did contribute to economic rationality, but not as directly as one might suppose. The importance of early English writings on trade is that they breached, even as they recognized, the natural-law distinction between convenience and necessity. They resembled Continental political economy in their concern with the "mercantilist" themes of balance of trade and the enhancement of treasure, and some of them were preoccupied with royal revenues in particular. Also, like writings on political economy, they frequently breached the Aristotelian distinction between politics and household administration by comparing the realm to a family.[26] But these early writings on trade were not political economy in the style of Montchrétien's *Traicté de l'Oeconomie Politique*, insofar as they were not really concerned with public administration, at least not of the state. They cleaved to the traditional distinction between internal and long-distance trade, and they focused on the latter. Thus if they were concerned with administration it was with a kind of imperial rather than state administration; they argued the collateral benefits or banes of a merchant regime. In writings on trade from the 1620s, these benefits were not cast in the language of "interest" because they were not juridical matters. Some forty years later, however, trade was easily assimilated to the discourse of a public or national interest.

How did these writings move in the direction of monistic interest? They contributed to the conception of a measurable good of the whole that blurred the line between necessity and convenience and was not centered on any state apparatus. This development is present in Thomas Mun's *A Discourse of Trade* (1621). Mun was a London merchant, and his treatise was a response to writings attacking the East India Company for depleting national treasure in the pursuit of foreign goods. That his work was an apology for a mercantile monopoly is not insignificant: early English imperialism was an affair of "private" chartered companies, and so could foster a conception of the augmentation of a whole not centered in the state. (England, the seat of a triple monarchy, can be said to have had an empire before it had a state.) Mun not only referred to national stock rather than treasure, and did so without referring to the royal household or royal administration; he even discussed benefits or banes to "Christendom" as well as to England. Like his contemporaries, Mun assumed the need for what we now call a favorable balance of trade and warned of the dangers of corruption by luxury imports. However, in defense of the East India Company he did more than insist that Eastern goods would be bought from "the Turks" at higher prices if not brought over directly, he also explicitly defended the importance of many of the items consumed. Drugs and spices, for example, are not "to surfeit, or to please a lickorish taste." They are "desired . . . by so many Nations . . . as things most necessarie to preserve their health, and to cure their diseases."[27] These commodities were (apparently) not only goods, they were needs. Later in the pamphlet Mun concedes that England could, "upon strickt tearmes of need," be self-sufficient: "But to live well, to flourish and grow rich, wee must finde meanes by Trade, to vent our superfluities; therewith to furnish and adorne us with the Treasure and those necessarie wares, which forreine Nations do afford: and here industry must begin to play his part, not onely to increase and guide the Trades abroad; but also to maintaine and multiply the Arts at home: for when either of these faile . . . then doth the Common-wealth abate and growes poore."[28] Mun repeatedly makes the distinction between necessity and convenience only to erase it again: "the riches or sufficiencie of every Kingdome, State, or Common-wealth, consisteth in the possession of those things, which are needfull for a civill life."[29] Mun's distinction and conflation is displayed in his frequent referral to goods without which one can survive, but which, he maintains, have a "necessarie use."

In *A Discourse of Trade* Mun offers proof of the company's role in augmenting the stock of treasure and useful goods by calculating and representing their total *value* numerically—contrasting this total with, for example, the amount that went to the Ottomans in the previous overland trade. In this use of aggregate figures to represent something called "value" in circulation, and in his understanding of the source of this value in the "industry" of England's inhabitants coupled with more efficient trade, Mun's work is strikingly modern. It is also striking for seeming to suggest that foreign trade and the company can meet police goals of the care and discipline of inhabitants without mediation by a state apparatus:

> It is both naturall and just, that every Kingdome, State, or Common-wealth, should feede and cherish up the Native people of all degrees and conditions whatsoever, to their preservation of life and health, with such meanes and moderation, as their plentie shall affoord; and this is not onely due to them in the time of their aboad at home, but also upon all occasions of voyages into other Countries beyond the Seas, wherein they shall be imployed for their owne maintenance, and for the good of the Common-wealth.[30]

Mun praises foreign trade in part for keeping people employed, for their own sakes and England's. Although some mariners die at sea, new men replace them in a process that benefits both them and a polity otherwise harmed by masterless men:

> Landmen . . . in one voyage prove good Marriners to serve the Kingdome and Commonwealth, unto which many of them were a burthen before

they obtained this employment[.] And thus is the Kingdome purged of desperate and unruly people, who being kept in awe by the good discipline at Sea, do often change their former course of life; and so advance their fortunes.[31]

According to Mun, then, employment in trade contributes simultaneously to national stock, national peace, and self-improvement.

By the 1640s the benefits of trade could be expressed in the new language of interest, but not yet, it seems, as a monistic interest. In 1647 Henry Parker—the most important of Parliament's polemicists in its early battle for public support—wrote an apology for the Merchant Adventurers against attacks on their exclusive rights to trade in various districts abroad. In the dedicatory letter to his fellow merchants, Parker invokes a common rather than aggregate interest: "I perceived your interest was the same as the Common interest of all Merchants, and that could have no termination, but in the common interest of our Nation." The treatise begins with the claim that what is good for the Merchant Adventurers is good for England, and thus everyone has a kind of stake in their trade: "My Lord *Cook* in his Commentary upon our Great Charter (where the Merchants contentment is so prudently provided for) tels us, that Traffick is the Merchants livelihood, and that the livelihood of the Merchant is the life of the Common-weal, such as the King himself, and every Subject of the Land has an interest in."[32] Parker argues the benefits of trade in general, but his main concern is to defend an "ordered" trade, and in particular, the kind of trading monopoly possessed by his association. In his arguments against free trade, it becomes clear that Parker's language of common interest is not so much a monistic interest but refers instead to that which is common among overlapping interests. To take away exclusive trading rights in the name of liberty would be analogous to taking away exclusive land rights, and:

> If all Land-inclosures were every where layde open, and all evidences cancelled, upon which mens private interests, and proprieties depend, many poore men would expect to have their conditions meliorated; yet undoubtedly their expectations at last would faile them; and together with community in all things a generall confusion of all persons, and things would breade in to the fatall destruction both of poore and rich.
>
> Our common Proverbe puts us rightly in mind, that he which dwells every where, dwells no where: that every mans interest is no mans intrest, & that every mans businesse is no mans busines: now this being true in matters of Husbandry, and in all other Interests, and negotiations, why should it not be as true in matters of commerce . . . ?[33]

Parker renders free trade equivalent to communism, and defends mobile property on the model of real property. How can it be, though, that every subject "has an interest" in trade, if "every man's interest is no man's intrest"? An ordered trade is of benefit, it seems, to each and all. But the ambiguities of Parker's uses of "interest" show that it does not name what we might think it names. Interest here does not resemble the aggregates that we encountered in chapters 3 and 4 on Shaftesbury and Bentham. It is still sufficiently tied to its juridical origins, still sufficiently partial and overlapping, that it does not invoke the fungible abstraction of exhaustive generalized benefit that is monistic interest. If that abstraction could even be named it was still not known as a goal that governs conduct; instead such a good was not yet present here.

Background and Beginnings II:
New Proprietary Interests

Where did monistic interest as a governing abstraction come from, if not from the discourse on trade? By calculating benefit as an aggregate measure and eroding the distinction between necessity and convenience, early English writings on trade did supply crucial elements of a monistic interest not centered in the state. However, trade lacked the ruling element that was present in reason of state and that is essential to the economic rationality of monistic interest.[34] It is my contention that we find evidence of the origins of economic rationality in local mutations of the language of "interest" itself, mutations that were galvanized by the contemporary crisis of religious and political settlement. Interest broke free of the constraints of juridical discourse to become a forward-looking descriptive and prescriptive language of universal government. Most important here was the fusion of a newly imported reason of state with the rebellious millennialism of militant Protestantism. This fusion precipitated an interest that joined self and whole, and their necessities and conveniences, in a continuous project unencumbered by the institutional constraints of state.

When Parker uses "interest" to refer to property in land, he hews to a juridical sense that had expanded, extended, and transformed in ways very important to the polemics of the 1640s. The language of interest broadened considerably under the pressure of the remarkable events of 1640–60: elite crisis and rupture, civil wars, republican revolution, dictatorship, and Restoration. The immediate background to these events is primarily to be found in two closely intertwined problems of governmental "settlement." The first was the problem of the unraveling of the Elizabethan settlement of church-government. Dissenters both within and outside the Establishment were repelled by what they saw as the church's persistently "Romish" qualities: its bishops, forms of worship, iconography, and so forth. It is difficult to overstate the role that hatred for the Church of Rome played in English political thought and practice from the sixteenth century through the nineteenth. The fuel in the early seventeenth century came mostly from the memorialization of Queen Mary's brief ("bloody") sixteenth-century Catholic restoration, from reports of the shifting worldwide battle with Jesuits and other counter-Reformation forces, and from the confirmation through the thwarted Gunpowder Plot of 1605 of the enemy's presence, aims, and power. When James's son Charles I ascended to the throne in 1625 he augured for many a building conspiracy to hand over English souls to Rome. Charles was a weak supporter at best of Protestant causes abroad, and he married the devoutly Catholic Henrietta Maria of Spain, whose children would be heirs to the throne. Catholics were increasingly present at court. And there were strong signs of backsliding at the highest levels of the church. Charles's archbishop Laud, installed in 1633, preached an anti-predestinarian doctrine that seemed to reverse a united Protestant emphasis on faith over works; he was cast by dissenters as a mini-pope. Thus when the Duke of Rohan's interest of princes and states entered English discourse in the climate of 1640, England's "interest" was more than likely to be construed as a pan-Protestant interest arrayed against a single enemy within and without, an enemy that included at least a portion of what might pass for the English state at this time.[35]

Meanwhile, Charles's relationship with many of England's leading lords and commoners had seriously deteriorated, for reasons that included but went beyond confessional conflicts. In the late twenties he exacerbated the throne's already bad relations with Parliament, and shut it down for the entire decade of the thirties, refusing to work with it for the traditional purposes of making law and raising money. Taxation was perhaps the most sensitive issue as Charles extended the royal prerogative to extract tribute without parliamentary approval. During both James's and Charles's reigns, resisting members of the ruling stratum of England were defeated in the courts of justice in a series of prominent trials. The nobility and gentry, who in their localities were often themselves all-powerful patriarchs, increasingly felt vulnerable to royal caprice not only in their goods but in their persons. And many powerful men of London—city of ready money, Continental refugees, and religious heterodoxy—were even more alienated from the Crown. Emboldened by new common-law narratives of their ancient privileges, many members of Parliament and their supporters saw their king's actions as sliding toward tyranny. While the opposition tended, in the way of the age of absolutism, to train its criticism on nefarious advisors, it was clear to many of its members that settled traditions of state government were imperiled, traditions constituting the rights and privileges that to their minds distinguished them as Englishmen. Here again, the first notions of a general or public interest were mapped onto constituencies outside what might be called the state; in fact, it would not be long before the king and his allies were cast as a private interest in conflict with the public.[36]

It is by no means anachronistic to speak of an English nation at this time. That England was a nation before it was a state in the modern sense is key to its housing of an "interest" that was not tied to a ruling apparatus of state. The Reformation itself, and the impassioned Protestant exile literature of Mary's reign, had given new urgency to English nationalism.[37] Englishness and its Protestant mission were then bolstered by the island defense from a huge Spanish armada and by new Irish and other overseas campaigns. Opposition to the practices of the highest spiritual and temporal authorities was figured in nationalist terms. England, for example, was the biblical chosen nation, or the beleaguered victim of the Norman yoke. Puritanism and parliamentarism (understood loosely as broad tendencies) were mutually reinforcing in a dynamic that claimed rather than opposed England's church and monarchy. Toward both institutions, the opposition could see its project simultaneously as radically reformist and conservatively restorative. Increasingly stressed and suppressed, rebellious tendencies rose up and found expression in Parliament when Charles was pressed by his financial needs to reconvene it in 1640. In 1641 the Irish Catholic rebellion further inflamed Puritans and Parliament, who were not confident of the Crown's firmness in defending the English nation and its mission. Opposition doctrines proliferated, especially but not exclusively in London, when in 1642 royal government and censorship collapsed and the first civil war began. As the decade wore on, the perspectives of the politicized parts of the nation would explode in completely unanticipated kaleidoscopic variety, as the continual foundering of parliamentary attempts to reunite the church occasioned an imperfect but extensive *de facto* toleration.

John Goodwin, a Puritan who preached on "The Saints Interest in God," was a leading separatist minister of London in the 1630s and early 1640s. Conforming just enough to be allowed to continue to preach, he was what came to be known as an "Independent," politically allied with the leading opposition Dissenters (who came to be known as "Presbyterians") but opposed to their goal of imposing a uniform discipline on a reformed Church of England.[38] In Goodwin's sermons we can see some of the tendencies that became increasingly prevalent in the insurgent theology of the day—subtle breaks with Calvinism implying that any of the faithful who opened themselves to be sufficiently purified by the word of God might join the elect. Goodwin's interest in God, like other interests of the day, is a "propriety," or property. But this is a property to which any man or woman might have title. All interests benefit their proprietors. Goodwin implies that the benefit brought by material interests is small because one-sided, and that much greater benefit is realized through the "natural" and "civil" relations of mutual interest that obtain between man and wife, father and son, and prince and subject. But people are frail and contingencies are such that these benefits always fall short of their promise: not so with God. The individual who makes a genuine covenant with God—the saint who gives himself or herself fully to God—effectively joins with the omnipotence of the other party to the relation, and can reasonably expect infinite benefit from this interest; that is its promise, and its promise is necessarily fulfilled. Goodwin qualifies this assertion by arguing that all relations are governed by law, and that it is only lawful benefit in each case that one can reap.[39] This qualification distinguished his doctrine from an antinomianism that might view grace as liberating its recipient from the limits of carnal custom and law.

But the "saints" interest in God is clearly the *saints'* interest in God. The chapter is titled "Wherein the nature and importance of that propriety, or interest which the Church hath in God, is declared."[40] And the occasion for the sermon was the annual remembrance of the discovery of the Catholic Gunpowder Plot of 1605, "that great Deliverance which that great God of *ours* wrought for this Nation."[41] Goodwin preaches on Psalms 68:10, "He that is our God, is the God of salvation, and unto God the Lord belong the issues of death."[42] Goodwin tells his congregation that according to this text they have a special interest in the god with whom they have covenanted (he is truly theirs), and they can with all confidence expect from him salvation, a salvation from or out of death itself.[43] The thwarting of the Gunpowder Plot demonstrates the truth of this, and reveals the meaning of Psalms 87:2, "The Lord loveth the gates of Sion, more then all the dwellings of Jacob." It is England and the English saints that the lord loves so, He "loveth more to be praised by us, then any other Nation under heaven; the English Incense is in heaven . . . preferred before that of other Lands: it makes the sweetest perfume and savour in the Nostrils of God." Considering the nation's deliverance from the popish plot of 1605, "What other construction can all the world make"?[44]

With the translation of Rohan's *Of the Interest of the Princes and States of Christendom* in 1640, a spate of "interest of England" texts appeared; this topic would again be the subject of many pre- and post-Restoration tracts. In the early tracts we find a kind of reason of state, but one that is infused with the Protestant mission in a way not symmetrical with the theological charge of Continental reason of state. Cardinal Richelieu, after all, would undertake cross-confessional alliances in pursuit of the interest of France; *The Interest of England* (1642) by William Constantine is subtitled "How it Consists in Unity of the Protestant Religion" and is aimed squarely, if "moderately," at the Catholic enemy within and without.[45] After John Goodwin's attention to England's deliverance by God from the Gunpowder Plot, we should not be surprised to find what look to be interest-of-state sermons. Thus Thomas Goodwin, a more prominent Independent minister and no relation to John, preached a Fast sermon to Parliament in 1646 on *The Great Interest of States and Kingdomes*. Goodwin comments at length on a wealth of biblical history demonstrating the downfall of all states and kingdoms that treat their saints badly. The fundamental interest of state is the interest of the saints, which is the interest of God. Goodwin cites Rohan on the need for English unity, and exhorts his audience to remember that "THE SAINTS OF ENGLAND ARE THE INTEREST OF ENGLAND. Write this upon your walls, to have it in your eye in all your consultations, never to swerve from it for any other interest whatsoever."[46] Thus for Constantine, Goodwin, and many others, English "state" interest was not really state interest at all; it was the interest of a church-nation. This national interest could readily be conceived as a single continuous and future-oriented pursuit; it was none other than the interest of God. And for the saints, taken singly or together, it was ultimately their only true interest.

Continental reason of state was newly resonant in an England falling into civil war, but because of this condition it refracted into a doctrinal plurality. Its systematization of the natural law of necessity was a factor in the growth of natural-rights theories, which were grounded in the right of preservation.[47] The justly famous doctrines of individual right of the 1640s were not the most prominent contemporary rights doctrines; these did not concern individual rights, but instead the right of the people collectively to act to preserve themselves if the instrument of their preservation, the sovereign, abandoned or turned against them.[48] This collective right of preservation was also called the "public interest," which translated the *salus populi* of Cicero.[49] But who were "the people" whose representatives were entitled in this time of emergency to take matters into their own hands? They were all those who had an *interest* in the realm—that is, a sufficient proprietary stake in its preservation. In a sense, then, they were all interested parties to the equivalent of a suit at law, with the king and his retainers and rabble as defendants and God as judge. Thus interest of state would not only join with the saints' interest in God, it would also join with a more traditional proprietary interest and forge a new synthesis. Just as princes were thought to be disciplined and directed by the interest of state to preserve and augment their states, subjects were thought to be disciplined by their proprietary interests to act in the service of these interests. In a domestic political context this implied that interest would sustain their judgment on matters affecting the realm in which they had a stake.

Rohan's governing interest from *Of the Interest of the Princes and States of Christendom* appeared in many places, suggesting in different ways that individuals' or parties' interests would direct their affairs. We can even find a direct transposition of his interest of state onto parties to the civil wars, in a way that faithfully imitated his complete lack of concern with right.[50] But for the most part the existential insights and directives of Rohan's treatise and other new humanist literatures were grafted onto existing juridical relations, in a kind of new constitutional hybrid of power and right. And so we see a number of arguments from different perspectives claiming that those with interests constitute a bulwark against the twin evils of tyranny and anarchy.[51] Some of these were Polybian "balance" arguments, with different interests checking or stabilizing one another.[52] These plural, as opposed to monistic, interest schemes remained very important to English political thought throughout the seventeenth century and beyond. In them, interest is usually a sort of guarantor of virtue or the fulfillment of duty, if not on the part of the individual or party then for the realm as a whole. In this sense interest may well oppose passion or conscience, in the mode of reason of state. But these interests do not exhibit the monism and abstraction of interest of state. They are instead a kind of recasting of civil relations, one that sees these relations not only through a juridical lens, but also as what we might call social forces.

Interest pluralism represented a significant and lasting development, and is perhaps the signal contribution of what has been called English Machiavellianism.[53] For our purposes, however, the more important development from the transplantation of reason of state to the England of the 1640s was the rise of an animating general interest of a Protestant nation intent on reforming its ruling institutions. With this development a prospective and monistic self and public interest did begin to emerge, one that was not necessarily incompatible with, but could fuel and be fueled by, the energetics of sufficiently dynamic plural interests. I have already noted that the early discourse on trade carried some of the elements important to my story: it breached the distinction between necessity and convenience, it posited an aggregate good, and its good was not the good of a state. But even though the discourse was partly concerned with the virtues of the merchant and the disciplining effects of sea labor, it did not make any intimate connection with the interior lives of individuals, and its goals were not in any way exhaustive of public or private purposes. The discourse on trade posited "value" as an aggregate good, but this value was embodied in useful articles and treasure and so it was a very limited abstraction, tied to the circulation of things. The good pursued by early English trade was quite distant from Benthamic interest. It did not posit self and whole as economies, and it did not govern selves through themselves. The pursuit of trade was not yet even identified with the pursuit of interest. Instead, an increasingly mainstream millennialism was the more important vehicle for the emergence of a genuinely economic rationality, governing its saints intimately and exhaustively in pursuit of an individual and collective good potentially abstracted from all existing specific relations and interests. This was not the pursuit of a utopia or other fixed abstraction. On the contrary, neither the makeup of the coming kingdom of Christ nor the route to it was clear, and Christ's servants took their bearings continually from a proliferation of signs and unfolding portentous events.[54]

The peculiar mappings of interest during the English civil wars produced a host of theoretical and practical tensions. Perhaps the most dramatic tension was that between more constitutionalist and traditionalist uses and formulations, and those that reflected a suspicion of the fallen character of all civil arrangements—a suspicion present among the more antinomian saints. The tension is most evident in those elements of the opposition that were most free with the language of the public interest, those who would eventually kill the king in its name. According to Pocock, "the abortive revolutions were the work of an army—a unique phenomenon in itself—inspired by millenarian hopes which were only half accepted." This army, the Parliament's New Model Army, was "led by legally educated lesser gentry profoundly split. . . . With half their minds they were radical saints; with the other half they were conservative reformers."[55] These tensions were on full display in the New Model Army's internal Putney debates of 1647. Despite these tensions we also find there a powerful background consensus, a consensus about the supremacy of the "public interest." The Putney debates illustrate how this mobile abstraction could join necessity and convenience, individual and collective, and present and future in a novel and most consequential governmental rationale.

Interests and the Public Interest at Putney

"Presbyterians" led the initial rebellion against Charles. Toward the middle of the 1640s and beyond, Independents and other "schismatics," who were marginal at the beginning of the first civil war, would gain greatly in power and converts, especially because of their numbers in the radicalizing New Model Army that defeated the Royalists in the first civil war. This army, which refused Parliament's order to disband after the victory, and which fought the loyalist (Presbyterian) Scots in the second civil war, eventually conquered Parliament itself, purging it of everyone suspected of seeking a rapprochement with Charles, including most early leaders of the rebellion.[56] The New Model Army was the major force behind the trial and execution of the king and the abolition of the monarchy and House of Lords; one of its generals, Oliver Cromwell, would rule the Protectorate that followed the short-lived republican Commonwealth.

The Clarke manuscripts from Putney display the power of a new and still fluid vocabulary of interest. They are transcriptions of meetings held in the autumn of 1647 to discuss the obligations, conditions, and direction of the New Model Army in light of Parliament's order to disband, and in light of unaddressed grievances over pay and political reform. The discussion on the first day was taken up with the question of "engagements," promises or covenants, and what if anything could justify breaking them. The second day was largely devoted to a discussion of constitutional reform and the franchise in particular. The transcripts from Putney have all the elements of crisis political theory, as the participants attempted to come to terms with the role of a newly politicized army under fluid and dangerous conditions. While only a few of the voices of revolutionary England were represented, it is clear that there were big divisions among the speakers, who have been broadly characterized as "Grandee" officers, civilian "Levellers," and officers and rank-and-file "Agitators" allied with the Levellers. These debates were replete with the vocabulary of interest. Interest was a shared language of the participants, who shared many assumptions, but there were differences in usage that correspond to strong differences of analysis and principle. The discussions nicely illustrate the flexibility and limits of a changing language of interest and its relationship to basic conflicts in what we would now characterize as seventeenth-century political theory. They also chart the vicissitudes of a potent form of rule: an encompassing interest tied directly to conscience. The participants have *this* interest in common. It is a completely compelling interest, yet acknowledged by their own arguments to be dangerously destabilizing, and the problem of how to identify, apply, and contain it weaves through the entire proceedings. A solution of sorts is implied in the appearance of the public interest as a new constitutional interest. Here a general interest is glimpsed that unlike the exceptional *salus populi* is continuously present, and that cautiously demotes the importance of existing entanglements in its purposive connection with the conscientious striving of individuals.

A quick reading of the two days of debates over promise breaking and the vote might suggest a clear lineup of sides. The Grandees and the Levellers agree on the law of preservation and the supremacy of the *salus populi*, they agree that promises need to be broken when survival is at stake, but the Grandees suspect that the Levellers are ready to break their promises for purposes that fall short of preservation. And the Grandees and the Levellers agree on the need for substantial regime reform, but the Grandees insist that the franchise be divided equally among holders of landed estates, while the Levellers wish to extend it to include all free men. What this reading misses, however, is the substantial problems and potential solutions that are posed by the vocabulary of interest. If it is agreed that preservation is an interest, then the distinction between preservation and augmentation or necessity and convenience is erased. And if it is agreed that the vote must be grounded in interest and that interest names very different kinds of property, then the distinction among relevant kinds of property is blurred. Finally, if it is agreed that one's ultimate interest is the saints' interest in God, which is the public interest and is apprehended through conscience, then a secular reading of these debates misses the contribution made by both sides to the assembling of the elements of a new governing rationality.

Cromwell's aide Henry Ireton, who dominates these debates, tries to exercise care and consistency in his use of the language of interest, aware as he is of its pitfalls. He is a sophisticated political thinker with a coherent vision of the new constitutional interest pluralism developed in the early 1640s. His is the voice most consistently opposed to precipitous action and radical reform. But when trying to convince his interlocutors of his sincerity and lack of prior partisan "engagement," he illustrates the consensus position of the soldiers, that they are not merely Parliament's army but God's army: "I look upon this Army as having carried with it hitherto the name of God, and having carried with it hitherto the interest of the people of God, and the interest which is God's interest, the honour of his name, the good and freedom and safety and happiness of his people." In the same speech he gets specific about what this commitment must have entailed for him and for all those assembled—a readiness, if called upon, to obey even the most unreasonable orders of his Commander: "Whatever I find the work of God tending to, I should desire quietly to submit to. If God saw it good to destroy, not only King and Lords, but all distinctions of degrees—nay if it go further, to destroy all property, that there's no such thing left, that there be nothing at all of civil constitution left in the kingdom—if I see the hand of God in it I hope I shall with quietness acquiesce, and submit to it, and not resist it."[57] While he is less likely than some of his colleagues and subordinates to see God's interest in disrupting fundamental civil distinctions, he readily acknowledges that this interest is what they are serving, and that all other considerations have to be swept away before it.

Ireton's use of the language of interest echoes John Goodwin's mutual interest of God and his saints, but this interest seems to have dispensed with the requirement that its benefits be lawful. And it has been mobilized, so that familiar rhetorics of purification are used to characterize the army's violence. For example, a sermon preached at Putney speaks of the coming rule of the saints, which entails both inward and outward revolution. Individuals will be wholly transformed in the "new creation," as will church and state. "Outward form" will be dropped, conscience freed from the constraints of the established church, and righteousness brought to government. The renewal of the state will involve "first, in respect of the persons ruling, [that] they shall be such as are acquainted with, and have an interest in, the righteous God." Spiritual and temporal oppressions will be removed so that "justice and righteousness may flow down abundantly without respect of persons." All of this is the "great interest of God, the public good."[58]

By no means is this manner of speaking confined to sermons, however. The debates themselves are replete with this kind of talk, which is renewed at great points of contentiousness as a reminder of the assembly's greater purpose. Apocalyptic rhetoric is most frequent among the Fifth Monarchy men at Putney, whose speeches strike the modern reader, but not the other participants, as out of place. Lieutenant Colonel Goffe takes it for granted that they are an army of saints battling Antichrist in the last days before the coming reign of Christ: " 'Tis true the kings have been instruments to cast off the Pope's supremacy, but we may see if they have not put themselves into the same state. . . . Certainly, this is a mystery of iniquity. Now Jesus Christ his work in the last days is to destroy this mystery of iniquity; . . . Now the word doth hold out in the Revelation, that in this work of Jesus Christ he shall have a company of Saints to follow him." The existing order, its state churches bound up in the "interest of states," is under assault from the army of Christ. The assembled are the saints, and their constant and taxing task is to read the will of God so as to be the instrument of, and not an impediment to, his work.[59] This millenarian vision may appear to be radically "voluntarist," but the equation between the will of God, God's interest, and the interest of the people foreshadows the "rationalist" national felicity of postwar natural theology. Crucial to the transition are potentials present in this new prospective and elastic governing abstraction of interest. This interest overwhelms the distinction between necessity and convenience; it replaces intermittent natural-law necessity by continuous subservience to a better tomorrow. And it links the interior of the individual to a global project that can just as easily be posed against as with the ruling apparatus of state. But in its millenarian form it is dangerously volatile, subject to the changing conscientious conclusions of discrete gatherings of saints. Interest can, however, be rationalized, and arguments that modify it in this direction are present at Putney. They are present alongside attempts to reinstate the distinctions that interest threatens. And the gestures away from apocalypse and toward past distinctions and future articulations of interest are present on both sides of the debates.

We have seen the potential effects of the interest of God on traditional civil bonds. There are other bonds as well that will not withstand it. Very little stands as more sacred for these saints than their engagements, the promises or covenants that they enter into. It is, after all, a covenant that binds them to their God, a bond that they have freely chosen and committed never to break. And so the topic of the first day's debate is the army's engagement to the authority of Parliament. When can an engagement, or oath, be broken; and specifically, can particulars of the *Solemn Engagement of the Army* to Parliament be broken under the present circumstances? This poses an extremely difficult problem: engagements are sworn and signed in the presence of God—breaking them not only endangers the soul, it dishonors the very name of God. But keeping this engagement may give strength to that power that is the source of the "mystery of iniquity" to be destroyed by Christ's army. Everyone at Putney agrees that engagements are to be respected if at all possible, but also that God, their ultimate master, may command the breaking of any engagement. There are disagreements over what has been promised, and whether those promises have been or should be broken, and on what evidence.

The debate over engagements illustrates what happens to the doctrine of necessity when it is translated into terms of interest, and not contained by the criteria of state interest, but expressed as a public interest identical with God's interest. Initial skirmishes between Ireton and the civilian Leveller John Wildman take up and continue a pamphlet war over the meaning of the army's engagement to Parliament. The greatest points of contention are the conditions under which the army agreed to disband, and the matter of the "interests" of king and Lords and their consistency with the safety—or, at times, "interest"—of the people. The safety of the people is paramount; this public good is the "great interest of God"; it would, according to different interpretations, be grounds for the breaking of engagements. The Agitator Everard is freest with these grounds, saying that engagements can be broken "in case they . . . proved unjust, and that it might [so] appear to [one's] conscience. Whatsoever hopes or obligations I should be bound unto, if afterwards God should reveal himself, I would break it speedily, if it were an hundred a day." Wildman carefully amends him in an attempt to qualify conscience with the requisites of the traditional law of necessity: "Provided that what is done [by others] tends to destruction, either [to] self-destruction or to . . . my neighbour especially." Cromwell concurs with Wildman but questions his judgment of the present case, because if his judgment is not well grounded "whether it be lawful to break a covenant upon our own doubts and fears, will be the issue."[60] These disagreements betray a basic consensus over the proper grounds for oath breaking. If directed by God through their consciences to act on behalf of God's interest, which is the paramount matter of public interest, these soldiers must do no other even if contrary engagements have been sworn. It seems that we can know this interest according to the old law of necessity or other criteria of judgment but, as participants on both sides have suggested, God might ask us to do something for reasons that are less than clear.

If God's interest potentially justifies the suspension or transformation of any existing juridical order, how can order possibly be sustained? Perhaps it can be sustained on the basis of a new conception of interest. This is suggested by the second day's discussion of the franchise, which has justly received substantial attention for its display of stark political differences over constitutional reform. Here we see the pressure put on the traditional juridical sense of interest, and how it might give way not to God's commands but to a new political rationality. Again, this possibility appears on both sides of the debate and is evident from mutations in the language of interest. The debate over the franchise springs from the reading of a paper called *An Agreement of the People*, containing constitutional demands drafted by army agitators and civilian Levellers calling for religious toleration, broad suffrage, and equal representation. In response to the reading Ireton objects to the egalitarian implications of the document, and introduces a distinction between civil and natural right. According to Ireton, instituting equality among current constitutional electors is fine, but broadening the electoral base to mere "inhabitants" of England is a dangerous importation of principles of natural right. Ireton asserts that the current arrangement has existed from time immemorial, and that this arrangement would be completely destroyed by the Leveller interpretation of the document.[61] He charges that the Leveller version of "birthright" is a natural right, on the basis of which all engagements could and would be broken. Claiming that this right "is no right at all," Ireton argues:

I think that no person hath a right to an interest or share in the disposing of the affairs of the kingdom, and in determining or choosing those that shall determine what laws we shall be ruled by here—no person hath a right to this, that hath not a permanent fixed interest in this kingdom, and those persons together are properly the represented of this kingdom, and consequently are [also] to make up the representers of this kingdom, who taken together do comprehend whatsoever is of real or permanent interest in the kingdom.[62]

Ireton insists on the stakeholder definition of the people that we encountered in the crisis of 1642—the holders, it seems, of real property or other exclusive privileges who together make up the combined interest of the realm. He goes on to call the individual interest, or constituent part, a "local interest." The "meanest" of these—those that "hath but forty shillings a year"—can have "as great voice" as the greatest, but to allow others a role would be "to take away all property and interest that any man hath either in land by inheritance, or in estate by possession, or anything else."[63]

Colonel Rainborough, the highest-ranking Leveller sympathizer, responds by noting that many members of the Army may have lost property during the fighting:

I will be bound to say that many a man whose zeal and affection to God and this kingdom hath carried him forth in this cause, hath so spent his estate that . . . he shall not hold up his head, if when his estate is lost, and not worth forty shillings a year, a man shall not have any interest. And there are many other ways by which [the] estates men have (if that be the rule which God in his providence does use) do fall to decay. A man, when he hath an estate, hath an interest in making laws, [but] when he hath none, he hath no power in it; so that a man cannot lose that which he hath for the maintenance of his family but he must [also] lose that which God and nature hath given him! . . . Every man born in England cannot, ought not, neither by the Law of God nor the Law of Nature, to be exempted from the choice of those who are to make laws for him to live under, and for him, for aught I know, to lose his life under.[64]

The soldiers should not have to sacrifice without representation; this is their birthright. Ireton's suspicions are justified as God, nature, and life are opposed to his arguments from property and civil constitution. Rainborough's suggestion here is that the interest in making laws is actually God-given. It is the exercise of reason: "I do think that the main cause why Almighty God gave men reason, it was that they should make use of that reason, and that they should improve it for that end and purpose that God gave it them."[65] The only alternative would be fully to submit to human laws, and all present at the Putney debates could see how absurdly corrupt the present system of representation was.

Ireton, in reply, repeats his argument that expansion of the electorate equals the destruction of property. In the course of this argument he elaborates on the meaning of "interest" and the importance of its *locality*: "I mean by permanent . . . local, that . . . is not [able to be removed] anywhere else. As for instance, he that hath a freehold, and that freehold cannot be removed out of the kingdom; and so there's a . . . corporation, a place which hath the privilege of a market and trading, which if you should allow to all places equally, I do not see how you could preserve any peace in the kingdom, and that is the reason why in the constitution we have but some few market towns."[66] Thus the individual freeholder "is tied to that place, . . . his livelihood depends on it." And "that man hath an interest, hath a permanent interest there, upon which he may live, and live a freeman without dependence." Rainborough's invocation of a law of nature raises the disorderly specter of an elector of whom it will be said that "whatever interest he hath he may carry about with him."[67] Any principle that would allow a voice in elections to "men that have no interest but the interest of breathing"[68] will lead to anarchy.

Interest in these accounts appears to be a kind of "propriety," or property (the word is modernized in this edition of the transcripts). Ireton argues that property and interest arise from the civil constitution, and not the law of nature. Rainborough, who has already implied that God is the source of a man's interest, argues that his position does not mean that property could be destroyed; property is, after all, enshrined by the eighth commandment against theft. When once again making the argument that the "right of nature" is a slippery slope, Ireton challenges his opponents: "Show me what you will stop at; wherein you will fence any man in a property by this rule." Rainborough responds by suggesting that the property that grounds the vote must be different from Ireton's interest, because otherwise he would "desire to know how this comes to be a property in some men, and not in others."[69] Not only does it seem that the origin of this crucial property is contested, its site is as well. This difference over the site of property corresponds with a difference in the use of "interest." Frequent Leveller uses of the word seem to indicate a natural property of individuals that is not *in* anything other than one's self.[70]

For Ireton, a movable interest is suspect in its capacity as a movable property.

He wants to exclude from the franchise those whose interest is "the same equally everywhere." This formulation appears to equate interest as natural right with a money; he refers to those who "may have as much interest, in another kingdom as here."[71] Money illustrates the dangers of natural right: "If [a man] hath money, his money is as good in another place as here; he hath nothing that doth locally fix him to this kingdom."[72] The fear of money is fear of an interest that is a mobile property that, even if not resident in the self, is as potentially disruptive of the constitutional order. Neither money nor property in oneself, nor even birthright, do anything to attach the interested to a locality; thus they threaten to erase the distinction between those who have a stake in the realm and those who do not.

It is tempting to read this debate as a clash between declining aristocratic and rising bourgeois values. It seems as if the divide between Grandees and Levellers in the Putney debates marks a transition toward an emergent natural rights-based "possessive individualism," where interest and property are two of many concepts undergoing transformation.[73] But if there is a new individuation going on here, it is very much tied to a new collective. And although the tension between real and mobile property is important to the ways in which interest seems to get unmoored or reanchored, it certainly cannot easily be mapped onto opposing parties.

In fact, the very flexibility of the language of interest subverts the coherence of Ireton's critique. Colonel Rich, in support of Ireton, suggests that if the electorate is expanded, "those that have no interest in the kingdom will make it their interest to choose those that have no interest." They may "by law, not in a confusion, destroy property."[74] There is a consequentialist argument to be made against the *Agreement*, and not just one of destruction by disorder, but of methodical destruction by interested parties (in a new sense of interest) who do not have an interest (in the old sense) in the kingdom. Ireton too begins to use the language of the Levellers when he speaks of those "who have the interest of this kingdom in them."[75] And when Rainborough in frustration abandons debate about constitution and natural right and asks Ireton what the soldiers fought for if not their rights and those of the people, Ireton is pushed to blur his position in curious ways. Interests proliferate in what could be, with a change of syntax, a twenty-first-century endorsement of upward mobility—a statement about opportunity, the rule of law, and individual expectations as motive for political action:

> Every man that was born [in the country, that] is a denizen in it, that hath a freedom, he was capable of trading to get money, to get estates by; and

therefore this man, I think, had a great deal of reason to build up such a foundation of interest to himself: that is, that the will of one man should not be a law, but that the law of this kingdom should be by a choice of persons to represent, and that choice to be made by, the generality of the kingdom. Here was a right that induced men to fight, and those men that had this interest, though this be not the utmost interest that other men have, yet they had *some* interest.[76]

Interest, which Ireton had throughout deployed as a category of distinction for purposes of exclusion, is suddenly inclusive. It is in fact the *means* of inclusion. Ireton's statement deploys a kind of self-interest that serves as both justification and motivation. Without it, the actions of the propertyless majority of soldiers might simply serve the rebellious interests of their immediate superiors. Or without it, the enthusiasm growing in the ranks that moves them to study their Revelations, and listen together for God and follow wherever He leads, would have to be openly sanctioned.[77] Although Ireton has made statements endorsing this enthusiasm, he and Cromwell as commanders have been anxious to contain and mediate divine leadership by, for example, insisting on reasons for breaking engagements. Otherwise groups of soldiers might see their mission as the immediate execution of whatever they read from the mind of God. But Ireton also has to beat back a Leveller rationalism founded in natural right. Interest emerges as a category that provides a grounding for constitutional claims for or against civil arrangements that can be invoked without recourse to natural right or divine command. And its ground, unlike that of the Ancient Constitution and its settled conveniences, is the future.

On the third day of debate, after repeating the requirement not to act by means, such as oath breaking, that would dishonor God's name, Cromwell reiterates the emergency exception upon which all are agreed. But he does so in a way that allows for the supremacy of a public interest that goes beyond mere preservation: "On the other hand, I have but this to say: that those who do apprehend obligations lying upon them . . . that they would clearly come to this resolution, that if they found in their judgments and consciences that those engagements led to anything which really cannot consist with the liberty and safety and public interest of this nation, they would . . . not . . . oppose any other that would do better for the nation than they will do."[78] Because of the reach of the language of interest, Cromwell's words justify oath breaking for national augmentation as well as preservation. Again, this position anticipates a standard for judgment that can mediate conscience. Protecting the public interest is not simply a matter of obeying a seemingly arbitrary command from God; it will not entail Everard's one hundred oath violations per day. But if Cromwell and Ireton were concerned to put brakes on their opponents, by looking back to civil interests and the natural law distinction between convenience and necessity, then their arguments might, in a sense, have won the battle but lost the war.

Of course Cromwell's and Ireton's real war was with Charles, and with those among their allies, including some of their friends and foes at Putney, who would still look for national reconciliation after the coming second civil war. And the new rationale of interest was useful for casting Charles's leadership in an exceedingly poor light. The remarkable and unprecedented trial of Charles I, engineered in large part by Cromwell himself, would accuse him, among other things, of acting against the public interest: "All the said wicked designs, wars, and evil practices of him, the said Charles Stuart, were still carried on for the advancement and upholding of the personal interest of will, power, and pretended prerogative to himself and his family, against the public interest, common right, liberty, justice, and peace of the people of this nation."[79] This statement, from Charles's sentencing of 1649, promotes the new language of interest to a place alongside the traditional vocabulary of English political thought.

One could argue that Charles's sentence still refers to interest as the *salus populi*. But public safety is a negative and exceptional check on the civil constitution and civil affairs; Cromwell's public interest is something that the constitution might be continuously directed toward fostering through positive measures. The "safety of the people" calls forth a higher law, a "law of nature and nations," a law of necessity. The "interest of the people" calls forth no law at all. It is a rhetoric that initially moves beyond civil authority and natural law to seek the will of God, a will that might be rationalized by tying it to a constant goal, the maximization of convenience, the realization of something "better." But convenience has no measure; any convenience that can be maximized is no longer "convenience" in Hooker's sense, if it is convenience at all. Interest assimilates the very necessity with which convenience had formerly been contrasted. Matters of interest include matters of both necessity and convenience; the distinction between these is lost. The public interest—interest of the kingdom, national interest, interest of the people—is a trump over civil law in the way that the law of nature is for Hooker, but it is not limited to an exceptional role. Even when natural law is transformed from exception to foundation, as it is for example in the work of the Restoration theorist Richard Cumberland, it is limited in ways that interest is not.[80] That is because interest does not have the determinacy and inflexibility of law. It governs without limit by precedent or code.

How, though, does the public interest govern? For the armed saints at Putney, the pursuit of this new interest is a kind of maximizing behavior, and behavior that is wholly in their interest. It has an introspective component as well. But the ways in which this pursuit can be said to be maximizing and self-regarding and introspective are most peculiar. The interest that governs the rebels is a command from God, and it is not apprehended by reflection, unless we consider listening to the voice of conscience, often listening together in prayer, to be a kind of reflection. Although the interest of God can be more or less fulfilled if not maximized, and although it is simultaneously the saints' interest, it makes more sense to say that to follow the command of God, to make oneself into his instrument, is simply to do the thing that is necessary and best in every way. And for these theological voluntarists acting in eschatological time, God's commands may be intermittent, unprecedented, even unreasonable. Such commands would normally be exceptional, but the saints find themselves under exceptional and pressing circumstances. On all these points, all the participants at Putney are agreed. Several would like to maintain some of the criteria for distinguishing the commands of God, criteria that come out of the contrast between necessity and convenience, and between the natural and the civil. But the public interest sweeps these distinctions away, and even though it reaches for criteria, for a standard with which to mediate divine rule, it does not yet provide clear criteria of its own. Many of the saints see themselves as engaged in a millennial showdown with the Antichrist, one where the end of the world is imminent. But others are not so sure. And even those who are confident of godly victory are ambivalent about the conditions of this rule.

Stabilizing Interest

Charles I is executed in the name of interest, but interest will call Charles II to the throne. In the tension between the consensus over their mission and the specifics of its ramifications for civil affairs, the members of the New Model Army come close to generating a new constitutional standard. They are the army in the field whose invocation of *salus populi* matches the context of Cicero's slogan, but they are a very peculiar army, because not only are they defending against an "external" enemy that threatens the *res publica*, but they themselves are a revolutionary army seeking to transform the very thing they are defending. Their differences over what they are constructing and defending are grounded in a consensus over whom they are fighting for, the English people and their God. The New Model Army could be seen as the guarantor of the interest of Goodwin's proto-rational theology—not unlawfully deciding on or rushing benefits from the people's covenant with God, but securing the national covenant itself (it is the means by which God secures the contract, securing his church as he did in 1605). But if they are God's army then they are acting from and for the end of time itself, and acting directly from God's will to a purpose yet unknown, and, as they all acknowledge, this might mean doing things that are simply impossible to make sense of in any terms available to them. The specter of this very present possibility, and concern that their consciences might not be synchronized if and when the time comes, make the idea of the public interest as we understand it look like a very agreeable standard. At moments of dialogue the public interest serves, as it were, as a check on the army's status as a divine agent of destruction, and so contributes a third term to Pocock's "half radical, half conservative" characterization, with a more rationalist orientation toward the future. The soldiers grope together toward something that stands for the advance of the individual and collective welfare of themselves and their people, something other than natural right or the Ancient Constitution that would ground a critique of existing arrangements and conditions.

This standard needs a measure, and it began to get one in the ensuing years. In the 1650s interest became a more systematic language of political theory. James Harrington's *Oceana* of 1657 articulated a sophisticated republican interest pluralism. More important for our purposes, Matthew Wren's monarchist critique of *Oceana* translated Hobbesian arguments into a kind of interest monism. According to Wren, in the state of nature there was no interest of mankind distinct from the parts, "yet since the Institution of Government, Men are obliged besides, nay in many Cases above, their own Private Interest, to advance the Publique or Common One." Without some divestiture of private interest, government is too weak to provide protection. But "by this protection and benefit of Lawes, Every Mans power and Interest which He had parted with, comes home to him again with Increase."[81] Wren offers elements of the new monistic interest constitutionalism hinted at by Ireton, in which measures of interest are implied in a kind of economic model of the social contract.

During the 1650s the monistic language of interest was normalized. For those parties shut out of the politics of the Interregnum, the public interest was one route back in. Whereas Royalists, for example, had only rarely argued in these terms in the 1640s, by the eve of the Restoration claims from across the political spectrum were made in terms of a public or national interest, which became a fixture of controversialist literature. Arguments for bringing in Charles II to resolve the political crisis of 1659 were made in terms of the general interest; interest justified the Restoration itself.[82] After the Restoration, one measure developed for this interest came from the discourse of trade, as trade became prominent in "interest of England" writings. The standards provided by the discourse of trade are a measure of national welfare, and they serve the purposes of simultaneously aiding and disciplining the new prince. And so Samuel Fortrey is one of many to combine trade and conscience, arguing that if Charles's agents deal too harshly with nonconformists and their property, the kingdom will increasingly become impoverished and the prince weakened.[83] Other arguments were less focused on the relationship between prosperity and princely power, valuing prosperity for its own sake. These writings on the "interest of England" were mostly domestic in orientation, and if they now tended to recognize the central importance of protecting the government, they often did so as part of an interest grounded outside it. Soon a new political arithmetic would appear, which helped to provide this interest with a metric, amid the emergence of new epistemological standards that elevated the status of its probable knowledge.[84] Arguments in terms of prosperity would mix with more familiar Whiggish appeals to the rights of Englishmen. Thus William Penn could argue for toleration in terms of rights, constitutional balance, princely power, and national prosperity, all in the name of the interest of England.[85]

The Restoration left the problems of Protestant fratricide unresolved. Even through the filter of an effective censorship, the continuing conflicts over religious and political settlement shone through. Nonconformists were "schismaticks" fomenting "faction," the government was guilty of "popery" and "arbitrary government." We can see the Glorious Revolution of 1688 as marking the victory of liberty and property and the conquest of absolutism by an enduring constitutional interest pluralism. We can also see it as marking the emergence of an English state apparatus, whose philosopher is less the John Locke of the *Two Treatises of Government* than the Locke of the *Essay Concerning Human Understanding* and the *Letter Concerning Toleration*. Before the Glorious Revolution, the problem of Protestant fratricide was addressed through several writings on "natural religion." Partisans of natural religion tended to be "latitudinarian": their solution to the difficulties posed by religious difference was not Locke's famous separation of civil and spiritual interests, but the identification of a number of "things indifferent" to salvation that could point in two directions at once. For instance, if it can be established that many of the forms of religious observance ordered by the prince are indifferent to salvation, one might as well observe them in order, as Hooker pleaded, not to disturb the English church. Or perhaps if they are so indifferent, the prince and everyone else might as well allow their variety to proliferate undisturbed. Locke's own trajectory in his contributions to the toleration controversy was a move from the first to the second of these alternatives.[86] But natural religion was not only relevant to the problem of toleration in this way. Natural religion was rational religion; it developed a regulative ethic that could steer a course between the disastrous alternatives of atheism and radical enthusiasm. The roots of this family of doctrines predate the 1640s. Its theorists were quietly active in the universities during the Interregnum, and it came into prominence as Establishment theology in the latter part of the reign of Charles II. In the use of "interest" made by the theorists of natural religion we see the first appearance of an abstract, stable, reflexive, and prospective conception of interest in English writing, one that consistently motivates the individual in a manner contributing to his own good and to the interest of the whole.

It is worth recalling who the targets of the work of natural religion were. On the one side we have the "atheistical" Hobbes, arguing the nonexistence of natural human order and the purely emotive or political grounds of judgments of good and evil. On the other side we have the "enthusiasts," steering the covenant of faith into a collision course with all "carnal" law and institutions. Both were thought to be a threat to order. "Hobbists" spread a corrosive skepticism that unleashed the dangerous instrumentality of an immoral interest of self unmoored to any greater purpose. "Enthusiasts" spread an infectious dogmatism that encouraged factional interests, aggravated the already fractured unity of the church, and reopened the wounds of war and regicide. Granted, this latter charge might be leveled against the mainstream party of Presbyterians, who were instrumental in restoring king and church yet whose opponents never tired of recalling how disloyal they had been to the martyred Charles I.[87] But the actions of Presbyterians and others in 1660 were motivated in large part by fear of "phanatiques," and enthusiasm was an ecumenical target for many decades to come.

A glance at a not untypical Fifth Monarchist pamphlet offers a reminder of what was so troubling to so many about the most animated consciences among their fellow subjects. Here is how a participant remembers the civil wars and urges a completion of their mission, from the vantage point of the crisis of 1659:

> It is well known to many, that both the spiritual and visible Interest of Christ hath begun to shine forth more of late in this Nation, and God hath

given more visible testimonies in a way of owning of it here then in any other Nations besides: So soon as this Interest and Cause was placed among us, what a series of changes did presently flow in upon us?

A deliverance from the yoaks of Tyranny and Persecution, unto a condition of meer outward liberty and quiet, was not the chief Result in[t]ended us in our changes, but that God wou'd thereby bring us both Church and State under a more immediate Government to his Son . . . . If the Lord has thus kindled a Refining fire among us, let us take heed how we quench it, till our purification, thereby preparing us unto that Kingdom and Glory that is drawing near.

The Lord hath taken new and extraordinary wayes with us; besides that peculiar eye that hath watched over the English Nation, in former times, to save it from the blood-thirsty Rage of Antichristian Adversaries, their Invasions from abroad, and Conspiracies at home: God has of late made this Nation, as it were, a Stage, whereupon he came forth . . . ; here began the Horns of Antichrist to be thrown down.[88]

The interest of Christ demands the continued purification of saints and realm. The revolution is definitively not about fighting for civil interests or against religious persecution; it is about preparing for the rule of Christ, and there is yet much work to be done. Various partisans of "outward liberty and quiet," exhausted from the instability of those years, had much to fear from such a vision.

If the millenarian interest of God contributed to sectarian violence, the latitudinarian response was to rationalize this eschatology in a regulative ethic also generated from an immanent and transcendent monistic interest. Although related in spirit and sources to modern natural-law theory, latitudinarianism incorporated the new experimental knowledge, and so its self and public interest were potentially dynamic and open to contingent calculation and verification. Thus John Wilkins, Anglican bishop and founding member of the Royal Society, is a particularly emblematic figure. His *Of the Principles and Duties of Natural Religion* is among the first in a number of texts of the period to recommend the sober and industrious pursuit of a transcendental self-interest that simultaneously contributes to the interest of the whole. As John Tillotson writes in a preface, it is "an effectual antidote against the pernicious Doctrines of the *Antinomians*, and of all other *Libertine-Enthusiasts* whatsoever." Tillotson praises the text for demonstrating "that *Religion* and *Happiness*, our *Duty* and our *Interest*, are really but one and the same thing considered under several notions."[89]

Wilkins is concerned with the destruction and perversion of conscience. Atheism destroys it, and enthusiasm perverts it.[90] Natural religion, on the other hand, enlists conscience in a project of self-government by demonstrating the wisdom of the dutiful life: "how much it is, upon all accounts, [men's] chief happiness and interest to lead a religious and virtuous course of life."[91] The first book of Wilkins's treatise begins the discussion of duty with a cutting-edge epistemological discussion of kinds of evidence and types of certainty. The second book discusses the wisdom of duty, considering man alone and in society. What distinguishes human beings from other animals is a specific prospective orientation, their "*Apprehension of a Deity*" and their "*expectation of a future state after this life*."[92] When we combine this specific, reasonable expectation and apprehension with a reasonable assumption of self-interest, we see that the wisdom of practicing duties is in their conformity with this interest: "Now 'tis the usual course of men to apply themselves to that as their chief business, by which their interest is most promoted, and which may most conduce to that main end which they propose to themselves. And can any thing be more reasonable, than for that to be the chief *business* of a man's life, which is the chief end of his *Being*?"[93] If men would focus on their own interest in this world and the next, and calculate rewards and punishments concerning things important rather than indifferent to their eternal happiness, they would see the wisdom of quietly practicing the basic duties of a natural religion that are key to their well-being, both alone and in society with others.[94]

What is remarkable about these texts is how they combined the reasonable calculation of commensurables with an infinitely prospective vision that bridges the gap between this world and the next. With the notions of happiness with which they worked—a perspective that we now label "theological utilitarianism"—they succeeded in constructing a scheme of value not tied, in the way of the trade tracts of the time, to the circulation of material goods.[95] Natural religion's "interest" had the potentially infinite scope of millenarian interest, but combined it with an individuation and stability that anticipated Shaftesburean and Benthamic interest. Natural religion was well suited to the new national metrics of interest. Its scheme of value was not tied to the state, even as it argued the service that its insights performed for good government. Writers on natural religion advertised the ordered contributions of the pious man, compared to the destructiveness of the impious and of the pervertedly pious. Civil and natural order were impossible, it was feared, without the assurance that good things will happen to good people and bad things to bad people, and without God as inspector general. This was key to the new interest constitution of self and society. At the turn of the century, by contrast, we have secular assurances from Shaftesbury's introspector, and from the example of Daniel Defoe's shopkeeper, who knows he is going to see his customers again. In Bentham's vision the situation is once again changed, as society is held together by individuals behaving prudently amid multiple instruments of security, instruments that can work sufficiently well in contexts of anonymity. For all their differences, however, these perspectives commonly posit selves as economies in pursuit of the future, conforming through their calculations to the broader arrangements that structure their interests.[96]

Much is made of the distinction between even an aggressively rational religion and secular rationalism. It seems to many observers that the self who includes an afterlife in determinations of interest is vastly different from the one who does not—that there is a kind of transcendental divide between them. But these forms of economic rationality have much more in common with one another than either does with enthusiasm or common-law constitutionalism. Both this believer and this nonbeliever set mobile time-horizons for their calculations of cost and benefit. And it would be a mistake to underestimate the potential power and reach of the rational imagination of the "secular" utilitarian. According to Gary Becker, for example, the possibilities of risk assessment are such that in an important sense, almost every death is a suicide.[97] Thus the economic actor, like the prudently conscientious one, is effectively immortal: already present at the scene of his own death, and refusing the possibility of another.

7   The Economic Polity

The late-seventeenth-century latitudinarian conscience no longer listened for the voice of God. Instead it understood God's rules as the foundation for expectations and apprehensions of the future, in order to calculate a route to individual and collective felicity. Conscience was transformed into an organ of imagination. In "Governing Conduct," James Tully revisits Nietzsche's puzzle of a "modern subject, who is both calculable in his behaviour . . . and sovereign, the bearer of rights and responsibility." He challenges Nietzsche's emphasis on conscience as the basis for predictable agency: "If my study [of Locke and his context] is correct, just the opposite is true. The new practice of governing was an attack on the conscience, as both too radical and too submissive, and an effort to create habits that would replace the conscience and guide conduct."[1] This is a crucial insight for the study of early modern English political theory and practice. Whether we think of the seventeenth-century saints as free or chained, they were, for a time, notoriously unpredictable. If *my* study is correct, the imagination is the faculty that gradually displaces conscience: it proves to be both less radical and less submissive, and so much more suited to an economic government by and for interest.

I have argued that economy needs to be reconceptualized, and reconceptualized as government. Economy pursues a goal of monistic interest that balances, through the imagination, the various considerations, "material" as well as "spiritual," of a choosing, prospective individual. But its rationality—

economic rationality—is not merely instrumental; it subsumes ends as well as means, and so it requires a more extensive discipline, one not governed by a sovereign instrumentality. I have illustrated through Bentham how economic government structures the imaginings of the imagination that it relies on: the economic polity generates as it arranges the expectations that drive it. And I have demonstrated that economy as government has origins in reason of state and in the conscience-driven pursuit of the public interest. Economic rationality is a specific kind of political rationality. It is not the encroachment on politics of a market that did not yet exist, and it is less a characteristic or effect of self-interest than it is its organizing presupposition.

Bentham posits the agency and materiality of the imagination even as he denigrates the imaginary in relation to the real; thus he both confounds and reinforces the oppositions in social science between matters of value and matters of fact. Bentham's rule of interest defies instrumentality with a governing rationality that subsumes individual and collective wills, and this challenges philosophical models of liberal and democratic sovereignty. Bentham's reforms aim at harmonizing expectations through legislative tactics that shape and fix the very expectations they harmonize; this approach confounds, even as it exploits, popular and theoretical attachments to the priority of the expectant and choosing agent. Economic government is demonstrated by, and explicated in, Bentham's work. Bentham develops economic rationality as an omnibus political logic, challenging our associations of economy with particular practices and particular locations. And this development has been taken up and refined by neoliberal practitioners of the new "imperial" economics.[2]

The conundrums posed by Bentham have contributed to his contemporary neglect as a political theorist. Neoliberal trends in theory and practice are similarly puzzling, and their analysis is similarly in danger of neglect. Neoliberal trends are best understood, I argue, through a focus on the governmental rationality that I have identified. The story of economic rationality offered here suggests that it has been a part of liberalism from the beginning. In the Introduction I claimed that neoliberalism renews economic rationality in part by reoccupying liberal assumptions, reoccupying them, so to speak, from within. But I also claimed that Bentham, the paradigmatic theorist of economic government, was a touchstone for previous transformations of the liberal state. There seems to be a tension between these claims. Is Bentham a kind of protean figure, able to be claimed as a forebear by political, social, and economic reformers from across the political spectrum? And if so, what is notable about his neoliberal appropriation?

Perhaps the most problematic of my claims about Bentham and neoliberalism is that Bentham is a kind of anti-juridical theorist of jurisprudence, and that the neoliberal colonization of the juridical is continuous with Bentham's. After all, Bentham was a great codifier: he was famously hostile to the common law and wrote voluminous amounts of proposed legal code. The contemporary law-and-economics movement, on the other hand, embraces and affirms the common law, and most of its adherents are very suspicious of statutory law.[3] The historical Bentham was undeniably a prominent ally of the modernizing forces, movements, and individuals most responsible for building the nineteenth-century British state. And it appears that contemporary neoliberals are striving to dismantle this state wherever they encounter it.

Bentham was a great state builder, but he was also a great critic of the state. Perhaps the same can be said of contemporary neoliberals. The opposition between Bentham and neoliberalism results from too great a focus on the state as such.[4] The previous chapter argued that a distinctive diffuse and decentered reason of state was advanced in the name of a godly individual and collective interest crucial to the building of the first English state. I hope that my account has helped to estrange the reader from any understanding of this state as a sovereign agent or instrument. There remains, however, a powerful tension between Bentham the writer of sovereign code and the Bentham I have emphasized—the developer of a flexible rationality of government, the theorist of what he at one time called "indirect legislation." My focus on the latter has provocatively ignored the extent to which even projects of indirect rule are figured by Bentham himself as legislative projects in the traditional sense: projects emanating from a sovereign law-making body. Although it is quite possible and reasonable to object to my reading of Bentham by assembling all the evidence that he was engaged in a normative project of state building, it is still important to understand his Pannomial efforts within the broader context of his thought and his milieu. As I stressed in chapter 4, Bentham was writing before the dawn of social science, before we were comfortably assumed to be integrated into "social systems" that regulate and harmonize our behaviors. In fact, the closest approximation to such a social system during his lifetime was the church. It was a core position of anti-toleration arguments in the late eighteenth century and the early nineteenth that without the Establishment the nation would crumble, and so nonconformity was really a kind of political separatism or worse, anarchism. For Bentham and his contemporaries, our notion of society as a kind of law-governed second nature was new, if present at all. The possibly authorless laws of nature did not have a corollary in civil affairs. Bentham wrote at the cusp of the discovery of the social.

Bentham himself refused the phrase "natural law" even with reference to the physical world: laws had authors, nature did not. Even if society were a second nature, it would not have laws but simply regularities. According to Bentham, society's laws issue from bodies with coercive power such as Parliament and, lamentably, the church. This is not to say that he thought society chaotic; the opposition here is not between order and chaos, but between badly authored and well authored order. (Badly authored order can produce chaos.) The most significant evolution in Bentham's thought over his long writing life was a growing conviction—probably reached as a result of his repeated frustrations at the nonadoption of his Panopticon proposal—that bad authorship of laws was deliberate, not accidental. In his later years, Bentham understood this authorship to produce not only chaos and waste but sinister order as well; it involved organizing the affairs of the many to serve the interest of the few. Bentham's code increasingly aimed at rewriting this relationship, which explains the extent of his later emphasis on constitutional code in particular. Penal code and civil code would continue to be as important as before, but there would be little possibility of their adoption, and little guarantee for their maintenance, if a system wasn't designed that could break sinister interest and keep it from reassembling.

And so Bentham's ambitious code making seems to represent a powerful remnant of sovereignty in his work. But it is worth reiterating that this sovereignty is very different from the tradition in which it is often placed: that of Hobbesian command. In contrast to Bentham, Hobbes maintained that the law obligates subjects in a fundamental way. According to Hobbes, law obligates because it is authorized by the subject, who consents to sovereign rule. For Bentham, on the other hand, the subject's obligation to any law is nothing more or less than the interest that it creates in its obedience. According to Bentham, even democratic sovereignty in no way implies the citizen-subject's authorization of the laws; at no point does sovereignty trump utility. And so for Bentham the test of any code, including his own, will be the severe test of its continuing utility. This will be a test according to observable and measurable criteria, a test of the various direct and collateral effects of the laws on those they govern. If a law is inadequately sanctioned it will be disobeyed; if it is in this or another respect uneconomical instead of economical it must be changed or abandoned. These standards are of course crucially relative: a good law is no longer good in relation to a better alternative, and the aptitude of a law is its aptitude in relation to an existing regime of expectations that would doubtless be disturbed by legal change.[5]

Now the kind of inquiry that assesses and measures these relations of costs and benefits is in no way fixed or given. And the unit of cost and benefit is not exactly given, either. As standards, Bentham's "happiness" or "unhappiness," "pleasure" or "pain," must guide translations of diverse phenomena into weights for a numeric scale that arranges the elements of a prospective economy in relation to one another. Bentham wrote at a time when a number of scientific disciplines emerged, the usefulness of which he understood but which did not themselves govern his thinking. Bentham and his contemporaries did not think in terms of social systems because the various disciplines that have discovered and codified these systems had not yet arisen. Bentham's principle of economy—the principle that in all affairs it is best to govern them toward the greatest benefit at the least cost—remains in large part a formal and not a representational principle.[6] And by this I mean that economy is for Bentham strictly a mode of proceeding rather than a thing, and so as a mode of proceeding it does not take its bearings from a picture of economic activity. Although Bentham's economy is strikingly monistic, and although it links with and reproduces an individual economic rationality through a science of the self and its springs of action, the principle is in important ways pre-disciplinary and capable of entertaining possibly competing representations of society. Should those representations produce or confirm social regularities not in need of maintenance through code, the pertinent code would be considered wasteful and thus be scrapped. Bentham is by no means committed to code for its own sake, and his work on indirect legislation anticipates the possibility that the "allied sanctions" might, in all sorts of venues, govern more economically than political measures. Most likely, as I've suggested, this insight recommends using discoveries of regularities to graft code onto them. Epidemiological discoveries, for example, should inspire a critique of any pertinent code and its modification or replacement with more efficient measures, assuming full sensitivity to the various costs of change as reported by other disciplines. The idea in each case is to produce welcome and avoid unwelcome collateral effects. Bentham's own examples of indirect legislation stress the benefits to be gained from trading a central police for the mobilization of subjects to police one another.[7] In realms ranging from public health to corporate governance, insights from the disciplines can be used to craft code mandating transparency and the dispersal of information, producing maximally productive systems of mutual surveillance.

My focus on disciplines is not concerned with the production of "disciplined" and "normalized" subjects but with the production of the policies that govern subjects whose disciplining and normalizing I here take for granted.

According to Bentham's *Chrestomathia*, "discipline" names any useful art and science.[8] Although the differentiation between art and science is not strict, sciences study practical causation, or causation with a view to intervention, and arts are practices of intervention based on scientific knowledge. Thus the designation "art-and-science": not only can the two not be strictly separated, it would never make sense to practice an art without its science or vice versa. What becomes crucial to a form of government like Bentham's, oriented as it is to the maximization of interest, are the sciences that study what we might call social causation (which include what we call natural as well as social sciences), and the arts that intervene on the basis of these studies. Consider his penchant for the medical metaphor. Benthamic government, like all the disciplines that serve it, is therapeutic. Thus Bentham is open to being informed by several old and new arts-and-sciences, including some, like the arts-and-sciences of rhetoric, architecture, and penology, that seem quite far removed from what we think of as "economic" concerns. It is simply crucial that these be pressed into service for an art of government aimed at harmonizing and maximizing the totality of relations within an imagined economy: "The several disciplines, being each of them a means of happiness or well-being, considered with relation to mankind taken in the aggregate, the thing to be desired with a view to their happiness, is, that the quantity of *disciplines* should at all times be as great as possible. Say for shortness,—subservient to the maximum of *happiness*, is the maximum of *disciplines*."[9] Thus Benthamic interest could justify proliferating and inevitably competing norms. It could justify the great disciplinary governmentalities that grew out of the profusion of new arts and sciences associated with the discovery of the social, with their accompanying elevation of the justicial status of the professions, of associations of statisticians, physicians, social workers, and so on. Since the rise of economics, and the emergence of "the economy," economy is no longer a formal principle. It has become subject to competing, and increasingly homogeneous, representations. Typically, macroeconomic representations allow for a diversity of factors to be relevant to the calculation of benefit or bane, but are likely to exclude whatever lies outside their representation of "the economy." It would seem that microeconomics, and especially the new imperial economics, would be reversing this trend: for Becker, as for Bentham, every question is in a sense an economic one. But whereas Bentham's conception of the value sought by economic government, utility, is a notoriously open one, utility for contemporary economics is strictly defined in terms of preferences. This representation of value and the disciplinary attachment to markets as proofs and maximizing distributors of utilities is of some consequence. For contemporary economics, the expansion of the empire of choice is almost by definition good. So long as the opening of a horizon of choice doesn't seriously allow an agent to threaten the utilities of others, it is a great candidate for increasing efficiency and aggregate utility. This disciplinary definition of utility points to the biggest difference between Benthamic legal reform and the law-and-economics movement. Bentham wanted to govern everything in accordance with economy; the law-and-economics movement wants to govern everything in accordance with economics. The ascendancy of a particular representation of economy helps to explain the strategic difference over statutes. Law-and-economics theorists deride statutory law for Benthamic reasons; statutes result from, protect, and promote sinister interest, or what economists call "rent-seeking" behavior. But the preemptive strike against statutory law—simply assuming, without verification, that it is suspect—is governed by the distinction between state and market, and by a belief in the relative efficiency of the latter. It also relies on numerous other assumptions that Bentham did not make, most importantly the assumption that any number of spheres, if not governed by statute, will be governed by the systematic reign of equilibrating markets. The representational norm that governs many neoliberal renewals of Benthamic government is the assurance of the latent existence of markets wherever they are not manifest. And if the targeted practices do not automatically organize themselves "efficiently" following *laissez-faire* measures, a more active *laissez-faire* using policy and statute, if necessary, will be recommended to produce the conditions in which the latent markets can appear.

In the twenty-first century, Bentham still looms large as a legal theorist, but he was relatively ineffective as a legal reformer.[10] His proliferation of code was not, in the end, nearly as important as the governmental spirit of his project. That spirit, by never viewing the law as any kind of end in itself, maintains the subservience of the law to the formal principle of economy. It is a spirit that spurred the growth of what we call the policy sciences, which, as arts-and-sciences of government, are some of our most important sources of indirect legislation. Insofar as these sciences come under the sway of microeconomic representations of efficiency, economic government increasingly becomes government by economics. Bentham himself violated the formality of his own conception of economy whenever he emphasized the "four ends" of government: security, subsistence, abundance, and equality. Twentieth-century macroeconomics had room for all of these in its representations, which explains how its Benthamism could justify the welfare state. Contemporary microeconomics and its extrapolations, by contrast, are not concerned with subsistence and equality; they are focused on abundance and tend to take security for granted.

But the problem of security is fundamental to neoliberal practice because neoliberal reforms enhance what is fundamental to Bentham's project: government through, by, and for expectations. This mode of government has been enhanced by cultivating the choosing subject, by developing new technologies of choice in a number of different venues. Bentham was well aware of the uses of choice, and much of his "policy" work anticipates contemporary privatizing rhetorics. However, Bentham tended to be clearer than many of today's proponents of choice about the role and mechanics of the individual imagination in technologies of choice, and clearer about the governmental purpose of their implementation. Consider his scheme for managing prisons under a contract system, which has all the advantages of "private economy" plus "publicity." In this scheme, publicity is more than a public check on the manager's activities: it is a means to preemptive self-auditing: "To enable the public to look at his accounts, a man must look at them himself. No man travels quietly on in the road to ruin with the picture of it before his eyes."[11] And with contract management, individual managers will set their own standards, and these are higher than any that could be imposed on them. On salary they won't work as hard: "Will they screw up diligence and ingenuity to their highest pitch? Never while man is man: a man himself can never know what he could get, unless the profit is his own. What a man has got and pocketed, or thrown away, you may punish him for: can you punish him for the extra profit which, for want of a peculiar measure of industry and ingenuity . . . he failed of getting?"[12] Bentham is always frank in acknowledging that *laissez-faire* measures are measures of government: "Power and inclination beget action: unite them, the end is accomplished, the business done. To effect this union in each instance is the great art and the great study of Government."[13] Neoliberal government renews this project to, in F. A. Hayek's words, "dispense with the need of conscious control and . . . provide inducements which will make individuals do the desirable things without anyone having to tell them what to do."[14] But not only does this government narrow the scope of the "desirable" in its service to economics: its libertarian rhetoric mystifies its own governmental project.

According to neoliberalism, choice is thought to introduce efficiency into a number of areas; today it is being introduced into areas where Bentham himself would hesitate, including security systems themselves. Here utility is maximized by introducing new "prices" for reduction of risk that allow those, for example, who value the reduction less to raise their risk and devote more resources toward other goods. I have argued that American political theory is ill equipped to conduct a critique of choice because it focuses instead on a critique of government, and does not recognize government through choice. But scholars such as Nikolas Rose have identified technologies of choice as key to a government of "advanced liberalism," one that governs through a new "prudentialism."[15] This prudentialism, which relegates to individual calculation everything from health to personal safety, to education, to degree of employment, to old-age pensions, has enabled "public" and "private" institutions to shift a variety of functions to an ever-busier choosing agent, and has multiplied insecurities for every new horizon of decision. These insecurities, as burdensome to individuals as they might appear to be, are figured by choice theorists to be productive insecurities that contribute to the maximization of expectations across the aggregate whole.

But across which aggregate whole? Writing in the context of the building of the nation-state, Bentham for the most part assumed that the aggregate "community" of his concern—the "party whose interest is in question" whose utility was to be maximized—was the population within the nation-state's borders. However, the extent to which his thinking is devoid not only of reason of state but of nationalism is remarkable; the generality of his language suggests the potential adaptability of his standard to any aggregate and to any scene of government. "Public" and "private" planners today seem similarly to be leaving the nation-state behind in order to build a global security regime. In its renewal of monistic interest neoliberal theory can join with neo-imperial practice to attack national sovereignties and economies themselves as partial interests; these interests stand between selves and the designated aggregate, and thus concern for them promotes sinister interest at the expense of efficiency. Contemporary government intensifies the reflexive interest-relation; its expansion of freedom of choice is necessarily an expansion of imagineering, self-inspection, mutual surveillance, and relentless commensurability.

It should be clear from my analysis that I do not believe that Bentham's government by and for expected happiness was really about happiness; it was instead about government. But the term "happiness" as an interest measure provided a critical language with which to make this very point. With expected happiness it still made sense to talk about how the endless drive for efficiency could cause unhappiness; the claims of the disgruntled about growing inequalities, hidden costs, exploitation, and unnecessary suffering could still be heard. Today's polity of expected utility, on the other hand, provides no such language. Left to its own terms, its proceedings are in a sense unassailable, because the economic polity always already casts all contestations as simple matters of preference and choice. Perhaps by redescribing preference and choice as the effects and instruments of government, we can begin to question the conditions of economic rule.

149

Notes

1 Introduction

1   The attack on and self-defense of society are Polanyian themes (Karl Polanyi, *The Great Transformation* [New York: Rinehart, 1944]) that are enjoying a revival in contemporary critiques of neoliberalism. (For one of many fine examples of this work see Maurice Glasman, *Unnecessary Suffering* [London: Verso, 1996]; see also the late political speeches and writings of Pierre Bourdieu collected in *Acts of Resistance: Against the Tyranny of the Market*, trans. Richard Nice [New York: New Press, 1998]). These are not my themes. Although this study takes considerable theoretical inspiration from Polanyi and more generally from the tradition of grand sociology from Marx through Mauss, it maintains a historicist distance from many of that tradition's central categories, including "society" itself. Such skepticism is the hallmark of "governmentality" studies (see *The Foucault Effect: Studies in Governmentality* [Chicago: University of Chicago Press, 1991] and previous and subsequent work by its contributors and others). This is not, however, itself such a study, in that I merely investigate a specific governmental rationality.

2   Anthony, Earl of Shaftesbury, *An Inquiry concerning Virtue, or Merit*, in Shaftesbury, *Characteristicks of Men, Manners, Opinions, Times*, ed. Philip Ayres (Oxford: Clarendon, 1999), vol. I, p. 247 (II.ii.1).

3   Jeremy Bentham, *A Table of the Springs of Action* ("Explanations"), in Bentham, *Deontology Together with A Table of the Springs of Action and The Article On Utilitarianism*, ed. Amnon Goldworth (Oxford: Clarendon, 1983), p. 90.

4   James Coleman, *Foundations of Social Theory* (Cambridge: Harvard University Press, 1990), p. 504.

5   "Shaftesbury and Bentham" is misleading. With the exception of Bentham, this is not an

author-driven study: my work on Shaftesbury in chapter 3 treats the somewhat anomalous *Inquiry*. On its anomalousness, see Lawrence Klein, *Shaftesbury and the Culture of Politeness* (Cambridge: Cambridge University Press, 1994).

6 "Interest" was initially a legal term, as in the Roman law *id quod interest*, which asks "what is the share?" This usage, which seems to be the first appearance of a noun variant of *interesse* (before this it might mean to matter or to make a difference), most frequently addressed the resolution of disputes involving compensation for damages. The answer to the question demanded the assessment of specific relations and circumstances rather than the application of a rule; this would only change when *interest* came to function as a vehicle for usury payment, payment which under prohibition could only be sanctioned as compensation for damages. See the entry for "Interesse" in Otto Brunner, Werner Conze, and Reinhart Kosel-leck eds., *Geschichtliche Grundbegriffe: Historisches Lexikon zur politisch-sozialen Sprache in Deutschland* (Stuttgart: Klett-Cotta, 1982), vol. 3, especially pp. 306–10 (Ernst Wolfgang Orth, "Lateinische Grundbedeutungen von 'interesse' bis in die frühe Neuzeit"). See also the *Oxford English Dictionary* entry for "interest" and Albert O. Hirschman, "From Euphemism to Tau-tology," in *Rival Views of Market Society* (New York: Viking, 1986), pp. 35–55. There are unrelated but close antecedents, for example the Greek word transliterated as *sympheron* and the Latin *utilitas*, both of which are sometimes translated as "interest." "Utility" has come to mean something like monistic interest, but this is less a translation of *utilitas* than a retransla-tion of interest.

On the rise of the psychological sense of interest see Martin Heidegger's lament in the opening lecture of *What Is Called Thinking?*, trans. Fred D. Wieck and J. Glenn Gray (New York: Harper and Row, 1968): "Nobody will deny that there is an interest in philosophy today. But—is there anything at all left today in which man does not take an interest, in the sense in which he understands 'interest'? Interest, *interesse*, means to be among and in the midst of things, or to be at the center of a thing and to stay with it. But today's interest accepts as valid only what is interesting. And interesting is the sort of thing that can freely be regarded as indifferent the next moment, and be displaced by something else, which then concerns us just as little as what went before (p. 5)."

7 In *An Introduction to the Principles of Morals and Legislation*, to be "material" means to matter. "Discourse" is Bentham's term, and denotes speech and writing. See Bentham, *An Introduc-tion to the Principles of Morals and Legislation*, ed. J. H. Burns and H. L. A. Hart (London: Athlone, 1970), pp. 74, 76, and *passim*.

8 Ibid., p. 45, and *A Table of the Springs of Action* ("Explanations"), p. 89.

9 The distinction between direct and indirect legislation is one from Bentham's early work that he did not keep. I write "direct and indirect legislation" to give an idea of how broad Ben-tham's vision of government is, and to stress that it involves much more than law as law is usually understood. Indirect legislation seems to be everything that can be done to achieve a legislative end through indirect means (means other than a statute aimed squarely at the problem), including the buttressing of existing sanctions, legal as well as "social," and the triggering of remote effects. My reading of Bentham as a theorist of indirect legislation follows Fred Rosen in viewing Benthamic measures as "instruments of security across a wide spec-trum of law and policy" (Rosen, *Bentham, Byron, and Greece* [Oxford: Oxford University Press, 1992], p. 34). Even the most direct Benthamic code acts indirectly, as it relies on subjects to choose what is in their interest. See notes 10 and 31 to chapter 4, below.

10 David Hume, *A Treatise of Human Nature*, ed. Peter H. Nidditch, 2nd edition (Oxford: Oxford University Press, 1978), p. 415.

11 Even such an astute and independent critic as André Gorz is confined by these assumptions. His *Critique of Economic Reason* (trans. Gillian Handyside and Chris Turner [London: Verso, 1989]) remains attached to a critical-theory narrative that conflates economic rationality with "cognitive-instrumental" rationality (he calls it a "particular form" of this rationality—p. 107). Gorz acknowledges that he is following Horkheimer, Adorno, and Habermas here (p. 108n). Horkheimer's and Adorno's work is of course significantly less Kantian than Habermas's, but their critiques of instrumental reason perform a similar conflation.

12 One preoccupation for economic theorists is the stability of these preference economies. For critics the greatest preoccupation is the reduction performed by the commensurability thesis. An excellent philosophical critique that incorporates and extends much of the analytic literature on this topic is Elizabeth Anderson's *Value in Ethics and Economics* (Cambridge: Harvard University Press, 1993).

13 The huge literature in behavioral economics has no critical bearing on this argument, which is about the specificity of economic reason and its effects—not about its descriptive realism or instrumentality, or about its prescriptive limitations or limits.

14 For Bentham's constitutional theory, see Jeremy Bentham, *First Principles Preparatory to Constitutional Code*, ed. Philip Schofield (Oxford: Clarendon, 1989), *The Collected Works of Jeremy Bentham*, especially chs. 1 and 2 of "Constitutional Code Rationale," pp. 229–43. For a primer on law and economics see Richard Posner, *Economic Analysis of Law*, 5th edition (New York: Aspen, 1998). Law and economics is not a uniform tradition; my references are to Posner's neoliberalism.

15 F. A. Hayek advocates a juridical or "nomocratic" over a "telocratic" order (a distinction borrowed from Michael Oakeshott) and condemns economization, but when he gets specific he reduces law to a tool of economic government:

> The task of rules of just conduct can thus only be to tell people which expectations they can count on and which not. The development of such rules will evidently involve a continuous interaction between the rules of law and expectations: while new rules will be laid down to protect existing expectations, every new rule will also tend to create new expectation. . . . In an external environment which constantly changes and in which consequently some individuals will always be discovering new facts, and where we want them to make use of this new knowledge, it is clearly impossible to protect all expectations. . . .Which expectations ought to be protected must therefore depend on how we can maximize the fulfilment of expectations as a whole.

Hayek, *Rules and Order*, vol. 1 of *Law, Legislation, and Liberty* (Chicago, University of Chicago Press, 1973), pp. 102–3. That Hayek, a fierce critic of Bentham and utilitarianism, is Benthamic is well demonstrated by Allison Dube in *The Theme of Acquisitiveness in Bentham's Political Thought* (New York: Garland, 1991), pp. 198–313.

16 Michel Foucault, "Governmentality," "*Omnes et Singulatim*: Toward a Critique of Political Reason," and "The Subject and Power," in Foucault, *Power*, ed. James D. Faubion, trans. Robert Hurley and others (New York: New Press, 2000), vol. 3 of *Essential Works of Foucault, 1954–84*, ed. Paul Rabinow, pp. 201–22, 298–325, 326–48. See also Michel Foucault, *Discipline and Punish: The Birth of the Prison*, trans. Alan Sheridan (New York: Vintage, 1979) and *History of Sexuality*, vol. 1, *An Introduction*, trans. Robert Hurley (New York: Vintage, 1980).

For relevant course summaries, see "Security, Territory, and Population" and "The Birth of Biopolitics," *Ethics: Subjectivity and Truth*, vol. 1 of *The Essential Works of Michel Foucault* (New York: New Press, 1997), pp. 67–79. Foucault seems to have established a much sharper discontinuity than I do between state and economic rationality, locating a somewhat differently characterized liberal political reason in eighteenth-century civil society's critique of state knowledge. Note that the seventeenth-century "public interest" that I analyze in chapter 6 was initially, among other things, a critique of civil interests, and that Bentham's critique of the state does not posit a civil society.

17 See "L'Oeil du Pouvoir," interview with Foucault in Jeremy Bentham, *Le Panoptique* (Paris: Pierre Belfond, 1977), pp. 9–31, and Foucault, *Discipline and Punish*, pp. 195–228, and compare Gertrude Himmelfarb, "Jeremy Bentham's Haunted House," in *Victorian Minds* (Chicago: Ivan R. Dee, 1995), pp. 32–81.

18 A stance friendly to statutory rights and liberties and hostile to natural rights is present already in Bentham's early writings on Blackstone; see Jeremy Bentham, *A Comment on the Commentaries and a Fragment on Government*, ed. J. H. Burns and H. L. A. Hart (London: Athlone, 1977). Bentham's most famous critique of natural rights is "Nonsense upon Stilts" (formerly known as "Anarchical Fallacies") in Jeremy Bentham, *Rights, Representation, and Reform: Nonsense upon Stilts and Other Writings on the French Revolution*, ed. Philip Schofield, Catherine Pease-Watkin, and Cyprian Blamires (Oxford: Clarendon, 2002). A few writings with prominent libertarian moments and themes include "Of Indirect Legislation" and "Offences against Oneself," *Journal of Homosexuality* 3:4 and 4:1 (1978); *Defence of Usury*, in W. Stark ed., *Jeremy Bentham's Economic Writings* (London: George Allen and Unwin, 1952–54), vol. 1; "On the Liberty of the Press and Public Discussion," in Jeremy Bentham, *Works of Jeremy Bentham*, ed. John Bowring (Edinburgh: William Tait, 1838–43), vol. 2; and "Radicalism Not Dangerous," *Works of Jeremy Bentham*, vol. 3. Bentham sometimes opposed imperialism on what we now might call libertarian as well as economic grounds, and his attacks on Church and State would become especially fierce by the 1820s.

19 See Jeremy Bentham, *Panopticon: Postscript*, part 2, *Containing a Plan of Management for a Panopticon Penitentiary-House* (London, 1791).

20 Early contributions include Colin Gordon, "Governmental Rationality: An Introduction," in *The Foucault Effect*, especially pp. 43–44, and Nikolas Rose, "Governing the Enterprise Self," in Paul Heelas and Paul Morris, eds., *The Values of the Enterprise Culture: The Moral Debate* (London: Routledge, 1992), revised as ch. 7 of Rose, *Inventing Our Selves: Psychology, Power, and Personhood* (Cambridge: Cambridge University Press, 1996). On human capital, see Gary Becker, *Human Capital*, 3rd edition (Chicago, University of Chicago Press, 1993).

One exception to the absence of such analysis on the American scene is Barbara Cruikshank, "Revolutions Within: Self-Government and Self-Esteem," in Andrew Barry, Thomas Osborne, and Nikolas Rose, eds., *Foucault and Political Reason* (Chicago: University of Chicago Press, 1996). There exists now an extensive "governmentality" literature and networks of researchers who have written several books and articles on the emergence of neoliberal government, many of which treat the activation of choice.

21 See Barbara Cruikshank, *The Will to Empower: Democratic Citizens and Other Subjects* (Ithaca: Cornell University Press, 1999).

22 Bentham, *First Principles Preparatory to Constitutional Code*, p. 234.

23 Antonio Negri and Michael Hardt have recently offered an intriguing analysis of the contemporary global regime as a de-centered empire. Theirs is a very different project from mine that tells a different history relying on different assumptions, particularly in their focus on sovereignty and in their articulation and advocacy of an insurgent political program. But what my study has in common with theirs is an attempt to narrate a prehistory of contemporary neoliberal government so as to better appreciate it in its specificity, in particular to account for the puzzle of "capitalist sovereignty" and the mobilization of affect in what they, following Gilles Deleuze and Felix Guattari, call the "society of control." Perhaps attention to monistic interest can further illuminate the phenomena they describe. See Hardt and Negri, *Empire* (Cambridge: Harvard University Press, 2000).

24 Reason of state is receiving much new attention from historians of political thought. See for example Maurizio Viroli, *From Politics to Reason of State* (Cambridge: Cambridge University Press, 1992), Richard Tuck, *Philosophy and Government, 1572–1651* (Cambridge: Cambridge University Press, 1993), Peter N. Miller, *Defining the Common Good* (Cambridge: Cambridge University Press, 1994), and Anthony Pagden, *Lords of All the World: Ideologies of Empire in Spain, Britain and France, c.1500–c.1800* (New Haven: Yale University Press, 1995). These excellent studies explore the importance of humanism and the topic of necessity, but have little to say about convenience and how necessity and convenience are merged in reason of state's "preservation and augmentation." The "modern" natural lawyers (Grotius, Selden, Hobbes, et al.) were, through their reformulations of the doctrine of necessity, important in eroding the distinction between necessity and convenience. This is especially true of later less voluntarist theorists such as Cumberland and Pufendorf, and is why Cumberland has often been identified as the first modern utilitarian.

25 Reason of state's qualities as a new rationality entailing a distinctive knowledge and ethic are treated by Friedrich Meinecke in *Die Idee der Staatsräson in der neueren Geschichte* (1927), tendentiously translated as *Machiavellism* (New Haven: Yale University Press, 1957).

26 Richard Tuck, *The Rights of War and Peace: Political Thought and the International Order from Grotius to Kant* (Oxford: Oxford University Press, 1999).

27 Albert O. Hirschman notes this connection between state interest and self-interest but deemphasizes it in favor of a focus on the passions. I engage his stimulating essay in chapter 2. See Hirschman, *The Passions and the Interests: Arguments for Capitalism before Its Triumph* (Princeton: Princeton University Press, 1977), p. 12.

28 A useful way to understand the contrast between sovereignty and economy is to compare the objects of justice and police as identified by Adam Smith at the outset of his lectures on jurisprudence: "The four great objects of law are Justice, Police, Revenue, and Arms. The object of Justice is the security from injury, and it is the foundation of civil government. The objects of Police are the cheapness of commodities, public security, and cleanliness, if the two last were not too minute for a lecture of this kind. Under this head we will consider the opulence of a state." Smith, *Lectures on Jurisprudence*, ed. R. L. Meek, D. D. Raphael, and P. G. Stein (Oxford: Clarendon, 1978), p. 398 (report dated 1766). For prominent neoliberal redefinitions of justice in terms of policing see Richard Epstein, *Takings: Private Property and the Power of Eminent Domain* (Cambridge: Harvard University Press, 1985), and William M. Landes and Richard A. Posner, *The Economic Structure of Tort Law* (Cambridge: Harvard University Press, 1987).

29 These shifts are being tracked by researchers who do close and conceptually innovative work on specific areas of legal change. See for example Evan McKenzie, *Privatopia* (New Haven: Yale University Press, 1994), Alfred C. Aman Jr., "The Globalizing State: A Future-Oriented Perspective on the Public/Private Distinction, Federalism, and Democracy," *Vanderbilt Journal of Transnational Law* 31:769 (1998), and Bill Maurer, "Forget Locke? From Proprietor to Risk-Bearer in New Logics of Finance," *Public Culture* 11:2 (1999). Thanks to Louis Howe for alerting me to Aman's essay.

30 I myself, of course, draw extensively from recent research in the history of political thought, which has generated a number of significant challenges to earlier Whiggish accounts. Contextualist work on early modern European politics has proved especially useful. But I want to emphasize the difference that a focus on interest, as opposed to rights and virtue, can make. I also risk deploying a historical method that is less wedded than newer histories of political thought are to the concerns of contemporaries. In my more historical chapters 5 and 6, I focus on shifts in framing that often fall outside the scope of political history and so are at least off-center from the main content of contemporary controversialist literatures. My project is itself Whig history in the strict Butterfield sense; it takes its bearings entirely from present-day puzzles and predicaments.

31 Interest and the public interest were also prominent concerns for pluralist theory and its critics in American political science.

32 John Rawls, *A Theory of Justice* (Cambridge: Harvard University Press, 1971), pp. 22–27, 33, and rev. edition (1999) pp. 19–24, 28.

33 Rawls comes closest to directly embracing monistic interest in his early formulations of "primary goods," which have been significantly refined since the initial publication of *A Theory of Justice*.

34 Bonnie Honig, *Political Theory and the Displacement of Politics* (Ithaca: Cornell University Press, 1993), pp. 126–61.

35 See ibid., pp. 205–6, and Bonnie Honig, "Toward an Agonistic Feminism: Hannah Arendt and the Politics of Identity," in Honig, ed., *Feminist Interpretations of Hannah Arendt* (University Park: Pennsylvania State University Press, 1995), p. 160. Honig tempers somewhat her embrace of the prospective with an ambivalence toward remorse and regret; see *Political Theory and the Displacement of Politics*, pp. 224–25n.

36 Joseph Raz, *The Morality of Freedom* (Oxford: Oxford University Press 1987).

37 On the roots, meaning, and consequences of the hegemony of normative theorizing in contemporary North American political theory, see Sophia Mihic, "Flirtations with Wissenschaft: Thinking Thinking and Thinking Politics in, and Out of, the Work of Hannah Arendt" (Ph.D. diss., Johns Hopkins University, 2000).

38 Raz, *The Morality of Freedom*, p. 320.

39 Even the manuscript that was posthumously published by Bentham's executors as his treatise on morals, the *Deontology*, is in fact another treatise on government—arguably a branch of what he earlier called "indirect legislation." (Thus true moralists are important educators or landscapers of prospects: see Bentham's discussion of why we should bother with a discourse on ethics when we know that people will always pursue pleasure and avoid pain regardless, *Deontology Together with A Table of the Springs of Action and The Article on Utilitarianism*, pp. 149–50). Here Bentham's normative philosophizing tends to be as laconic and dismissive as in

An Introduction to the Principles of Morals and Legislation. See for example the brief chapters 1 and 2 of the *Introduction*—"Of the Principle of Utility" and "Of Principles Adverse to That of Utility"—and sections like "*Summum Bonum*: Consummate Nonsense," "Virtue What: According to Principle of Utility," and "Virtue What: According to Aristotle and Oxford" in the *Deontology* (pp. 134–47, 154–63). The *Deontology*'s brief "Justice: Its Relation to the Three Primary Virtues" (pp. 219–22) is even questionable as a section heading (p. 219n); Bentham often reserves the word for reference to systems of justice.

40 Robert Putnam, *Making Democracy Work* (Cambridge: Harvard University Press, 1993), pp. 163–85. Putnam's particular criteria for distinguishing beneficial networks have come under attack especially in response to his American work. See for example Michael Shapiro, "Bowling Blind," *Theory and Event* 1:1 (1997, on-line). For a range of appropriations and criticisms, see Robert K. Fullinwider, ed., *Civil Society, Democracy, and Civic Renewal* (Lanham, Md.: Rowman and Littlefield, 1999).

41 See for example Richard A. Posner, *The Problems of Jurisprudence* (Cambridge: Harvard University Press, 1990), p. 357.

42 For a history of liberalism that is attentive to this trajectory see Ian Shapiro, *The Evolution of Rights in Liberal Theory* (Cambridge: Cambridge University Press, 1986).

43 On the four ends of security, subsistence, abundance, and equality, see for example Jeremy Bentham, "Pannomial Fragments," in Bentham, *Works of Jeremy Bentham*, vol. 2.

44 "Indirect Legislation," University College London Bentham Collection, boxes 87 and 62. For an analysis of this essay see Stephen G. Engelmann, "'Of Indirect Legislation': Bentham's Liberal Government," *Polity* 35:3 (spring 2003).

45 In conversation, Ike Balbus made the fascinating observation that Bentham's "auto-icon"—his successful scheme to have himself stuffed for posterity after death—is indicative of a utilitarian incapacity to confront mourning. Anyone who doubts that microeconomics is insensitive to loss *qua* loss should consult the literature on "loss aversion" or the "endowment effect," in which researchers puzzle over why experimental subjects consistently demand more to give up a good than they would be willing to pay to acquire that same good, in apparent violation of the theory of consumer behavior. In other words, people "irrationally" value what they have more highly by virtue of the fact that they have it. See Daniel Kahneman, Jack Knetsch, and Richard H. Thaler, "Anomalies: The Endowment Effect, Loss Aversion and Status Quo Bias," *Journal of Economic Perspectives* 5:193–206 (1991). (The evidence prompts these authors, in an aside, to acknowledge a distinction from classical economics that has generally been erased in neoclassical theory: that between use-value and exchange-value [p. 200n].) Bentham himself was at least sensitive to loss as such, but he tellingly formulated it entirely in terms of expectations. See for example Bentham, *Works of Jeremy Bentham*, "Principles of the Civil Code," vol. 1, p. 325; Bentham, "Supply without Burthen," *Jeremy Bentham's Economic Writings*, vol. 1, pp. 290–92; and Bentham, "On Retrenchment," *Official Aptitude Maximized, Expense Minimized*, ed. Philip Schofield (Oxford: Clarendon, 1993), pp. 342–67.

46 On risk and governmentality, see *Economy and Society* 29:4 (2000), a special issue devoted to the topic.

47 "Struggle over incommensurables" does not imply either the presence or absence of any of a range of practices from consensus-formation to bargaining to political violence.

48 My focus on interest overlaps with the strong tendencies of two of the usual suspects in

accounts of the origins of liberalism: Thomas Hobbes (in accounts emphasizing political jurisprudence) and Adam Smith (in accounts emphasizing political economy). Prominent in each is the role of the imagination and a concern with governance and security that links individuals more or less directly to political order. But Hobbes and Smith each have strong countervailing tendencies to Benthamism; in the following chapters scattered treatments and notes will argue why they and especially John Locke and David Hume are not theorists of monistic interest. In any case, "liberalism" is anachronistic for all of these figures, as it should be, I think, for Bentham. I'm suggesting not that Bentham is a liberal, but that many of our familiar liberalisms (unlike the theories of Hobbes, Smith, and others) are Benthamic.

2 Against the Usual Story

1 Albert O. Hirschman, *The Passions and the Interests: Arguments for Capitalism before Its Triumph* (Princeton: Princeton University Press, 1977, 1997).

2 On *lo stato*, see J. H. Hexter, "*Il Principe* and *lo stato*," *Studies in the Renaissance* 4 (1957): 113–38; J. G. A. Pocock, *The Machiavellian Moment* (Princeton: Princeton University Press, 1975), pp. 175–76; Harvey C. Mansfield, "On the Impersonality of the Modern State: A Comment on Machiavelli's Use of *Stato*," *American Political Science Review*, Dec. 1983; Machiavelli, *The Prince*, ed. Quentin Skinner and Russell Price, trans. Russell Price (Cambridge: Cambridge University Press, 1988), appendix B, "Notes on the Vocabulary of *The Prince*," pp. 102–3; Quentin Skinner, "The State," in Terence Ball, James Farr, and Russell L. Hanson, *Political Innovation and Conceptual Change* (Cambridge: Cambridge University Press, 1989), pp. 90–131; Maurizio Viroli, "Machiavelli and the Republican Idea of Politics," in Gisela Bock, Quentin Skinner, and Maurizio Viroli eds., *Machiavelli and Republicanism* (Cambridge: Cambridge University Press, 1990), pp. 143–71, especially p. 163n.

3 This is seen especially in the contrast between *The Prince* and *The Discourses*. Viroli follows other scholars in noting that "Machiavelli never uses the word *politico* or its equivalent in *The Prince*" (Viroli, "Machiavelli and the Republican Idea of Politics," in Bock, Skinner, and Viroli, eds., *Machiavelli and Republicanism*, p. 160).

4 Situating and thus constraining Machiavellian princes is what such otherwise widely divergent texts as Innocent Gentillet's *Discours sur les Moyens de Bien Gouverner* (1576), Jean Bodin's *Six Livres de la République* (1576), and Henri, duc de Rohan's *De l'interest des Princes et Estats de la Chrestienté* (1634) have in common.

5 Such a subjection is already possible in early references where the state simply refers to the monarch's status. For some of these references, see Skinner, "The State." Interest as a new constraint is Hirschman's theme; on the constraint of monarchs in particular see *The Passions and the Interests*, pp. 34–35.

6 See Friedrich Meinecke, *Machiavellism* (New Haven: Yale University Press, 1957), chapter 6, "The Doctrine of the Best Interest of the State in France at the Time of Richelieu," pp. 146–95.

7 On the growth of the human sciences in relation to a project of liberal government see Mary Poovey, *A History of the Modern Fact: Problems of Knowledge in the Sciences of Wealth and Society* (Chicago: University of Chicago Press, 1998). See also Ian Hacking's indispensable pair of books on the history of probability, *The Emergence of Probability* (Cambridge: Cambridge University Press, 1975) and *The Taming of Chance* (Cambridge: Cambridge University Press, 1990).

8   This way of reading Hobbes is developed by William Connolly in *Political Theory and Modernity* (New York: Basil Blackwell, 1988). Connolly pointedly identifies interest as a program, rather than a premise, in Hobbes's work. See p. 28 and chapter 2, *passim*.

9   For example, in chapter 14 of *Leviathan* the right of nature is introduced before the law of nature, but this right is grounded in its end, the goal of preservation that is the foundation of all right and all duty. See Thomas Hobbes, *Leviathan*, ed. C. B. Macpherson (London: Penguin, 1968), pp. 189–90. This common foundation doesn't suggest that Hobbes is at all inconsistent in his opposition between natural right and law, an interpretive controversy raised by H. Warrender and addressed by Richard Tuck in *Natural Rights Theories: Their Origin and Development* (Cambridge: Cambridge University Press, 1979), pp. 119–32. For one thing, Hobbes quite consistently maintains that I alone am the judge of what I require for my preservation. Tuck argues that Hobbes's early *Elements of Law* is here different from the later work and closer to John Selden and the Tew Circle, suggesting a right of nature not limited by the end of preservation; Tuck links this to a lack of any right of resistance for preservation that is also shared by Selden. But he acknowledges that the *Elements* is ambiguous on resistance (p. 120), and the passage he quotes to confirm detachment of the exercise of the right of nature from any judgment of needfulness for preservation doesn't quite support this case: "Every man by nature hath right to all things, that is to say, to do whatsoever he listeth to whom he listeth, to possess, use, and enjoy all things he will and can. For seeing all things he willeth, must therefore be good unto him in his own judgement, because he willeth them; and may tend to his preservation some time or other; or he may judge so . . . : it followeth that all things may rightly also be done by him." *Elements* I.14.10, quoted in Tuck, *Natural Rights Theories*, pp. 120–21.

10 It is in keeping, for example, with Richard Hooker's formulation (discussed in chapter 6), as well as with a number of other Thomist and humanist arguments from necessity.

11 See Quentin Skinner, "Conquest and Consent: Thomas Hobbes and the Engagement Controversy," in G. E. Alymer, ed., *The Interregnum: The Quest for Settlement, 1646–1660* (London: Macmillan, 1973), pp. 79–98, and W. H. Greenleaf, *Order, Empiricism, and Politics: Two Traditions of English Political Thought, 1500–1700* (London: University of London, 1964). Tuck places Hobbes in the midst of the "modern" natural law tradition of seventeenth-century theorists from Grotius and Selden to Pufendorf and Locke; see "The 'Modern' Theory of Natural Law," in *The Languages of Political Theory in Early-Modern Europe*, ed. Anthony Pagden (Cambridge: Cambridge University Press, 1987), pp. 99–119. For a provocative emphasis on the continuity between Hobbes's theorizing and Elizabethan conceptions of order see "Theatricality and Power," in Christopher Pye, *The Regal Phantasm: Shakespeare and the Politics of Spectacle* (London: Routledge, 1990), pp. 43–81.

12 This is generally but not always the case, because of the opening to rebellion allowed by Hobbes (in *Leviathan*, ch. 21, p. 272). According to Hobbes, I may unilaterally withdraw my allegiance to the regime if I perceive a threat from it, or perhaps even if I consider it inadequate or irrelevant to my self-preservation. But it must be *my* life that is somehow imperiled before I can act.

13 This is highly debatable, because some interpreters have found in Hobbes's texts prescriptions for very little in matters of government, leaving the conduct of conduct for the most part outside the sphere of sovereign concern—see for example Richard Flathman, *Thomas Hobbes: Skepticism, Individuality, and Chastened Politics* (Newbury Park: Sage, 1993). Others have seen

there prescriptions for integrating all individuals under a utilitarian sovereign who directs all conduct toward more commodious living. For an approach that breaks this impasse with a reading of Hobbes as a theorist not of sovereignty but of government, see Melissa A. Orlie, *Living Ethically, Acting Politically* (Ithaca: Cornell University Press, 1997), especially pp. 35–60.

14 Hobbes, *Leviathan*, ch. 6, p. 127.

15 This is akin to the distinction between a "rule utilitarian" and a "deontological" approach to ethics. The rule utilitarian approach, however concerned with rules, remains consequentialist.

16 Hobbes, *Leviathan*, ch. 15, pp. 202–5. Granted, this too can be given a utilitarian gloss—as it is by much of the new literature on trust—but all such glosses ignore how seriously "engagements" are taken in this time and place. The sanctity of promising among Hobbes's contemporaries, its relationship to divine law, is further explored in the discussion of the Putney debates in chapter 6.

17 Hobbes, *Leviathan*, ch. 18, p. 232.

18 Hobbes, *Leviathan*, author's introduction, pp. 81–82. The tension between Hobbes the mechanist and Hobbes the jurist is a central preoccupation of Leo Strauss's commentary. See Strauss, *The Political Philosophy of Hobbes: Its Basis and Its Genesis* (Oxford: Clarendon, 1936). For an interpretation of this tension and the need for an affective supplement in seventeenth-century contract theory generally, see Victoria Kahn, "The Duty to Love: Passion and Obligation in Early Modern Political Theory," *Representations* 68 (fall 1999).

19 This is consistent with a significant expansion of the purview of "jurisprudence" for Hume and his successors. Thus Adam Smith's jurisprudence includes police, which itself includes not only the regulation of sanitation and the like but the regulation of "cheapness or plenty." In other words, Smithian political economy is a branch of jurisprudence. See Adam Smith, *Lectures on Jurisprudence*, ed. R. L Meek, D. D. Raphael, and P. G. Stein (Oxford: Oxford University Press, 1978), editors' introduction, p. 26. On the appropriation of Smith by modern economics, see Keith Tribe, *Land, Labour and Economic Discourse* (London: Routledge and Kegan Paul, 1978), especially "The Structure of Political Oeconomy" and "The Formation of Economic Discourse" (chapters 5 and 6, pp. 80–145), as well as *Genealogies of Capitalism* (Atlantic Highlands, N.J.: Humanities Press, 1981), especially "The 'Histories' of Economic Discourse" (chapter 4, pp. 121–52).

20 David Hume, "Of the Original Contract," in Hume, *Essays Moral, Political, and Literary*, ed. Eugene F. Miller (Indianapolis: Liberty Fund, 1985), pp. 465–87.

21 Colin Gordon, "Government Rationality: An Introduction," in G. Burchell, C. Gordon, and P. Miller eds., *The Foucault Effect: Studies in Governmentality* (Chicago: University of Chicago Press, 1991), p. 21.

22 See David Hume, *A Treatise of Human Nature*, ed. Peter H. Nidditch (2nd edition; Oxford: Oxford University Press, 1978), especially book 2, "Of the Passions."

23 "Of the Origins of Government" in ibid., book 3, "Of Morals." See Graham Burchell, "Peculiar Interests: Civil Society and Governing 'The System of Natural Liberty,' " in Burchell et al., *The Foucault Effect*, pp. 119–50.

24 Thus Adam Ferguson: "If we are asked therefore, Where the state of nature is to be found? we may answer, It is here." Ferguson, *An Essay on the History of Civil Society*, ed. Fania Oz-Salzberger (Cambridge: Cambridge University Press, 1995), p. 14.

25 Hume, *A Treatise of Human Nature*, p. 536.

26 Ibid., p. 418. Cf. Hobbes on "the Schooles," p. 25, above.

27 Hume's *An Enquiry Concerning the Principles of Morals* doesn't carry forward the elaborate analysis of the passions from the *Treatise*, but there's no reason to think that he abandoned these fundamentals. Knud Haakonssen calls it "a complete illusion to see the later work as an approach towards the utilitarianism of a later age." Haakonssen, *The Science of a Legislator: The Natural Jurisprudence of David Hume and Adam Smith* (Cambridge: Cambridge University Press, 1981), pp. 5–6.

28 Hirschman, *The Passions and the Interests*, pp. 40–41.

29 He also considers the possible influence of the longstanding use of "interest" to denote the profit from money lending. On this interest, see Albert O. Hirschman, "The Concept of Interest: From Euphemism to Tautology," in *Rival Views of Market Society* (New York: Viking, 1986), pp. 35–55.

30 Hirschman, *The Passions and the Interests*, pp. 110–11, quoting Adam Smith, *The Wealth of Nations*, ed. E Cannan (New York: Modern Library, 1937), pp. 594–95, Hirschman's emphasis.

31 François, Duc de La Rochefoucauld, *Maxims*, trans. Leonard Tancock (Harmondsworth: Penguin, 1959). La Rochefoucauld can be seen as part of a broader skeptical French literature including Montaigne and Nicole that focuses on the importance of self-love. See Nannerl Keohane, *Philosophy and the State in France* (Princeton: Princeton University Press, 1980). Keohane's erudite study is largely about the category of interest, which she promotes as an alternative foundation for democratic order.

32 See the citations from La Rochefoucauld's *Maxims* in the entry on "Interesse" in Otto Brunner, Werner Conze, and Reinhart Koselleck, eds., *Geschichtliche Grundbegriffe: Historisches Lexikon zur politisch-sozialen Sprache in Deutschland* (Stuttgart: Klett-Cotta, 1982), vol. 3, pp. 320–21.

33 The complex story of interest on the Continent, its aesthetic dimension, and the emergence in aesthetics of disinterested interest—a kind of monistic interest that triumphs over mere interests—is introduced in ibid., especially under the headings "Kunst" and "Der Interessebegriff in der Philosophie des 18. Jahrhunderts," pp. 325–36 (Ernst Wolfgang Orth).

34 This imagination is of course not exclusively visual.

35 For an introduction to Becker, see *The Economic Approach to Human Behavior* (Chicago: University of Chicago Press, 1976). A book that well illustrates Becker's ambitions for the reach of the microeconomic model is *A Treatise on the Family*, 2nd edition (Cambridge: Harvard University Press, 1991), where he extends it to cover household and even nonhuman relations.

36 Timothy Mitchell, in a forthcoming article, argues that "the economy" is actually a twentieth-century construction. See Mitchell, "Origins and Limits of the Modern Idea of the Economy," in George Steinmetz ed., *The Politics of Method in the Human Sciences* (Durham: Duke University Press, forthcoming).

37 My use of the masculine pronoun is appropriate for the period under consideration, but not for Becker. The question of the gendering of *homo economicus* is an extremely complex one. A good starting place that addresses the historical coincidence of the attack on patriarchy and the domestication of English women, as well as the persistence of kinship-derived domination in an increasingly unisex contemporary American market, is Linda Nicholson's *Gender and History* (New York: Columbia University Press, 1985). A fascinating moment in the gender history of monistic interest is William Thompson's *Appeal of One Half the Human Race* (1825;

New York: B. Franklin, 1970), which ventriloquizes a woman's response to James Mill's exclusion of women from the suffrage in the *Essay on Government*. As in Mill's *Essay*, the argument is couched in terms of monistic interest.

3 Virtuous Economies

1 Anthony Ashley Cooper, 3rd Earl of Shaftesbury, *An Inquiry Concerning Virtue, or Merit* (hereafter cited as *Inquiry*), in Shaftesbury, *Characteristicks of Men, Manners, Opinions, Times*, ed. Philip Ayres (Oxford: Clarendon, 1999), vol. I, pp. 189–274. The *Characteristicks* was first printed in 1711, the *Inquiry* in 1699 as *The Inquiry Concerning Virtue*. The early version was printed without Shaftesbury's permission and differs significantly from the approved work. Much of the material treated below is also present in the early *Inquiry*; for comparison see Anthony Ashley Cooper, third earl of Shaftesbury, *Standard Edition: Complete Works, Selected Letters, and Posthumous Writings*, ed. Gerd Hemmerich, Wolfram Benda, and Ulrich Schödlbauer, vol. 2, part 2 (Stuttgart: Frommann-Holzboog, 1981), which presents both versions on opposite pages. Shaftesbury was the grandson of the first earl, a prominent legislator (a leader in the movement to exclude the Catholic James II from the throne, and of other agitations leading to the Glorious Revolution of 1688) and patron of Locke; Locke tutored the third earl. The *Inquiry* is an early and in some respects anomalous work.

2 Thus the *Inquiry* stands at the beginning of L. A. Selby-Bigge's nineteenth-century anthology; see Selby-Bigge, ed., *British Moralists: Being Selections from Writers Principally of the Eighteenth Century* (Indianapolis: Bobbs-Merrill, 1964 [one-volume reprint of the 1897 Oxford University Press edition]). And it earns early mention in Mary Poovey's chapter on "Experimental Moral Philosophy and the Problems of Liberal Governmentality" in Poovey, *A History of the Modern Fact* (Chicago: University of Chicago Press, 1998), pp. 144–213.

3 Lawrence E. Klein, "Shaftesbury, Politeness and the Politics of Religion," in Nicholas Phillipson and Quentin Skinner, eds., *Political Discourse in Early Modern Britain* (Cambridge: Cambridge University Press, 1993), pp. 283–301; I borrow "polite Whiggism" from J. G. A. Pocock's "The Varieties of Whiggism from Exclusion to Reform," in *Virtue, Commerce, and History* (Cambridge: Cambridge University Press, 1985), pp. 215–310. See generally Lawrence Klein's excellent *Shaftesbury and the Culture of Politeness* (Cambridge: Cambridge University Press, 1994). Klein acknowledges the dramatic contrast between the *Inquiry* and Shaftesbury's later work. "Indeed, from the standpoint of his mature outlook, *An Inquiry Concerning Virtue* was not polite philosophy at all" (p. 22). And "while mounting the *Inquiry* as the central text of *Characteristicks*, Shaftesbury framed it ironically and ambivalently. . . . Though the *Inquiry* defended human sociability, the text itself was somehow unsociable" (p.49). Although Klein does not problematize the self of Shaftesbury's *Inquiry* in his chapter devoted to the text—he refers to the 1699 version, whose mechanics of introspection are somewhat less developed—he follows up with an illuminating discussion of the problem of the self in Shaftesbury's contemporaneous notebooks (see pp. 48–80). My reading of the *Inquiry* is more compatible, then, with this latter chapter than it is with the former.

4 The historical and political status of the "public sphere" has been a subject of some contention in recent years, especially with the new debate over Jürgen Habermas's *Strukturwandel der Öffentlichkeit* (1962), published for the first time in English translation (by Thomas Burger with Frederick Lawrence) as *The Structural Transformation of the Public Sphere* in 1989 (Cam-

bridge: MIT Press). For a useful overview, see the opening of Nancy Fraser's "Rethinking the Public Sphere," published in two anthologies of public-sphere criticism: Craig Calhoun, ed., *Habermas and the Public Sphere* (Cambridge: MIT Press, 1992) and Bruce Robbins, ed., *The Phantom Public Sphere* (Minneapolis: University of Minnesota Press, 1993).

5 Shaftesbury's relationship to enthusiasm is discussed by Stanley Grean in *Shaftesbury's Philosophy of Religion and Ethics* (Athens: Ohio University Press, 1967), pp. 19–36.

6 Shaftesbury, *A Letter Concerning Enthusiasm*, in Shaftesbury, *Characteristicks of Men, Manners, Opinions, Times*, vol. I, p. 32 (section vii).

7 The first book of the *Inquiry* quite radically suggests that theism is a matter of degree, that it is not a prerequisite for virtue, and that the truth of Shaftesbury's doctrine does not depend on the existence of God.

8 See Pocock's "The varieties of Whiggism from Exclusion to Reform." "Scientific Whiggism" was coined by Duncan Forbes in *Hume's Philosophical Politics* (Cambridge: Cambridge University Press, 1976).

9 Francis Hutcheson, *An Essay on the Nature and Conduct of the Passions and Affections* (New York: Garland, 1971).

10 John Guillory's powerful critique of how these are confounded through the language of "aesthetic value" in contemporary criticism draws from the later Kantian problematic and from a particular reading of Bourdieu, and thus misses how in early British aesthetics, "economic" and aesthetic value are the same; "disinterestedness" for Shaftesbury, unlike for Kant, is equivalent to the interest of an existential whole. See Guillory, *Cultural Capital* (Chicago: University of Chicago Press, 1993).

11 *Inquiry*, pp. 196–99 (I.ii.1).

12 Metaphors suggesting a delicacy to sensibility and the potential danger in passions are scattered throughout the *Inquiry*, which is marked by a Stoical concern with the propriety of the temper.

13 *Inquiry*, p. 202 (I.ii.3).

14 *Inquiry*, p. 227 (II.i.1). This last is no ordinary organic metaphor. Body parts themselves have "interests"—for example, the eye will act independently to preserve itself by blinking (p. 233, II.i.3). And all organisms are systems, each with its own interest.

15 *Inquiry*, p. 228 (II.i.1). He also refers to the "separate Oeconomy of the Creature" (p. 257, II.ii.2).

16 *Inquiry*, p. 257 (II.ii.2). See note 35, below.

17 *Inquiry*, pp. 231–37 (II.i.3). This kind of classification, relatively absent in, for example, Hobbes and Locke, becomes a commonplace in the eighteenth century. Shaftesbury's conflation of the natural and the civil has the effect of naturalizing civil differences. For Shaftesbury and Bentham, these differences must be relocated in the "natural frame" of the typed individual (it should be said that this is not a central preoccupation for Bentham especially). This is also done more aggressively by Hume and other Scots theorists of civil society, but the ambiguous status of civil society, which is historical and relational even as it naturalizes the civil, can significantly mitigate the pernicious effects of this zoological move.

18 *Inquiry*, pp. 268–69 (II.ii.3).

19 *Inquiry*, p. 270 (II.ii.3).

20 *Inquiry*, pp. 241–42 (II.ii.1). Thus every prostitute knows how important it is to feign pleasure, p. 251 (II.ii.1).

21   *Inquiry*, p. 240 (II.ii.1).

22   Note that this model of virtuous pleasure best fits those acts that are executed by means of command of the labor of others. And note also what it suggests about the modern tradition of thinking about "egoism" and "altruism," insofar as that tradition is bound up with these introspective origins and its peculiar powers and pleasures.

23   *Inquiry*, p. 240 (II.ii.1).

24   *Inquiry*, p. 241 (II.ii.1).

25   Ibid.

26   *Inquiry*, pp. 243–44 (II.ii.1).

27   *Inquiry*, pp. 244–45 (II.ii.1).

28   *Inquiry*, p. 247 (II.ii.1).

29   *Inquiry*, p. 211 (I.iii.2).

30   "THERE are TWO Things, which to a rational Creature must be horridly offensive and grievous; *viz.* 'To have the Reflection in his Mind of any *unjust* Action or Behaviour, which he knows to be naturally *odious* and *ill-deserving*:' 'Or, of any foolish Action or Behaviour, which he knows to be prejudicial to his own *Interest* or *Happiness*.' "

   The former of these is alone properly call'd "CONSCIENCE." *Inquiry*, p. 247 (II.ii.1). But a little further on he writes: "Now as for that other part of Conscience, *viz.* the remembrance *of what was at any time unreasonably and foolishly done, in prejudice of one's real Interest or Happiness*." *Inquiry*, p. 250 (II.ii.1). Shaftesbury's system contributes to the construction of a particularly determinate distinction between prudence and morality—the prudence of a self-interested self and the morality of a socially interested self—and at the same time moralizes prudence and "prudentializes" morality through its aggressive naturalism. That the conflation of what he distinguishes is ultimately an extreme one is clear from the following on the system of the universe: "there can be no particular Being or System which is not either good or ill in that *general one* of the *Universe*: For if it be insignificant and of no use, it is a Fault or Imperfection, and consequently ill in the general System," p. 198 (I.ii.1). To interest, nothing whatsoever can be indifferent.

31   *Inquiry*, p. 247 (II.ii.1).

32   *Inquiry*, pp. 272–73 ("Conclusion").

33   Shaftesbury, *Characteristicks*, vol. 1, pp. 35–81, 83–186.

34   This ambivalence is expertly explored by David Marshall in the first three chapters of *The Figure of the Theater: Shaftesbury, Defoe, Adam Smith, and George Eliot* (New York: Columbia University Press, 1986). Marshall has very little to say about the *Inquiry*. I suspect he found it of little interest for illuminating the complex dynamics of theatricality that are the subject of his study.

35   This "interest" is not that discussed throughout the text, but is instead the name for one of the self-passions: "*Interest, or Desire* of those *Conveniences*, by which we are well *provided for*, and *maintain'd*" (p. 257 [222]). "Interest" as passion for convenience serves "interest" as the ruling principle of a self-economy comprehending both preservation and augmentation, or necessity and convenience. The greater prevalence of the latter interest in this and other contemporary sources supports the doubts raised in the last chapter about Hirschman's "countervailing passions" argument. See note 18, above. The greater prevalence of interest as ruling principle in this and other contemporary sources supports the doubts raised in the last chapter about Hirschman's "countervailing passion" argument.

36 *Inquiry*, p. 264 (II.ii.2).

37 "Such a one is in reality a self-oppressor, and lies heavier on himself than he can ever do on mankind." Ibid.

38 Ibid.

39 Consider the oft-cited opening to Smith's *The Theory of Moral Sentiments*: "Though our brother is upon the rack, as long as we ourselves are at our ease, our senses will never inform us of what he suffers. They never did, and never can, carry us beyond our own person, and it is by the imagination only that we can form any conception of what are his sensations. Neither can that faculty help us to this any other way, than by representing to us what would be our own, if we were in his case. It is the impressions of our own senses only, not those of his, which our imaginations copy." Adam Smith, *The Theory of Moral Sentiments*, ed. D. D. Raphael and A. L. Macfie (Oxford: Oxford University Press, 1976), p. 9.

40 Shaftesbury's monistic interest and Bentham's are aggregates in different ways. The very different relations between number and order in Shaftesbury and Bentham are captured by Poovey in *The History of the Modern Fact*, pp. 179, 375–76n.

41 Luc Ferry notes this with regard to Hume in *Homo Aestheticus*, trans. Robert de Loazia (Chicago: University of Chicago Press, 1993), pp. 53–62.

42 See W. C. Diamond, "Public Identity in Restoration England: From Prophetic to Economic" (Ph.D. diss., Johns Hopkins University, 1982).

43 *Inquiry*, pp. 221–22 (I.iii.3).

4 Imagining Interest

1 See David Hume, "Of the Original Contract," in *Essays Moral, Political, and Literary*, ed. Eugene F. Miller (Indianapolis: Liberty Fund, 1985), pp. 465–87; John Dinwiddy, *Bentham* (Oxford: Oxford University Press, 1989), p. 74; Douglas G. Long, "Taking Interests Seriously," *Rationality and Society* 3 (fall 1991): 343–64.

2 Werner Stark tells us: "The key to Bentham's philosophy of economics is, of course, the fact that he was a confirmed materialist," Jeremy Bentham, *Jeremy Bentham's Economic Writings*, ed. W. Stark (London: George Allen and Unwin, 1952–54), vol. 1, p. 16. See also Douglas G. Long, *Bentham on Liberty* (Toronto: University of Toronto Press, 1977), pp. 5–6. For a typical objection to the supposed reductionism of Benthamite psychology and morality, see Kevin L. Brown, "Comments on Long's 'Taking Interests Seriously,'" *Rationality and Society* 3 (winter 1991): 496–99. For a typical rational-choice reading of Bentham as a materialist forerunner of a now positivist program, in a defense of what they wrongly take to be his "experienced utility" against the contemporary "decision utility" paradigm, see Daniel Kahneman, Peter P. Wakker, and Rakesh Sarin, "Back to Bentham? Explorations of Experienced Utility," *Quarterly Journal of Economics*, May 1997, pp. 375–405. Douglas Long is, as far as I know, the only scholar to have explored the specific importance of the imagination in Bentham, in "The Secularized Imagination in Early Modern Political Thought: Hume, Smith and Bentham" (unpublished paper), Annual Meeting of the Canadian Political Science Association, 1997.

3 This is perhaps overstating the case, but some such mapping and contrast can be seen in the works surveyed by James E. Crimmins in "Contending Interpretations of Bentham's Utilitarianism," *Canadian Journal of Political Science / Revue canadienne de science politique* 29 (winter 1996): 751–77. The contrast between "natural" and "artificial" harmonies dates at least from

Elie Halévy's *La Formation du Radicalisme Philosophique* (1901; see *The Growth of Philosophical Radicalism*, trans. Mary Morris [Clifton, N.J., 1972], pp. 15–18); the libertarian critique is epitomized by F. A. Hayek's characterization of Bentham as a "constructivist rationalist" opposed to the "spontaneous order" of true liberalism (see "The Liberal Social Order," in *Studies in Philosophy, Politics and Economics* [Chicago, 1967], pp. 160–62). Defenses of Bentham's liberalism include Allison Dube's successful assimilation of Hayek to Bentham in *The Theme of Acquisitiveness in Bentham's Political Thought* (New York, 1991), pp. 198–313, Kelly's *Utilitarianism and Distributive Justice: Jeremy Bentham and the Civil Law* (Oxford: Oxford University Press, 1990), and Michael Quinn's "The Fallacy of Non-Interference: The Poor Panopticon and Equality of Opportunity," *Bentham Newsletter* 1 (1997, on-line). My treatment will inevitably be read by many as a strongly *dirigiste* interpretation of Bentham (see Dinwiddy, *Bentham*, p. 90), but this is a misreading based on an investment in the terms of this debate.

4   Jeremy Bentham, *Works of Jeremy Bentham* (hereafter *Works*), ed. John Bowring (Edinburgh: William Tait, 1838–43), vol. 2, p. 501 ("Anarchical Fallacies"). In the new edition of the *Collected Works* "Nonsense upon Stilts" has been restored as Bentham's title for this essay. See Jeremy Bentham, *Rights, Representation, and Reform: Nonsense upon Stilts and Other Writings on the French Revolution*, ed. Philip Schofield, Catherine Pease-Watkin, and Cyprian Blamires (Oxford: Clarendon, 2002).

5   Hanna Fenichel Pitkin, "Slippery Bentham: Some Neglected Cracks in the Foundation of Utilitarianism," *Political Theory* 18 (spring 1990): 104–31.

6   P. J. Kelly, *Utilitarianism and Distributive Justice*, especially pp. 79–94. On identity, see pp. 164–65; on pleasure and pain, see for example pp. 19, 77–78.

7   Examples of this recent work include David Lieberman, "Economy and Polity in Bentham's Science of Legislation," in Stefan Collini, Richard Whatmore, and Brian Young, eds., *Economy, Polity and Society: British Intellectual History, 1750–1950* (Cambridge: Cambridge University Press, 2000), and Philip Schofield, "La Arquitectura del Gobierno: Publicidad, Responsabilidad y Democracia Representativa en Jeremy Bentham," trans. M. Escamilla and J. J. Jiménez Sánchez, *Anales de la Cátedra Francisco Suárez* 34 (2000): 145–69.

8   Jeremy Bentham, *A Table of the Springs of Action* ("Explanations"), in *Deontology Together with A Table of the Springs of Action and The Article On Utilitarianism*, ed. Amnon Goldworth (Oxford: Clarendon, 1983), 90 (hereafter *Table*). Italics in this and all subsequent Bentham quotations are from the cited texts (and represent underlinings in manuscripts). Cf. Hobbes, *Leviathan*, ed. C. B. Macpherson (New York: Penguin, 1968), p. 118: "[T]he Imagination is the first internall beginning of all Voluntary Motion" (chapter 6).

9   *Table*, p. 92 ("Explanations").

10 Bentham's definition of law is both notoriously expansive and complicated by his distinction between direct and indirect legislation, which suggests a limited role for the state in tandem with limitless possibilities for governance. See Jeremy Bentham, *Of Laws in General*, ed. H. L. A. Hart (London: Athlone, 1970), pp. 1–3, 62, 245–6. Also see University College London Bentham Collection (hereafter UCLBC), box 87, pp. 2–3, and Jeremy Bentham, *An Introduction to the Principles of Morals and Legislation*, ed. J. H. Burns and H. L. A. Hart (London: Athlone, 1970), ch. 17, pars. 1–20 (hereafter *IPML*, citing chapter and paragraph because of the proliferation of editions), and see note 31, below. Bentham dropped indirect legislation as an explicit

category even as he became increasingly preoccupied from the late 1780s with those topics—such as political economy, the Panopticon, education, religion, and constitutional reform—that for the most part fall under it. Technically, direct legislation itself works indirectly by constructing and governing expectations; the civil law especially is about securing the conditions for the transactions that are regulated by it. "Bentham concentrated on the development of . . . instruments of security across a wide spectrum of law and policy. . . . [He] eschewed simple consequentialism in approaching the complex problems of law and politics. The legislator acted indirectly; he established the framework of security through law and public opinion." (F. Rosen, *Bentham, Byron, and Greece* [Oxford: Clarendon, 1992], pp. 34, 36). My own use of "indirect legislation" borrows and extends the term for a reconstruction of Bentham's project. It denotes the myriad sources, researches, and techniques developed by Bentham and reformers today that can supplement or substitute for the ostensibly more blunt and coercive and therefore inefficient and expensive means of state action. Even in his late work, these supplements might be referred to as "law"; see for example note 117, below, on the Public Opinion Tribunal, which suggests that what we call norms are a kind of law.

11   My thanks to Mark Canuel for stressing that prospects are landscaped points of view. Note also that prospect theory is a branch of game theory.

12   *IPML*, ch. 1, par. 2.

13   *Table*, p. 62 ("Uses").

14   *Table*, p. 99 ("Observations").

15   *IPML*, author's preface. My use of "logic of the will" in this chapter is controversial, much closer to Bentham's "thelematology" or psychological dynamics (*Table*, p. 71 ["Uses"]) than it is to the better-known formal aspects of imperation explicated by H. L. A. Hart (*Of Laws in General*, p. 15n; *IPML*, ch. 17, par. 29n; *Essays on Bentham: Jurisprudence and Political Theory* [Oxford: Oxford University Press, 1982], pp. 112–18). For an expansive and richly documented interpretation that combines these senses see Mary Mack, *Jeremy Bentham: An Odyssey of Ideas* (London: Heinemann, 1962): "[Bentham] hoped to create a logic of the will, a monumental and fully articulated structure rising from a foundation of fact, individual pleasures and pains, through ever-ascending orders of generality to the crowning abstraction, the normative Greatest Happiness principle" (p. 3). On thelematology and imperation see ibid., p. 164: "In 1831, when he was eighty-three, he made an outline. 'In man two faculties. 1. active—the will 2. passive—the understanding. . . . If to logic of the understanding the name of *Noology* be given, that of *Thelematology* may be given to the logic of the will. . . . *Nomography* the branch of thelematology which regards expression given to discourse employed by the superior to direct the conduct of the inferior.'" Citing Jeremy Bentham, Additional Manuscripts, British Museum, 33549, p. 28.

16   *IPML*, ch. 1, par. 1.

17   *IPML*, ch. 1, pars. 4–5.

18   I have translated the following from notes that Bentham wrote in 1828 under the heading "Deontology": "Si le bonheur d'un quelqu'un reçoit une augmentation, c'est de l'une ou l'autre de deux manières—1. par l'augmentation de la somme de ses plaisirs; ou 2. par la diminution de la somme de ses peines." Bentham, *Deontology Together with A Table of the Springs of Action and The Article On Utilitarianism*, p. 340 (appendix B: Definitions). Interest and happiness have the same makeup, but they are not synonyms. Interest has qualities that

make it, rather than happiness, the direct object of utilitarian concern: "But on every occasion the happiness of every individual is liable to come into competition with the happiness of every other. . . . Hence it is, that to serve for all occasions, instead of saying the greatest happiness of all, it becomes necessary to say the greatest happiness of the greatest number. If however instead of the word *happiness* the word *interest* is employed, the phrase universal interest may be employed as corresponding indifferently to the interest of the greatest number as to the interest of all." Bentham, *First Principles Preparatory to Constitutional Code*, ed. Philip Schofield (Oxford: Clarendon, 1989), p. 234.

19 On the reduction of all enjoyments to simple pleasures, see most prominently J. S. Mill, "Bentham," *Jeremy Bentham: Critical Assessments*, ed. Bhikhu Parekh, vol. 1. (London: Routledge, 1993), pp. 158–59. On the threat to respect for persons from the lumping together of different individuals' interests see most prominently John Rawls, *A Theory of Justice* (Cambridge: Harvard University Press, 1971), pp. 22–27, 33.

20 Bentham, *First Principles Preparatory to Constitutional Code*, p. 235.

21 Bentham, *Of Laws in General*, p. 133.

22 *Works*, vol. 1, pp. 308–9 ("Principles of the Civil Code").

23 If we must ask what this aggregate interest amounts to, since it is made up of such malleable intangibles, all that is clear is that it provides the following directives: (1) alter what works at cross-purposes, but (2) value security of fixed expectations above all else. "Bentham . . . held that there couldn't be a justification in natural law or natural justice of systems of property because what this would really be about was expectation, and expectation was neutral. So what was established might be quite arbitrary. Once this had happened, though, there is a good, non-arbitrary reason for maintaining it" (Ross Harrison, *Bentham* [London: Routledge and Kegan Paul, 1983], pp. 255–56). Generations of moral philosophers and normative political philosophers have been frustrated by Bentham's minimal attention to their concerns, and by their consequent inability to make clear sense of utility. "[T]hese ethical interpretations have obscured or trivialized the import of the principle of utility; they have invariably distracted readers from the purpose Bentham thought his principle would serve" (Nancy Rosenblum, *Bentham's Theory of the Modern State* [Cambridge: Harvard University Press, 1978], pp. 6–7). That purpose, as Rosenblum suggests, is a governmental one, the rationality of which is much closer to early-modern *raison d'état* than it is to the principles of normative theory (which is not to say that it is instrumental).

But for a powerful new ethical interpretation that opens to indeterminacy see Oren Ben-Dor, *Constitutional Limits and the Public Sphere: A Critical Study of Bentham's Constitutionalism* (Oxford: Hart, 2000): "Utility, for Bentham, did not aim at (providing an ideal for the substantive resolution of) moral questions, for example, to justify universally one substantive principle for the distribution of resources or rights. The enlightening thing about Utility was that it invoked, and constantly reverted back to, a basic human condition to explain moral possibilities" (p. 14n).

24 *IPML*, ch. 3, par. 1.

25 The great advantage of the *Table* (the core of which is a table, originally published on one spreadsheet) is that it graphically resolves all the temporal and causal confusions that are unavoidable in the more narrative structure of the *Introduction*. In this, and in its overall simplicity, the table can better serve through its publication as itself an effective piece of indirect legislation.

26   *IPML*, ch. 3, par. 2n.

27   Mack, *Jeremy Bentham*, pp. 242–43.

28   *IPML*, ch. 3, pars. 2–6.

29   For Bentham's plans regarding this text and what was written to follow it, and a statement of the relation between direct and indirect legislation, see *Of Laws in General*, pp. xxxi–xxxiii, 245–46.

30   *IPML*, ch. 3, par. 12.

31   This crucial essay of 1782—but the phrase "indirect legislation" is already in manuscript in 1773—has been published only in incomplete, embellished, and retranslated form (Bentham, *Works*, vol. 1, pp. 533–80; Bentham, *Theory of Legislation*, ed. P. E. L. Dumont, trans. R. Hildreth [London: Trübner, 1882], pp. 358–472). It comprehends a huge range of functions as functions of indirect government (even as it excludes some of them—such as political economy—from immediate consideration). The work throughout is proactive and preventive, and it includes a sustained discussion of "expedients against misrule" (UCLBC box 87, pp. 102–27) embodying early versions of Bentham's constitutional doctrine that he only fully developed in the 1820s. Because the work focuses on only one of its stated concerns (delinquency), it has been read mostly as a treatise on crime prevention, but I think this radically understates its importance. It is mostly in box 87 of the University College London Bentham Collection, but there is also material under this heading in boxes 62, 96, and 99.

32   *IPML*, ch. 1, par. 1.

33   *IPML*, ch. 3, par. 11.

34   *Table*, p. 76 (Introduction). See Bentham's peculiar twist on Samuel Johnson's rock-kicking response to the philosophical idealism of Bishop Berkeley: "Suppose the non-existence of corporeal substances—of any hard corporeal substance that stands opposite to you—make this supposition and as soon as you have made it, act upon it, pain, the perception of pain, will at once bear witness against you, and be your punishment, your condign punishment." Bentham, *De l'ontologie et autres textes sur les fictions*, ed. Philip Schofield, trans. Jean-Pierre Cléro and Christian Laval (Paris: Le Seuil, 1997), p. 182.

35   *IPML*, ch. 4, par. 2.

36   *IPML*, ch. 5, par. 1.

37   *Table*, pp. 75–76 (Introduction).

38   *IPML*, ch. 4, par. 8.

39   Cf. the maddening account in Bentham, *First Principles Preparatory to Constitutional Code*, p. 68: "On every occasion, the conduct of every human being will be determined by his own interest [fn. 'his own interest taken in its most extensive sense, that in which it is coextensive with the whole aggregate of pains and pleasures']: his own interest meaning according to his own conception of it, to the conception correct or incorrect entertained in relation to it by himself at the moment of action."

40   This prudence recalls the "art of measurement" of Plato's *Protagoras* 356d (*Protagoras*, trans. C. C. W. Taylor [Oxford: Clarendon, 1976, p. 50), and is a contemporary commonplace; see note 61, below.

41   *IPML*, ch. 7, par. 3; see also ch. 7, par. 23, and ch. 10, par. 2.

42   *Table*, pp. 91–92 ("Explanations"). Missing from this account is any hint of the open-ended and permanent interests that are catalogued in the *Table* correspondent to the catalogue of motives: for example, the "Interest of the GALL-BLADDER" (pursuing pleasures and avoiding

pains of antipathy) and the "Interest of the PILLOW" (avoiding the pains of labor), *Table*, p. 85 ("Table"). In the same text where we find this analysis, then, Bentham prominently deploys "interest" in a way that does not fit it.

43 That we are all always acting on the basis of calculations, no matter what our understanding of circumstances, is central to Bentham's formula. "Men calculate, some with less exactness, indeed, some with more: but all men calculate. I would not say, that even a madman does not calculate" (*IPML*, ch. 14, par. 28).

44 *IPML*, ch. 16, par. 27n.

45 UCLBC box 142, p. 200. I have removed a second "but" following "at best" in the manuscript. See also Bentham *Works*, vol. 1, p. 194. On the garden metaphor and debates inspired by Ernest Gellner over its meaning see Michael Crozier, "*Inter putatorem et vastitatem*: The Ambivalences of the Garden Metaphor in Modernity," in *The Left in Search of a Center*, ed. Crozier and Peter Murphy (Urbana: University of Illinois Press, 1996)—thanks to Ike Balbus for this reference. Crozier's ideal of a more English garden is close to Bentham's, despite Bentham's tendency here to make a sharp contrast with wilderness. Bentham's wilderness is no raw nature; instead it is improperly landscaped space, shaped haphazardly in accordance with ipsedixitism rather than utility.

46 This possibility is importantly dependent on the rare absence of nonpolitical—such as popular or religious—sanctions for particular acts. Landscaping through direct legislation is thus in practice inseparable from the landscaping through indirect legislation that involves supplementing and coordinating other sanctions.

47 *IPML*, ch. 14, par. 8.

48 *IPML*, ch. 17, par. 29n, 10–11.

49 H. L. A. Hart notes the distinction between Hobbes and Bentham on authority in a discussion of the theory of obligation in a command theory of law. While he is happy to join Bentham in a positivist abandonment of the framework of political jurisprudence, Hart relies on a tenet of Hobbes's that is missing from Bentham's theory and—according to Hart—required by it. This is the notion of an "authoritative legal reason," that a law-making command creates "peremptory" and "content-independent" reasons for its obedience. This is missing in Bentham, but it can't just be grafted on to his jurisprudence. Gerald J. Postema offers an ingenious interpretation of adjudication in Bentham, one that goes some way toward resolving tensions between utility and authority; but he thinks this solution ultimately fails (see Postema, *Bentham and the Common Law Tradition* [Oxford: Oxford University Press, 1986], pp. 440–64). What Hart seems unable to confront is the radicalism of Bentham's attack on the law: ultimately he is not an ally. For Bentham, law in Hart's sense is an obstruction to the reign of interest; it must be conquered and pressed into service as an artificial motive and securer of expectations. The law may grow in power, but it will decline in authority. See Hart, *Essays on Bentham*, pp. 253–55 and *passim*.

50 On Bentham and codification, completion, and British legal history see David Lieberman, *The Province of Legislation Determined* (Cambridge: Cambridge University Press, 1989).

51 *IPML*, ch. 6, par. 6n.

52 *IPML*, ch. 5, pars. 2–3. Note the absence of pains of power(lessness), which goes completely unremarked in the text. (Thanks to David Hasen for bringing this to my attention.)

53 The definition cited above from *IPML*, ch. 7, par. 3—"as either consist of pain or pleasure, or

have an influence in the production of pain or pleasure"—is referred back to throughout the remainder of the text. See also the fifth of Bentham's "instruments of invention and discovery": "Extension of the use made of the word *matter*, from the field of physics to the whole field of *psychics*, or *psychology*, including *ethics* and *politics*" (*Works*, vol. 3, p. 287).

54   *Table*, p. 76 ("Introduction"); *IPML*, ch. 3, par. 11.

55   *IPML*, ch. 5, pars. 5–9, 23–25.

56   *IPML*, ch. 5, par. 13.

57   *IPML*, ch. 5, par. 29.

58   *IPML*, ch. 10, par. 38n.

59   The question of Bentham's relationship to associationism is a complex one. In the note cited above he refers to Joseph Priestley's edition of Hartley's *Observations on Man*, rather than Hartley's own. This is relevant because Priestley's edition omits the extensive account of nervous vibration that in Hartley purports to give a strictly material grounding to the then widely acknowledged phenomenon of the mental association of ideas.

60   *IPML*, ch. 5, par. 33n.

61   " 'The greater the degree of affective force or influence with which the future operates in . . . [men's] mind in comparison of the present, the wider . . . is the distance between . . . [his] state of mind . . . and the state of mind of an inferior animal' " (UCLBC box 127, p. 288, quoted in Mack, *Jeremy Bentham*, p. 206). Thus the primary goal of the moralist and the pedagogue is to get their charges to properly weigh distant future in relation to immediate present pains and pleasures. The notion that this is a crucial component of civilized behavior and goal of the civilizing function is fairly common in the eighteenth century, but for Bentham it is fundamental.

62   *IPML*, ch. 5, par. 30.

63   *IPML*, ch. 5, pars. 30n, 14n.

64   For Bentham, what we call social science is always a governmental art-and-science. Political economy, for example, is to be considered "not only as a science but as an art." And it has a place on "the Map of Political Science," which itself encompasses "the entire field of the art of government." See Bentham, *Jeremy Bentham's Economic Writings*, vol. 3, pp. 305, 307 ("Institute of Political Economy"). On art-and-science see Mack, *Jeremy Bentham*, pp. 262–331.

65   *IPML*, ch. 7, par. 8.

66   *IPML*, ch. 8, par. 5n.

67   *IPML*, ch. 8, par. 2.

68   *IPML*, ch. 8, par. 6.

69   *IPML*, ch. 9, par. 10.

70   *IPML*, ch. 8, par. 13.

71   *IPML*, ch. 10, par. 2. Bentham frequently mixes organic and mechanistic metaphors.

72   *IPML*, ch. 10, par. 2.

73   *IPML*, ch. 10, par. 3.

74   *IPML*, ch. 10, par. 4.

75   See *Table*, pp. 79–86 ("Table") for lists of eulogisms and dyslogisms for each motive. As with "interest," Bentham defines "motive" in a way that should preclude the classification of the general human motives that are displayed in the Table.

76   *IPML*, ch. 10, pars. 5–6.

77 *IPML*, ch. 10, pars. 5–6.

78 *IPML*, ch. 10, par. 7.

79 *IPML*, ch. 10, par. 7n.

80 *IPML*, pp. 89–90 ("Explanations").

81 *Table*, p. 90 ("Explanations").

82 *IPML*, ch. 14, par. 28.

83 *IPML*, ch. 4, par. 8.

84 *Table*, p. 72 ("Uses").

85 *IPML*, ch. 10, par. 8.

86 *IPML*, ch. 7, pars. 11–12.

87 *IPML*, ch. 10, par. 8.

88 *IPML*, ch. 1, par. 1. This paragraph is not given a separate number, perhaps because it is itself "metaphor and declamation," inaugurating the antirhetorical rhetoric of the remainder of the *Introduction*.

89 *IPML*, ch. 16, par. 21.

90 See the lengthy and fascinating footnote concerning, among other things, the historical relationship between music and bad law—*IPML*, ch. 2, par. 11n.

91 Jeremy Bentham, *A Fragment on Government*, ed. J. H. Burns and H. L. A. Hart (Cambridge: Cambridge University Press, 1988), pp. 104–5.

92 I say "greater emphasis" because it was always his concern that governors be governed; this is the theme, for example, of the chapter on "expedients against misrule" in "Of Indirect Legislation" (UCLBC box 87, pp. 102–27). Here is the Bentham of 1822 on the Bentham of 1776: "At that time of day, so far as regards the general frame of the Government, scarcely in any one of those imperfections did the Author of the Fragment see the effect of any worse cause than inattention and prejudice: he saw not in them then, what the experience and observations of near fifty years have since taught him to see in them so plainly—the elaborately organized, and anxiously cherished and guarded products of sinister interest and artifice" (Bentham, *A Fragment on Government*, appendix A, p. 116).

93 The *Book of Fallacies* is a treatise in the "art of government," not only because its subject is specifically "political fallacies," but because it goes beyond what Bentham sees as the impartial and therefore merely instrumental treatment of rhetoric by classical humanists, who didn't distinguish between "promoting the purposes of the benefactor, and the purposes of the enemy of the human race" (*Works*, vol. 2, pp. 380–81).

94 According to "Institute of Political Economy" (1801–4), political economy is a branch of the art of government but is *distinct* from legislation. See Bentham, *Jeremy Bentham's Economic Writings*, vol. 3, p. 307, and note 64, above.

95 UCLBC box 87, p. 168.

96 UCLBC box 87, pp. 155–57, and Bentham, *Works*, vol. 1, pp. 555–56.

97 UCLBC box 87, p. 165.

98 UCLBC box 87, p. 18.

99 See UCLBC box 87, pp. 102–27.

100 Lyons is addressing a somewhat different set of concerns, but his remarks speak to my argument: "a social practise of driving on one side of the road rather than the other will be created (or reinforced) and that mode of driving will accordingly be . . . less hazardous. . . . The

difference of utilities will be *brought about* by legal sanctions, but the sanctions themselves do not enter into the relevant calculations" (David Lyons, *In the Interest of the Governed* [Oxford: Oxford University Press, 1973], p. 61, italics in original).

101   *IPML*, ch. 12, pars. 5ff.

102   UCLBC box 32, p. 1.

103   *IPML*, ch. 13, par. 2n.

104   *IPML*, ch. 15, par. 9. I have left out two parentheticals here that reinforce what I have called Bentham's theoretical legerdemain: "(or, in other words, the *apparent* punishment)" and "(the *real* punishment)."

105   *IPML*, ch. 15, par. 9.

106   *Works*, vol. 1, p. 549; UCLBC box 87, p. 137–38.

107   *Works*, vol. 1, p. 550; UCLBC box 87, p. 141. The manuscript makes the contrast and critique explicit: "At any rate not such a gloom, as is instilled with so little scruple, and which it is thought so necessary to be instilled by the terror of offences undefined and undefinable, to be punished by flames unquenchable, which only one out of the number can escape." See also on p. 138 the critique of the engravings of the Theresian code.

108   *Works*, vol. 1, p. 550; UCLBC box 87, p. 137. I can't find the "speaking image" reference in manuscript, but Bentham may be referring to it when he writes "I have observed elsewhere that a table of this sort ought in the manner of an almanack to make part of the furniture of every house."

109   Bentham, *Deontology*, in *Deontology Together with A Table of the Springs of Action and The Article On Utilitarianism*, p. 259.

110   Thus he is consistent in abandoning the antirhetorical rhetoric of utilitarian science when writing useful polemics or speeches. See for example Bentham, *Securities against Misrule and Other Constitutional Writings for Tripoli and Greece*, ed. Philip Schofield (Oxford: Clarendon, 1990), pp. 74–78.

111   Pitkin, "Slippery Bentham," p. 105.

112   UCLBC box 32, p. 149; *Works*, vol. 1, p. 337 ("Civil Code").

113   The sinister interest of the ruling class is capable not only of deploying bad direct legislation in its favor but also of generating a more durable and insidious "interest-begotten prejudice." This is bad indirect legislation; the prejudice that produces reverence for bad rulers works at cross-purposes with the proper landscaping function of the popular or moral sanction. See Bentham, *First Principles Preparatory to Constitutional Code*, pp. 180–83; Rosen, *Bentham, Byron, and Greece*, p. 62.

114   This governmental strategy of accommodating plural desires while containing plural involvements is manifest in the putatively simplifying assumptions of contemporary rational-choice theory. James S. Coleman, for example, insists on this monism of interest for the rational actor, and his is based, like Bentham's, in a relationship of identity. "The two parts of the structure of the simplest possible actor correspond to what I have called . . . the object self (receptor) and the acting self (actuator); interests constitute the linkage between the two" (Coleman, *Foundations of Social Theory* [Cambridge: Harvard University Press, 1990], p. 504).

115   These points—that Benthamic interest theory limits the possibilities of conduct by constructing an identity like Coleman's (see previous note) and by foregrounding viscerality—

are made by William Hazlitt in the first of his *Essays on the Principles of Human Action* (1805; Bristol: Thoemmes Antiquarian, 1990). See especially p. 17: "The interests of the being who acts, and of the being who suffers, are never one. . . . My real interest is not therefore something which I can handle, which is to be felt, or seen. . . . On the contrary, it is . . . by it's very nature the creature of reflection and imagination; and whatever can be made the subject of these, whether relating to ourselves or others, may also be the object of an interest powerful enough to become the motive of volition and action."

116   I owe this insight to a conversation with Sophia Mihic.

117   As does economy: "the economy" does not yet exist for Bentham and his contemporaries. "Culture" is not yet the abstract noun it will soon become; but part of Bentham's indirect legislation is devoted to ways to "culture" the nonpolitical sanctions (UCLBC box 87, pp. 18– 22, 25–28). The label "public opinion" for the popular sanction is first rejected out of a suspicion of the relevance of everything potentially named by it (*IPML*, ch. 3, par. 5n), but Bentham later recognizes a "public opinion tribunal" in his *Constitutional Code*: "ART. 4. Public Opinion may be considered as a system of law, emanating from the body of the people. . . . Able rulers lead it; prudent rulers lead or follow it; foolish rulers disregard it" (Bentham, *Constitutional Code*, vol. 1, ed. F. Rosen and J. H. Burns [Oxford: Clarendon, 1983], p. 36). Religion, on the other hand, was problematic in so far as it *was* a "social system," the Anglican Establishment: a system that generated sinister interest (see James E. Crimmins, *Secular Utilitarianism* [Oxford: Oxford University Press, 1990], pp. 182–201).

5   State Rationality

1   Michel Foucault, "Governmentality," in G. Burchell, C. Gordon, and P. Miller, eds., *The Foucault Effect: Studies in Governmentality* (Chicago: University of Chicago Press, 1991), p. 95.

2   See Jeremy Bentham, *Deontology*, in *Deontology Together with A Table of the Springs of Action and The Article on Utilitarianism*, ed. Amnon Goldworth (Oxford: Clarendon, 1983), p. 119.

3   See H. L. A. Hart, *Essays on Bentham: Jurisprudence and Political Theory* (Oxford: Oxford University Press, 1982), pp. 253–55. Also, see note 49 to chapter 4, above.

4   Thus, if this were all about voluntarism and rationalism, one might reasonably argue that it is an opposition that traces back to, for example, Plato's *Euthyphro* and *Protagoras*. But note that there is already a conflict between voluntarism and rationalism within sovereignty itself (as in the contrast between duty and desire), a conflict that reflects its theomorphism. My gloss on sovereignty ignores the much-explored paradoxes that sovereignty itself poses: the conundrum of a collective sovereignty, the rule of persons versus the rule of law, the role of the constituting versus the constituted power, the problem that the guarantee of sovereign order is a sovereign power that takes exception to it. Sovereignty has also been rightly criticized as a model inappropriate to republican and democratic politics, insistent as it is on the centrality of relations of command and obedience. These are all important concerns. But I hope to shift the focus to some extent away from sovereignty in an attempt to see a different mode of rule too often obscured by any treatment—critical or celebratory—that elevates sovereignty's profile.

5   Albert O. Hirschman, *The Passions and the Interests: Arguments for Capitalism Before Its Triumph* (Princeton: Princeton University Press, 1977), pp. 40–41.

6   "Suppose your own state at war with one more populous. *Per* Utility, you ought to sacrifice your own to the hostile state." Jeremy Bentham, *A Table of the Springs of Action*, in *Deontology Together with A Table of the Springs of Action and Article on Utilitarianism*, p. 37 ("Added Observations").

7   David Burchell, "How to Do Things with Cicero," unpublished paper, Rutgers Seminar in the History of the Book, spring 2001.

8   On contrasting styles, see Burchell, "How to Do Things With Cicero." Richard Tuck argues that reason of state is Tacitean. Peter Miller, however, notes that it relies at least as much on Cicero. See Richard Tuck, *Philosophy and Government: 1572–1651* (Cambridge: Cambridge University Press, 1993) and Peter Miller, *Defining the Common Good* (Cambridge: Cambridge University Press, 1994).

9   John Calvin, *Institutes of the Christian Religion*, ed. John T. McNeill, trans. Ford Lewis Battles (Philadelphia: Westminster, 1960), *Library of Christian Classics*, vol. 20, p. 35.

10   Michel de Montaigne, *The Complete Essays of Montaigne*, trans. Donald M. Frame (Stanford: Stanford University Press, 1958), pp. 2, 855, 857.

11   For example, he is put on trial by Apollo in Trajano Boccalini's satirical *The New-found Politicke*, trans. William Vaughan (London, 1626) and cited approvingly in Gabriel Naudé's *Considérations Politiques sur les Coups d'État* of 1639.

12   Lipsius's *De Constantia* was first printed in 1584.

13   Justus Lipsius, *Six Bookes of Politickes or Civil Doctrine*, trans. William Jones (Amsterdam: Da Capo, 1970 [London, 1594]). Lipsius cites from a number of Roman texts, and also uses occasional Biblical and Greek passages. Although these make up as much as half of the textual material, their framing and arrangement are very much his, and justify attributing everything in the work to "Lipsius." In the text, all the borrowed material is italicized.

14   Ibid., pp. 114–15.

15   Ibid., p. 117

16   Ibid., p. 119.

17   Ibid., p. 123.

18   *Salus populi suprema lex esto* is not from *On Duties* but rather *De Legibus*, in T. E. Page et al., eds., and Clinton Walker Keyes, trans., *De Re Publica / De Legibus* (Cambridge: Harvard University Press, 1948), p. 466 (book III, iii.8).

19   Lipsius, *Six Bookes of Politickes or Civil Doctrine*, p. 113. See Cicero, *On Duties*, ed. M. T. Griffin and E. M. Atkins (Cambridge: Cambridge University Press, 1991), pp. 101–47.

20   See for example Cicero's praise of Regulus, who kept a promise to the enemy in war when he knew that doing so would mean torture and death, even recommending against his own ransom as harmful to Rome. *On Duties*, pp. 138–42.

21   On the distinction between "for the sake of" and "in order to," see Hannah Arendt, *The Human Condition* (Chicago: University of Chicago Press, 1958), p. 154.

22   By no means am I saying that its translation into "public interest" alone transforms Cicero's public utility. Many conceptions of the public interest have drawn and continue to draw inspiration from it. My point is that we also live with another conception of the public interest, one that aggregates transformed private interests. Putting it bluntly, Cicero's *utilitas publica* is not utilitarian. (Neither, I think, is the "casuistical" private utility of his notorious seller who has limited duties to his buyer; it is a complete misreading of the distinction I'm

drawing between Cicero and utilitarianism to think that it implies Cicero's to be a more "altruistic" ethic.)

23 Montaigne, *The Complete Essays of Montaigne*, p. 607. Also, even if necessary, faith-breaking must not be done "without regret."

24 *The Political Testament of Cardinal Richelieu*, ed. and trans. Henry Bertram Hill (Madison: University of Wisconsin Press, 1961), pp. 34–35.

25 *The Political Testament of Cardinal Richelieu*, pp. 42, 88, 106–7.

26 Ibid., pp. 80–83, 94–102.

27 Ibid., pp. 76–79.

28 See for example Nannerl Keohane, *Philosophy and the State in France* (Princeton: Princeton University Press, 1980).

29 Lipsius, *Six Bookes of Politickes or Civil Doctrine*, p. 22.

30 Quoted in William F. Church, *Richelieu and Reason of State* (Princeton: Princeton University Press, 1972), p. 303.

31 The chapters on sovereignty are a small part of a work the last few books of which are not at all narrowly juridical. "Interest" for Bodin has a somewhat juridical sense that I explore in the English context in chapter 6, especially when used with regard to the distinction between laws and contract. "The prince is not subject to his own laws or to the laws of his predecessors, but only to his just and reasonable contracts in the observation of which his subjects in general or particular subjects have an interest." Jean Bodin, *On Sovereignty*, ed. Julian Franklin (Cambridge: Cambridge University Press), p. 14.

32 On the Dutch republicans see Roman Schnur, ed., *Staatsräson* (Berlin: Duncker und Humblot, 1975), pp. 233, 489, 500–501.

33 Lipsius, *Six Bookes of Politickes or Civil Doctrine*, pp. 12–13.

34 Ibid., p. 11.

35 Ibid., p. 12.

36 Ibid., pp. 13–15.

37 Ibid., pp. 41, 43.

38 Ibid., pp. 49–50.

39 Ibid., pp. 67–70.

40 Ibid., p. 82.

41 Ibid., p. 97.

42 Ibid., p. 102.

43 Ibid., p. 130.

44 Ibid., pp. 168, 170–71.

45 Ibid., p. 166. Rumor is discussed on p. 168.

46 This is true despite the importance for both Machiavelli and Lipsius of occasion (timing).

47 Giovanni Botero, *The Reason of State*, trans. P. J. Waley and D. P. Waley (New Haven: Yale University Press, 1956), pp. xiii–xiv.

48 Ibid., p. 3.

49 "Forms of knowledge" are introduced in ibid., p. 34, the opening to book 2.

50 Ibid., p. 3.

51 Ibid., p. 46.

52 Ibid., pp. 48–49.

53 Machiavelli does not consider wealth, except insofar as it is potentially corrupting.

54 Ibid., p. 134. This does not mean that a prince should accumulate riches for their own sake.

55 Ibid., pp. 142–43. This of course undercuts the metaphor of pastoral government even as it invokes it.

56 Botero, *The Reason of State*, pp. 145–46.

57 Ibid., pp. 151, 153–56.

58 Ibid., p. 155.

59 Ibid., pp. 150n, 155–56.

60 Gerhard Oestreich, *Neostoicism and the Early Modern State*, ed. Brigitta Oestreich and H. G. Koenigsberger, trans. David McLintock (Cambridge: Cambridge University Press, 1982), pp. 155–65.

61 Ibid., p. 161n.

62 See Michel Foucault, "*Omnes et Singulatim*: Toward a Critique of Political Reason," in Foucault, *Power*, ed. James D. Faubion, trans. Robert Hurley et al. (New York: New Press, 2000), vol. 3 of *Essential Works of Foucault, 1954–1984*, ed. Paul Rabinow, pp. 298–325.

63 Calvin, *Institutes of the Christian Religion*, p. 1229. On military discipline and its generalization see Oestreich, *Neostoicism and the Early Modern State* and Foucault, *Discipline and Punish: The Birth of the Prison*, trans. Alan Sheridan (New York: Vintage, 1979).

64 Antoine de Montchrétien, *Traité de l'Oeconomie Politique* (Paris: Marcel Riviere, 1920), pp. 31–32 (my translation—"la police" is not distinct from "la politique" until later in the seventeenth century).

65 For all of Adam Smith's eighteenth-century critique of the "mercantile system," this feature of political economy is continuous with his own police. Compare Smith:

> The man of system . . . seems to imagine that he can arrange the different members of a great society with as much ease as the hand arranges the different pieces upon a chessboard.[. . .] [B]ut [. . .] in the great chessboard of human society, every single piece has a principle of motion of its own, altogether different from that which the legislature might choose to impress upon it. If those two principles coincide and act in the same direction, the game of human society will go on easily and harmoniously, and is very likely to be happy and successful. If they are opposite or different, the game will go on miserably and the society must be at all times in the highest degree of disorder.

Smith, *The Theory of Moral Sentiments* (London, 1759), part 6, ch. 2, quoted in F. A. Hayek, *Rules and Order*, vol. 1 of *Law, Legislation, and Liberty* (Chicago: University of Chicago Press, 1973), p. 35.

66 See the section on "*l'exemple et des soins principaux du prince*" in Montchrestien, *Traité de l'Oeconomie Politique*, pp. 335–70.

67 See Peter Miller, *Defining the Common Good*, p. 27.

68 See Richard Tuck, "The 'Modern' Theory of Natural Law in Early-Modern Europe," in Anthony Pagden, ed., *The Languages of Political Theory in Early-Modern Europe* (Cambridge: Cambridge University Press, 1987), pp. 99–119.

69 Lipsius, *Six Bookes of Politickes or Civil Doctrine*, p. 23.

70 Quentin Skinner, *The Foundations of Modern Political Thought* (Cambridge: Cambridge University Press, 1978), vol. 2, p. 353. See also Quentin Skinner, "The State," in Terence Ball, James Farr, and Russell L. Hanson, *Political Innovation and Conceptual Change* (Cambridge: Cam-

bridge University Press, 1989), pp. 90–131. Skinner treats a number of different moments in the rise of a modern conception of the state, but he does not really contend with reason of state as such.

71 It seems to be in agreements involving republican states, such as the American states named in the Articles of Confederation, that we first see personified as juridical actors modern states explicitly (and not their nominal possessors, in this case citizens).

72 Interest thwarted by excessive ambition does, however, make an appearance in places in the text. See Duke of Rohan, *A Treatise of the Interest of Princes and States of Christendome*, trans. H. H. (Paris, 1640).

73 Duke of Rohan, *A Treatise of the Interest of the Princes and States of Christendome*, pp. 1–2.

74 Ibid., pp. 13, 34.

75 *"England is a mightie Animal, which can never dye except it kill it selfe."* Ibid., p. 35.

76 It *need* not take individual interest into account. Of course, some such articulation is possible and is present, at least in limited form, in Montchrétien's vision of public management cited above.

77 See Jeremy Bentham, *First Principles Preparatory to Constitutional Code*, ed. Philip Schofield (Oxford: Clarendon, 1989) and Bentham, *Constitutional Code*, vol. 1, F. Rosen and J. H. Burns, eds. (Oxford: Clarendon, 1983).

78 Again, this is not to say that state rationality does not construct points of interface with the conduct of subjects, which presumably it must do in all those proliferating areas where subjects' conduct is deemed to affect the interest of state.

6 The Public Interest

1 At least one contemporary political scientist has noticed this important distinction between game-theory and rational-choice approaches to the study of politics, although not exactly in these terms. See Barry O'Neill, *Honor, Symbols and War* (Ann Arbor: University of Michigan Press, 1999), pp. 253–62 (appendix A).

2 The most richly documented study of the public interest in seventeenth-century England is J. A. W. Gunn's *Politics and the Public Interest in the Seventeenth Century* (London: Routledge and Kegan Paul, 1969). Gunn's very useful volume is framed by a kind of Whig-history narrative that sees little connection, ultimately, between the public interest and the reason of state from which it derives (although Gunn is well aware of Rohan's importance in particular). Gunn sees the public interest as an "individualist" phenomenon (p. xi). A more recent study, also richly documented, that rightly rejects Gunn's narrative is Peter Miller's *Defining the Common Good: Empire, Religion and Philosophy in Eighteenth-Century Britain* (Cambridge: Cambridge University Press, 1994). Miller includes much on the uses of Cicero in the seventeenth century; he sees the importance of necessity to the discourse of interest, and thus interest's relationship to Reformation state- and empire-building. But he misses interest's intimate connection with individual conduct. Richard Tuck also links reason of state to the public interest and English interest-discourse more generally in *Philosophy and Government, 1572–1651* (Cambridge: Cambridge University Press, 1993). By connecting reason of state to natural rights, he gives the beginnings of an account of how these contrasting narratives of the public interest can be reconciled.

3   Richard Hooker, *Of the Laws of Ecclesiastical Polity*, preface and book 1, ed. Arthur Stephen McGrade (Cambridge: Cambridge University Press, 1989). In no way does Hooker deny the authority of the Bible, but none of those demanding a reformed discipline has shown "the deduction thereof out of scripture to be necessary." Instead it has been "but probably and conjecturally surmised" (pp. 113–14).

4   On the changing meanings of history, science, probability, and certainty, see Barbara Shapiro, *Probability and Certainty in Seventeenth-Century England* (Princeton: Princeton University Press, 1983).

5   See Ernest Tuveson, *Millennium and Utopia* (Berkeley: University of California Press, 1949) and Benedict Anderson, *Imagined Communities* (London: Verso, 1983).

6   Pocock, *The Machiavellian Moment* (Princeton: Princeton University Press, 1975), p. 338. Despite this caution, Pocock endorses the argument of Tuveson and others that—"in the long view," anyway—"it is possible to trace the mutation of the expected millennium or Third Age into that indefinite secular future which distinguishes the modern from the premodern sense of history (p. 46)."

7   Conscience, etymologically, is knowledge-with. On conscience see Gordon Schochet, "Persuading the Heart: Appeals to Conscience in the English Revolution," in *Historians and Ideologues: Essays in Honor of Donald R. Kelley*, ed. Anthony Grafton and J. H. M. Salmon (Rochester: University of Rochester Press, 2001), pp. 154–80.

8   This story of transformed republicanism, which is beyond the scope of this chapter, is implied in J. G. A. Pocock's analyses of the early-eighteenth-century "crisis of personality" and is detailed by Shelley Burtt in her analysis of the role of Trenchard and Gordon in the rise of a "privately-oriented" virtue. See Pocock, *The Machiavellian Moment* and *Virtue, Commerce, and History* (Cambridge: Cambridge University Press, 1985) and Burtt, *Virtue Transformed* (Cambridge: Cambridge University Press, 1982).

9   It is of course still better known as the century of natural rights and social contract.

10 Interest-plurality is linked to liberal governmentality in Graham Burchell's treatment of Hume and the Scottish Enlightenment. See Burchell, "Peculiar Interests: Civil Society and Governing 'The System of Natural Liberty,'" in Graham Burchell, Colin Gordon, and Peter Miller, eds., *The Foucault Effect: Studies in Governmentality* (Chicago: University of Chicago Press, 1991), pp. 119–50.

11 Hooker, *Of the Laws of Ecclesiastical Polity*, pp. 31–32.

12 Ibid., p. 62.

13 Ibid., pp. 107–9.

14 Ibid., p. 77.

15 Ibid., p. 78.

16 Ibid., pp. 80–81.

17 Ibid., p. 84.

18 Ibid., pp. 90–91.

19 Ibid., p. 88

20 Ibid., p. 63.

21 Ibid., p. 62.

22 Ibid., p. 96.

23 Sir John Davies, *Le Primer Report des Cases et Matters en Ley Resolues et Adiudges en les Courts*

del Roy en Ireland (1615), in David Wooten, ed., *Divine Right and Democracy* (New York: Viking Penguin, 1986), p. 131.

24 J. P. Kenyon, ed. *The Stuart Constitution, 1603–1688: Documents and Commentary*, 2nd edition (Cambridge: Cambridge University Press, 1986), p. 58.

25 Ibid., p. 38.

26 "A *Common-wealth* is like unto a *family*, the *father* or master whereof ought to sell more than he buyeth . . ." Edward Misselden, *Free Trade or the Meanes to Make Trade Florish* (London: 1622), pp. 11–12.

27 Thomas Mun, *A Discourse of Trade* (London, 1621), p. 6.

28 Ibid., p. 49.

29 Ibid., p. 50.

30 Ibid., pp. 33–34.

31 Ibid., pp. 36–37. The table of contents for this section reads as follows: "It breedeth more Marriners then it doth ordinarily consume, and disburtheneth the Kingdome of very many leude people."

32 Henry Parker, *Of a Free Trade* (London, 1647), dedication and p. 1.

33 Ibid., p. 7.

34 This managing aspect is not necessarily part of trade, and it is implied in the "economic" label itself.

35 For example see William Constantine, *The Interest of England* (London, 1642).

36 For this mapping of interest onto landed proprietors, see for example Henry Parker, *Observations on Some of His Majesty's Late Answers and Expresses* (London, 1642) and *The Observator Defended* (London, 1642).

John Warr contrasts the people's interest and the king's in *The Corruption and Deficiency of the Lawes* of 1649:

The rule of our English laws is as faulty as the rise. The rule of our laws may be referred to a twofold interest:

(1) The interest of the king, which was the great bias and rule of the law . . .

(2) The interest of the people, which (like a worm) when trod upon did turn again and in smaller iotas and diminutive parcels wound in itself into the texture of law, yet so as that the royal interest was above it and did frequently suppress it at its pleasure. The freedom which we have by the law owns its original to this interest of the people.

Wootton, ed., *Divine Right and Democracy*, p. 157.

37 Foxe's *Book of Martyrs* was, for a time, the second-best seller in England after the Bible. A sense of the passionately nationalist character of Protestant exile literature can be gleaned from John Poynet's *Politicke Power* (New York: Da Capo, 1972 [Geneva, 1556]).

38 He was actually forced out of the pulpit not by the episcopal church but by its reformers, yet he continued to gather in prayer with others, including the "Leveller" and freethinker William Walwyn, an early and consistent advocate of toleration. Ellen More, "John Goodwin and the Origins of the New Arminianism," *Journal of British Studies*, vol. 22, no. 1 (autumn 1982), pp. 50–70.

39 John Goodwin, *The Saints Interest in God: Opened in Severall Sermons, Preached Anniversarily upon the Fifth of November* (London, 1640), pp. 23–44.

40 Ibid., p. 23.

41 Ibid., p. 5.

42 Ibid., p. 1.

43 Ibid., pp. 20–22.

44 Ibid., pp. 7–9.

45 William Constantine, *The Interest of England* (London, 1642). One frequently sees moderating qualifications in texts calling for crackdowns on Catholics, in an attempt to avoid mirroring what their writers saw as the conscience-trampling, barbaric, and generally "Machiavellian" methods of the Counter-Reformation.

46 Thomas Goodwin, *The Great Interest of States and Kingdomes* (London, 1646), pp. 53–54. (The Fast Day is February 25, 1645, on the old calendar.)

47 Richard Tuck has traced a powerful relationship between the rights of states and the rights of individuals in *The Rights of War and Peace* (Oxford: Oxford University Press, 1999).

48 On natural rights, see Tuck, *Natural Rights Theories: Their Origin and Development* (Cambridge: Cambridge University Press, 1979). For a modified position that links natural-rights theories to reason of state see Tuck, *Philosophy and Government, 1572–1651*; also see note 2, above.

49 Henry Parker, *Observations on Some of His Majesty's Late Answers and Expresses* (London, 1642) and *The Observator Defended* (London, 1642).

50 Marchamont Nedham, *The Case of the Kingdom Stated* (London, 1647).

51 A dramatically absolutist use of this constitutional interest is displayed by Hobbes in the following passage from *De Cive* where, even though he would never of course call it a protection against "tyranny," he nevertheless offers reassurances to readers about the consequences of absolute sovereignty: "Lastly, since it was necessary for the preservation of ourselves to be subject to some *man* or *council*, we cannot on better condition be subject to any, than one whose interest depends upon our safety and welfare; and this then comes to pass when we are the inheritance of the ruler. For every man of his own accord endeavours the preservation of his inheritance." Thomas Hobbes, *De Cive*, 1651 English trans., ed. Howard Warrender (Oxford: Clarendon, 1983), "Dominion," ch. 10, par. 18. "Interest" here refers, as usual, to a property relation. The passage is part of a bold attempt to forge this relation, to forge this interest. And like so much in Hobbes, it produces an array of contrary effects. At the same time as the sovereign is made absolute to an unprecedented degree, his sovereignty is reduced by analogy to the status of a freeholder "every man."

52 Charles I, in *His Majesties Answer to the XIX Propositions of Both Houses of Parliament* (London, 1642), perhaps imprudently adopted the theory of balance. He mirrored Parliament's interest-constitutionalism with the following (p. 10): "The preservation of every Law concernse Us, those of obedience being not secure, when those of protection are violated; And we being most of any injured in the least violation of that, by which We enjoy the highest Right, and greatest benefits, and are therefore obliged to defend no lesse by our interest then by Our duty."

53 See Felix Raab, *The English Face of Machiavelli* (London: Routledge and Kegan Paul, 1964), J. G. A. Pocock, *The Machiavellian Moment* and Pocock, ed., *The Political Works of James Harrington* (Cambridge: Cambridge University Press, 1977), editor's introduction.

54 The spreading enthusiasm is not, for most, about the coming of a literal outward rule of Christ (as it may be for many Fifth Monarchists), but about an ongoing process of reform as

purification that involves both inner and outer transformation. See Michael Walzer, *The Revolution of the Saints* (Cambridge: Harvard University Press, 1965). Walzer rightly emphasizes the importance of Puritan discipline, and the discipline of the Army in particular, in accounting for the effectiveness of the saints.

55 Pocock, *The Machiavellian Moment*, p. 336.

56 We should not underestimate the monarchism of the opposition. Most "rebels" saw themselves as loyal subjects; perhaps this was even true of many who remained to prosecute the King. Ernst H. Kantorowicz, in *The King's Two Bodies: A Study in Medieval Political Theology* (Princeton: Princeton University Press, 1957), suggests that Charles Stuart was beheaded on behalf of Charles I (pp. 20–23).

57 A. S. P. Woodhouse, ed., *Puritanism and Liberty: Being the Army Debates (1647–49) from the Clarke Manuscripts* (3rd edition; London: J. M. Dent and Sons, 1986), p. 50.

58 Ibid., pp. 394–96.

59 Ibid., p. 40.

60 Ibid., p. 34.

61 Ibid., pp. 52–53.

62 Ibid., pp. 53–54.

63 Ibid., pp. 54–55.

64 Ibid., p. 56.

65 Ibid., p. 55.

66 Ibid., p. 57.

67 Ibid., p. 58.

68 Ibid., p. 59 (Cromwell's phrase).

69 Ibid., p. 63.

70 See for example ibid., pp. 6, 23, 34, 37.

71 Ibid., pp. 62–63.

72 Ibid., p. 67.

73 Although C. B. Macpherson notes the divisions over property at Putney, he wants to reduce their significance rather than make use of them—as I suggest he could—for his narrative. This results from, among other things, an overly narrow focus on the question of the Leveller franchise and its scope. See Macpherson, *The Political Theory of Possessive Individualism: Hobbes to Locke* (Oxford: Oxford University Press, 1962), especially pp. 137–59.

74 Woodhouse, *Puritanism and Liberty*, p. 63.

75 Ibid., p. 67.

76 Ibid., p. 72 (emphasis in text).

77 For an excellent source on the role of Scripture before, during, and after the wars see Christopher Hill, *The English Bible and the Seventeenth-Century Revolution* (New York: Penguin, 1993).

78 Woodhouse, *Puritanism and Liberty*, p. 107.

79 "The Sentence of the High Court of Justice upon the King," in S. R. Gardiner, ed., *The Constitutional Documents of the Puritan Revolution, 1625–1660* (3rd edition; Oxford: Clarendon, 1906), pp. 377–80.

80 I have suggested this already in chapter 2 with regard to Cumberland's far more subtle target, Hobbes, and his own transformation of necessity. Again, this does not mean that monistic

interest is not in certain respects considerably advanced by these theorists, and by the "modern natural law" tradition as a whole. It is with good reason that both Hobbes and Cumberland, for all their radical differences, have been identified as Bentham's seventeenth-century predecessors. See Richard Cumberland, *A Treatise of the Laws of Nature* (1727 English trans. of *De legibus naturae*, 1672).

81 This is actually from Wren's rejoinder to Harrington's response to Wren's critique of *Oceana*. Matthew Wren, *Monarchy Asserted, or the State of Monarchicall and Popular Government; in Vindication of the Considerations upon Mr. Harrington's Oceana*, 2nd edition (London, 1660), p. 49.

82 See for example John Fell, *The Interest of England Stated* (1659), which follows the style of Marchamont Nedham's direct transposition of Rohan's *Interest* to domestic politics, with the important difference that it posits an interest of the whole, which Nedham's *Case of the Kingdom Stated* (1647) rigorously eschewed. Nedham's response to Fell is noteworthy for its opening transposing Rohan to individuals rather than parties: "It is a Maxim among Politicians, That *Interest will not lie*: Which prudential saying hath a twofold sense, the improving whereof is very useful to a man, either in the conduct of his own Affairs, or in discerning the conduct and end of the Affairs and enterprises of other men." Nedham, *Interest Will Not Lie* (London, 1659), p. 3.

83 Samuel Fortrey, *England's Interest and Improvement* (Cambridge, 1663).

84 William Petty, *Five Essays in Political Arithmetick* (London, 1687).

85 William Penn, *England's Present Interest Discovered with Honour to the Prince and Safety to the People* (1675). Note that in the subtitle the "*Interest of the Government*" is a goal distinct from the "*Prosperity of the Kingdom*."

86 Kirstie M. McClure, "Difference, Diversity, and the Limits of Toleration," *Political Theory*, vol. 18 (1990): 361–91.

87 See for example Roger L'Estrange, *Interest Mistaken, or the Holy Cheat* (London, 1661). In the climate of the early 1660s, orthodox latitudinarians themselves were suspected by many to be dangerous to King and Church. See the defense by Simon Patrick, *A Brief Account of the New Sect of Latitude-Men* (London, 1662).

88 Thomas Higgenson, *Some Legible Characters of Faith and Love Towards the Blessed Cause and Kingdom of Christ: Worthy to be known and read of all men* (London, 1659), pp. 6, 8.

89 John Wilkins, *Of the Principles and Duties of Natural Religion* (London, 1675), "The Preface."

90 Ibid., pp. 294–95.

91 Ibid., p. 285.

92 Ibid., p. 288.

93 Ibid., p. 304.

94 Samuel Parker posits prospective goods of self and whole in a turgid treatise that appropriates and augments Cumberland's natural-law theory; he figures self-interest more explicitly than Wilkins as a sum of rewards and punishments over this life and the next. See *A Demonstration of the Divine Authority of the Law of Nature and of the Christian Religion* (London, 1681).

95 They anticipate, perhaps, the imminent appearance of Credit.

96 "These perspectives" should not be taken to include Defoe's.

97 Gary Becker, *The Economic Approach to Human Behavior* (Chicago: University of Chicago Press, 1976), p. 10.

1 James Tully, "Governing Conduct," in Edmund Leites, ed., *Conscience and Casuistry in Early Modern Europe* (Cambridge: Cambridge University Press, 1988), p. 13. The heart of Tully's study is a compelling governmental interpretation of Locke's *An Essay Concerning Human Understanding* in its successive drafts.

2 Gary Becker is a self-styled "economic imperialist." He has, of course, many nineteenth- and twentieth-century disciplinary antecedents. See for example Philip Wicksteed's popular textbook, *The Common Sense of Political Economy* (London: Macmillan, 1910), especially book 1, chapter 1.

3 See for example Richard Posner, *The Problems of Jurisprudence* (Cambridge: Harvard University Press, 1990), pp. 353–62.

4 "[M]aybe, after all, the state is no more than a composite reality and a mythicized abstraction.... Maybe what is really important ... for our present ... is not so much the *étatisation* of society, as the 'governmentalization' of the state." Michel Foucault, "Governmentality," in Graham Burchell, Colin Gordon, and Peter Miller, eds., *The Foucault Effect: Studies in Governmentality* (Chicago: University of Chicago Press, 1991), p. 103.

5 The care taken by Bentham with regard to expectations is well illustrated by *Supply without Burthen*, which proposes an abolition of oppressive taxes made up for by a change in estate law. See W. Stark, ed., *Jeremy Bentham's Economic Writings*, vol. 1 (London: George Allen and Unwin, 1952–54).

6 I owe this insight to a conversation with Mark Canuel.

7 This is especially important, of course, for policing any necessary central policing apparatus itself; thus the constitutional emphasis on *publicity*.

8 Jeremy Bentham, *Works of Jeremy Bentham*, ed. John Bowring (Edinburgh: William Tait, 1838–43), vol. 8, p. 27.

9 Ibid., p. 241.

10 David Lieberman, *The Province of Legislation Determined* (Cambridge: Cambridge University Press, 1989).

11 Jeremy Bentham, *Panopticon: Postscript*, part 2, *Containing a Plan of Management for a Panopticon Penitentiary-House* (London, 1791), p. 31.

12 Ibid., p. 35.

13 Ibid., pp. 23–24.

14 F. A. Hayek, "The Use of Knowledge in Society," in *Individualism and the Economic Order*, p. 88. I am taking the liberty of designating Hayek a neoliberal *avant la lettre*.

15 See Nikolas Rose, *Powers of Freedom* (Cambridge: Cambridge University Press, 1999), pp. 137–66. On risk and prudentialism see Pat O'Malley, "Risk and Responsibility," in Andrew Barry, Thomas Osborne, and Nikolas Rose, eds., *Foucault and Political Reason: Liberalism, Neoliberalism, and Rationalities of Government* (Chicago: University of Chicago Press, 1996).

Index

Bentham, Jeremy (*cont.*)
of government, 15, 147; on happiness, *see* happiness; and Hobbes, 144, 157–58 n. 48, 170 n. 49; illiberal image of, 3, 9, 157–58 n. 48, 165–66 n. 3; and the imagination, *see* imagination; and imperialism, 154 n. 18; junction-of-interests prescribing principle, 11, 54; and landscaping, 11, 51–52, 58, 64, 67, 70, 72, 75–76, 156 n. 39, 170 nn. 45–46, 173 n. 113; as liberal, 3, 6, 9, 16, 75, 81, 154 n. 18, 157–58 n. 48, 166 n. 3; logic of the will, 52, 54–55, 61, 63–64, 70, 167 n. 15; as materialist, 4–6, 48–51, 55–57, 59–60, 63, 68, 75–76, 142, 152 n. 7, 165 n. 2, 169 n. 34, 170–71 n. 53; on motive, 4, 37, 51–52, 54–56, 58, 60, 62–70, 72–73, 76, 171 n. 75; on natural law, 143–44, 168 n. 23; neo-liberalism and, 5, 8, 12, 14–16, 77, 142–43, 147–49; as normative theorist, 14, 156–57 n. 39, 168 n. 23; and Panopticon, 9, 144, 148; on penal law, 54, 72–74, 144; on pleasure and pain, 4–6, 44, 48, 50–51, 53–57, 59–62, 63–67, 69–70, 72–73, 74, 145, 169 n. 39, 170 n. 52, 170–71 n. 53, 171 n. 61; and Shaftesbury, 5, 13, 15–16, 19, 31–32, 35–36, 44, 45–46, 48, 77, 88, 99, 108, 117, 139–40, 151–52 n. 5, 163 n. 17, 165 n. 40; on sinister interest, *see* interest: sinister; and social science, 143; and the state, 15, 71–72, 81, 142, 149, 156 n. 16, 156 n. 18, 175 n. 6; and Stoicism, 83; as theorist of government, 12–14, 16, 37–38, 45–46, 48–76, 77–78, 100–103, 123, 140, 142–43, 147–49, 152 n. 7, 168 n. 23; on the understanding, 63, 69
Bentham Project, 50
Berkeley, George, 169 n. 34
Bible, 17, 82–83, 85, 106, 110, 119–21. *See also* Revelation, Book of
birthright, 128–29, 131
bishops, 110, 118, 138
Blackstone, William, 48
Blair, Tony, 2
Bodin, Jean, 90, 158 n. 4, 176 n. 31
Book of Fallacies (Bentham), 172 n. 93
Botero, Giovanni, 81, 91, 94–97
British moralists, 35
Butterfield, Herbert, 156 n. 30

Caesar, Julius, 86
Cairo, 97
calculation, 3, 9, 11, 16, 22–23, 25, 26, 50–51, 53, 58, 64, 70, 81–82, 88, 94, 101, 103, 104, 115, 138–40, 141, 146, 149, 170 n. 43
Calvin, Jean, 83–84, 86, 97, 110, 120
Canuel, Mark, 167 n. 11, 184 n. 6
Catholics, 83, 87, 106, 118–21. *See also* Church of Rome
censorship, 109, 119, 136
certainty, 43, 106, 110, 139; demonstrative vs. moral, 106. *See also* probability
Charles I, 105, 109, 118–19, 123–24, 133–34, 137; trial of, 124, 133, 181 n. 52, 182 n. 56
Charles II, 109, 134, 136–37
Chinese, 96
choice, 1, 2, 6, 9–11, 13, 16–17, 76, 103, 127, 129, 131–32, 142, 146, 148–49, 152 n. 9. *See also* rational choice
Chrestomathia (Bentham), 146
Christ, 123, 126–27, 137–38. *See also* God
Christendom, 86, 114. *See also* Europe; Ottomans
Church of England, English church, 38, 106, 109–10, 118–21, 126, 135, 137–38, 143–44. *See also* bishops; Establishment; Fifth Monarchists; Independents; Presbyterians; Protestants; Puritans; saints; schismatics
Church of Rome, 17, 73, 82, 110, 118, 126. *See also* Catholics; Jesuits; Reformation
Cicero, 82–85, 105–7, 121, 134, 175–76 n. 22
civil society, 8, 12, 14, 19, 27, 36–37, 102, 154 n. 16, 163 n. 17
civil war, 25, 94, 103, 121. *See also* English civil wars
Clarke manuscripts, 124
Clinton, Bill, 2
Coleman, James, 4, 173 nn. 114–15
collective action, problem of, 14, 18. *See also* rational choice
commensurability, 3–4, 6–7, 13, 16, 29, 36, 46, 53, 59, 86, 99, 101, 103, 104, 108, 139, 153 n. 12
commerce, 28, 31, 39, 44–45, 71, 96, 101, 116
common law, 112, 118, 140, 143
Commons, 112, 118. *See also* Parliament
competition, 12, 16, 17–18, 28, 71–72, 75

Renaissance, 79, 86; English, 110; Italian, 17

rent seeking, 147. *See also* interest: sinister

republic, 20, 81, 85–86, 90, 94, 102, 109, 117, 135, 179 n. 8

res publica, 134

Restoration, 107, 109, 117, 120, 133, 135–36

Revelation, Book of, 126, 132. *See also* Bible

rhetoric, 146, 172 n. 93

Richelieu, Cardinal, 87–91, 100, 107, 121

Rich, Nathaniel, 131

rights, 8–9, 12–14, 16, 18, 26–27, 36, 50, 52, 78, 113, 116, 119, 121–22, 128–29, 131–33, 136, 141

risk, 16, 140, 148

Rohan, Henri, duc de, 90, 100–102, 118, 120–22, 158 n. 4, 183 n. 82

Rose, Nikolas, 149

Rosen, Fred, 152 n. 9

Royalists, 105, 109, 124, 135

Royal Society, 138

rule of law, 2, 8, 37, 90, 131

saints, 107–8, 119–21, 123, 126–27, 134, 138, 141, 182 n. 54

Saints Interest in God, The (Goodwin, J.), 119–20

salus populi, 85–86, 105, 111, 121, 124–25, 133–34, 175 n. 18

salvation, 120, 136–37

sanctions, 25, 51, 54–55, 58, 72, 144–45, 170 n. 46; moral or popular, 54–55, 67, 71, 73; physical, 55, 57; political, 54–55, 72–73; religious, 54–55

schismatics, 123, 136

Scholasticism, 21, 25, 37

scientific revolution, 106

Scots, 124

Scottish Enlightenment, 12, 26–29, 39, 45

secrecy, 81, 84, 86, 96, 101

secularism, 17–18, 22, 34, 39, 87, 107, 125, 140

security, 4, 9, 12, 15–16, 23, 46, 51, 61, 70–73, 79, 140, 147–49, 152 n. 9

Selden, John, 159 n. 9

self-auditing, 148

self-help, 9–10

self-improvement, 116

self-interest, 3–6, 8, 11, 13, 15, 23–24, 27, 29–31, 36–37, 45–47, 75–76, 78, 82, 88, 101, 103, 107, 109, 122, 130, 132, 137–40, 142, 183 n. 94

self-love, 30, 161 n. 31

Seneca, 84

Sensus Communis: An Essay on the Freedom of Wit and Humour (Shaftesbury), 44

sermons, 109, 119–21, 126

settlement, 106, 108, 110, 117, 136

Shaftesbury, Anthony Ashley Cooper, third earl of: aesthetics, *see* aesthetics; Bentham and, *see* Bentham, Jeremy: and Shaftesbury; on interest, 33–34, 35–47, 77, 139, 164 n. 30, 165 n. 40; and introspection, 4, 27, 30–31, 33–34, 36, 39–44, 46, 48, 77, 140; as neo-Stoic, 83–84, 163 n. 12; on pain, 36–37, 41, 44, 46; on partiality, 42–43; on pleasure, 30, 33, 36, 37, 39–42, 44, 46; and theism, 163 n. 7; as theorist of public sphere, 38

Six Books of Politics (Lipsius), 84, 92, 94, 175 n. 13

Six Livres de la République (Bodin), 90, 176 n. 31

skepticism, 17, 35, 43–44, 88, 110, 137, 161 n. 31

Skinner, Quentin, 99

Smith, Adam, 28–30, 32, 39, 45, 155 n. 28, 157–58 n. 48, 160 n. 19, 165 n. 39, 177 n. 65

social capital, 14–15

social contract, 99, 135, 179 n. 9

social science, 15, 27, 36, 142–43, 146, 171 n. 64

society, 2–5, 12–14, 16, 25, 27–31, 34, 37–39, 42–45, 47, 75, 77, 79, 97, 102, 108–9, 139–40, 143–45

Solemn Engagement of the Army, 127

Soliloquy, or Advice to an Author (Shaftesbury), 44

solipsism, 38, 44, 48

sovereignty, 2, 7–12, 18, 21, 23–24, 26, 33, 36, 78, 82, 85, 89–90, 99–100, 102, 107, 112, 141–44, 155 n. 23, 174 n. 4; vs. monistic interest, 78–79, 155 n. 28

Spain, 30, 87, 89, 99, 118–19

spectatorship, 36–37, 41–46

state, 1–4, 6, 8–9, 11–12, 14–16, 17–18, 20–22, 24, 31, 38, 46, 49, 72, 78–82, 84–93, 95–103,

Stephen G. Engelmann is an assistant professor of
political science at the University of Illinois at Chicago.

Library of Congress Cataloging-in-Publication Data
Engelmann, Stephen G.
Imagining interest in political thought : origins of economic
rationality / Stephen G. Engelmann.
Includes bibliographical references.
ISBN 0-8223-3135-7 (cloth : alk. paper)
ISBN 0-8223-3122-5 (pbk. : alk. paper)
1. Liberalism. 2. Bentham, Jeremy, 1748–1832. 3. Self-interest.
4. Public interest. 5. Reason of state. I. Title.
JC574.E54 2003   320.51—dc21   2003003998